The Labour Party since

D0546351

Making Contemporary Britain Series

General Editor: Anthony Seldon
Consultant Editor: Peter Hennessy

The series *Making Contemporary Britain* is essential reading for students, as well as providing masterly overviews for the general reader. Each book in the series puts the central themes and problems of the specific topic into clear focus. The studies are written by leading authorities in their field, who integrate the latest research into the text but at the same time present the material in a clear, ordered fashion which can be read with value by those with no prior knowledge of the subject.

THE INSTITUTE OF CONTEMPORARY
BRITISH HISTORY

Senate House
Malet Street
London WC1H 7HU

WITHDRAWN
UTSA LIBRARIES

The Labour Party since 1945

Old Labour : New Labour

Eric Shaw

BLACKWELL
Publishers

Copyright © Eric Shaw 1996

The right of Eric Shaw to be identified as author of this work has been asserted in
accordance with the Copyright, Designs and Patents Act 1988.

First published 1996

Blackwell Publishers Ltd
108 Cowley Road
Oxford OX4 1JF

Blackwell Publishers Inc.
238 Main Street
Cambridge, Massachusetts 02142
USA

All rights reserved. Except for the quotation of short passages for the purposes of
criticism and review, no part of this publication may be reproduced, stored in a
retrieval system, or transmitted, in any form or by any means, electronic, mechanical,
photocopying, recording or otherwise, without the prior permission of the publisher.

Except in the United States of America, this book is sold subject to the condition that it
shall not, by way of trade or otherwise, be lent, resold, hired out, or otherwise circulated
without the publisher's prior consent in any form of binding or cover other than that
in which it is published and without a similar condition including this condition being
imposed on the subsequent purchaser.

British Library Cataloguing in Publication Data
A CIP catalogue record for this book is available from the British Library.

Library of Congress Cataloging-in-Publication Data
Shaw, Eric, 1949–
    The Labour Party since 1945 : old Labour : new Labour / Eric Shaw.
        p.   cm. — (Making contemporary Britain)
    Includes bibliographical references and index
    ISBN 0–631–19654–4. — ISBN 0–631–19655–2 (pbk.)
    1. Labour Party (Great Britain)—History.   2. Great Britain—
Politics and government—1945–   I. Title.   II. Series.
JN1129.L32S456   1996   95–37328
324.24107'09'045—dc20   CIP

Typeset in 10 on 12pt Ehrhardt
by Grahame & Grahame Editorial, Brighton, East Sussex

Printed in Great Britain by Hartnolls Limited, Bodmin, Cornwall
This book is printed on acid-free paper

Library
University of Texas
at San Antonio

Contents

Preface

The study is not, nor could it aspire to be in the space of a medium size volume, a comprehensive history of the Labour Party since 1945. Rather than covering a wide range of topics thinly it examines more fully a selected range of issues. This means that important matters have had to be omitted: for instance, little is said (directly at least) about the problem of Labour's faltering electoral fortunes. Instead, the book revolves around one central question: what has the Party been *about*, what objectives has it striven to realize? The (provisional) answer is Keynesian social democracy and the main thread running through the account is the rise, adoption and abandonment of this creed. After it had displaced traditional inter-war socialism (with its accent on public ownership, planning and social transformation) in the late 1940s it supplied Labour's main objectives: the pursuit of greater equality, social justice and full employment. It also provided the means: Keynesian management of aggregate demand to maintain high levels of employment and output and the use of progressively raised tax revenues to fund a large public sector from which collective goods (services or cash benefits) were distributed according to need rather than ability to pay.

Most recent studies of the Labour Party since 1945 have adopted a broad interpretive sweep, placing events and issues in a frame of reference that seeks to explain its trajectory (e.g. Elliott, 1993; Thompson, 1993. Earlier instances include Miliband, 1972; Coates, 1975). This approach is usually more stimulating than chronological accounts and these works contain many useful insights. But their explanatory value relies heavily on the adequacy of their frameworks and here the problem has been that they have rarely added a great deal new to our understanding of the dynamics of Labour's development. This study has preferred a less ambitious approach. It has sought to uncover the Party's purposes and priorities by analysing the choices it made on issues of seminal or strategic significance. Examples of these include the decision to undertake a huge rearmament programme in 1951, to maintain the value of the pound and to deflate rather than devalue in the 1960s, and its handling of the IMF Loan crisis in 1976. Since a party's character is only fully revealed by its actual behaviour – how it confronts the actual challenges of government – the book devotes considerable attention to Labour's three spells in office since 1945, though in the half century since the war this has accounted for only seventeen years.

Commentators in the media often claim that, until its recent 'modernization' Labour was outside the mainstream of western European social democracy because it was moored to an outdated economic collectivism, a socialism of a rather archaic stamp. This has recently been summed up in the concept of 'Old Labour'. 'Old Labour', it is argued, was deeply suspicious of market forces, which it sought to trammel by means of centralized economic planning and heavily interventionist policies. It 'tried to counter the injustices and failings of free market forces by substituting government for market' (Gordon Brown, transcript of speech 24 September 1994). Convinced of the superiority of public ownership it sought steadily to expand its frontiers at the expense of the private sector. It favoured the entrenchment of the power of the trade unions in government on the grounds that they represented the working class whose 'interests had a special legitimacy denied to other class interests' (Marquand, 1991: 25). Finally, it tended to be loose with the nation's finances, too often giving way to the temptations of the 'quick-fix' solution of 'tax, spend and borrow' rather than seeking more sober and considered approaches. The pages that follow suggest that this is not only a somewhat unflattering but, more to the point, rather poor portrait of 'Old Labour's' physiognomy, exaggerating certain of its features whilst neglecting others. The view expounded by this study is quite different: what distinguished Labour governments from their counterparts in northern Europe was less their collectivism than their *traditionalism*, that is the extent to which, in making key choices, their calculations were influenced by principles derived from the established and highly traditional national culture.

Chapter 1 traces Labour's programmatic and organizational development in its first four decades. Chapter 2 begins the more detailed exploration of its post-war history. It shows that, after 1947, neither planning nor public ownership played a significant role in its economic strategy, which was increasingly shaped by Keynesian ideas. It also contends that its impressive economic and social accomplishments were constricted by what we call the 'global mind-set', a view of British interests and identity that put great store on the maintenance of the UK's status as a world power. Chapter 3 sets down the main components of Keynesian social democracy, explains why it became Labour's ruling creed and then examines the basis upon which the hegemony of the Party's right, that espoused it, rested. Chapter 4 analyses the record of the 1964–70 Government. This was the only period in the so-called 'golden age of social democracy' of the 1950s and 1960s when Labour formed a government, yet when it departed from office it left behind a sense of hopes unfulfilled and promises abandoned. The turning-point was the Government's decision to give precedence to the defence of the pound over growth and social reform. The chapter suggests that the main reason for this choice, and therefore for its disappointing performance, was the impact of priorities derived from the global mind-set.

In the early 1970s the Party swung to the left and Keynesian social democracy came under fire from an opposing quarter – a resurgent traditional socialism. The outcome, as chapter 5 indicates, was that when it was unexpectedly returned to power in 1974 it was on the basis of manifesto pledged to extend public ownership, install a system of economic planning and, via the device of the Social Contract, to give to the unions a much enlarged role in government. But this challenge from the left was soon repulsed and the main theme of chapter 6 is the retreat from Keynesian social democracy to a semi-monetarist stance. We argue that the explanation lies less in the alleged internal contradictions or flaws of Keynesian social democracy than the emergence of a new global configuration of power far more hostile to the pursuit of progressive policies. The 1974–9 Labour Government found itself confronted by a coalition of the financial markets, the United States, the IMF, and elements within the Bank and even the Cabinet intent on tethering the Keynesian welfare state. The cuts in public spending which were, as a result, instigated by the Government and its failure to reduce unemployment from what was at the time regarded as a very high level led to a massive backlash after its fall from power. Chapter 7 discusses the temporary ascendancy of the left and its legacy of constitutional change and radicalized polices and then turns to the initial efforts made by Neil Kinnock, elected after Labour's total rout in the 1983 elections, to revive leadership control and return Labour to the political mainstream. After the Party received a further severe mauling in 1987, Kinnock embarked upon a major programme of (what came to be known as) modernization. In the organizational arena, this involved transforming Labour into a more centralized, tightly-managed and voter-oriented party; in the policy and ideological arena it took the form of the dilution or renunciation of Keynesian social democratic tenets. Modernization did not lead to electoral success but, after a brief interregnum under John Smith's leadership, the process was accelerated under Tony Blair. The outcome, half a century after Labour's great victory in 1945, was the emergence of 'New Labour', a party which differs strikingly from that which had embarked on the great post-war experiment. The modernizers' project, now nearing fruition, has been to shed what commentators often refer to as 'old ideological baggage' – and its emergence as the party that can manage capitalism more efficiently and humanely than the Conservatives.

I would like to acknowledge my thanks to the University of Stirling and the Carnegie Trust for the Universities of Scotland which provided assistance for the writing of this book. Thanks also to Nick Sigler for his willingness, as ever, to help. I owe my greatest debt of gratitude to my wife Susan for, once again (nearly always) displaying patience, understanding and forbearance.

Eric Shaw
July 1995

General Editor's Preface

The Institute of Contemporary British History's series *Making Contemporary Britain* is aimed directly at students and at others interested in learning more about topics in post-war British history. In the series, authors are less attempting to break new ground than presenting clear and balanced overviews of the state of knowledge on each of the topics.

The ICBH was founded in October 1986 with the objective of promoting the study of British history since 1945 at every level. To that end, it publishes books and a quarterly journal, *Contemporary Record*; it organizes seminars and conferences for school students, undergraduates, researchers and teachers of post-war history; and it runs a number of research programmes and other activities.

A central theme of the ICBH's work is that post-war history is too often neglected in British schools, institutes of higher education and beyond. The ICBH acknowledges the validity of the arguments against the study of recent history, notably the problems of bias, of overly subjective teaching and writing and the difficulties of perspective. But it believes that the values of studying post-war history outweigh the drawbacks, and that the health and future of a liberal democracy require that its citizens know more about the most recent past of their country than the limited knowledge possessed by British citizens, young and old, today. Indeed, the ICBH believes that the dangers of political indoctrination are higher where the young are *not* informed of the recent past.

The Labour Party has been more studied and written about than the Conservative Party (at least until the 1990s). Why then the need for another book on Labour's history, and one written at less length than some recent volumes?

The answer lies partly in the lack of any medium-length volume covering the Labour Party's fifty-year history since the seminal election victory of 1945. Such a long time span brings the Party's history sharply into focus. These were the years when Labour came of age: before 1939 it had always been a somewhat faltering force in British politics. For the twenty-five years after 1945 it seemed set to become the dominant fact, during the only time in the 'Conservative Century' when the Conservative Party hegemony has been challenged for a prolonged period.

The change to the Labour Party since the 1970s provides the other main rationale for this book. The author, a leading authority on the Labour Party, wisely eschewed an inclusive chronological approach, and has selected instead to focus on the transition from 'old' to 'new' Labour. During the period 1945–95 the Party adopted, maintained and then abandoned Keynesian social democracy, and then under three leaders after 1983, Neil Kinnock, John Smith and Tony Blair, shifted the Party decisively rightwards, abandoning many of the organizational bulwarks and needs of the traditional Labour Party.

As the Party approaches its centenary in 2000, this book will find an important place as a key text analysing exactly what the Labour Party has stood for over the last fifty years. The book illuminates not just the Labour Party, but the entire history of post-war Britain.

Anthony Seldon

1 The Early Years, 1900–1945

Formation of the Labour Party

In virtually every West European country the labour and socialist movement had political origins. Commonly inspired by some variant of Marxist theory, dedicated socialists formed mass-membership, class-based social democratic parties[1] and embarked on the task of mobilizing the working class through the building up of an array of organizations, including trade unions. For a generation, similar efforts were made in Britain, by such bodies as the Marxist Social Democratic Federation, the Socialist League and the ideologically more diverse Independent Labour Party (ILP). Compared to their comrades in Germany, France, Benelux and elsewhere they had the decided advantage of a working class which already constituted the majority of the population and a social milieu in which the main sociological barriers to socialist advance, a large peasantry and urban petit bourgeoisie, no longer existed. Yet decades of effort brought scant reward and by the 1890s many disillusioned socialists were reappraising their strategy.

What differentiated their experience from that of their continental counterparts was that, in Britain, unlike elsewhere, early industrialization and a relatively more open and pluralist political system had created conditions conducive to the emergence of influential and legally-recognized labour organizations which, in terms of size and membership, were far stronger than the socialist groupings. Leading figures within the ILP, most notably Keir Hardie, concluded that the only way in which a socialist party could be established was for socialists to dilute their identity and objectives and coalesce with the unions to form a broad-based Labour Party which could eventually be persuaded to adopt a socialist programme. Most union leaders were Liberal in orientation and initially reacted coolly to the blandishments of the ILP. However, by 1900 a sufficient number of unions had been convinced of the value of independent political action. They combined with the ILP, the Fabian Society and (briefly) the SDF to form a Labour Representation Committee (renamed Labour Party in 1906) which by 1909, with the affiliation of the largest union the Miners Federation of Great Britain (MFGB), included the bulk of unions.

The character of trade unionism was changing in the last twenty years of the nineteenth century. The unions had previously been preserves of the so-called 'aristocracy of labour' – highly-skilled, status-conscious and relatively well remunerated craftsmen – but an outburst of industrial unrest expanded unionization to the mass of semi- and unskilled workers. Strikes were often led by convinced socialists who began to rise within the union hierarchy, either in newly created general unions or within craft unions seeking to widen their basis of recruitment. In consequence, alongside the (often top-hatted and eminently respectable) 'Lib-Labbers' appeared a minority of younger, more militant and socialist-minded leaders. Yet the percolation of the unions by socialist ideas was probably the least of the reasons for their move towards independent political representation. The primary motivation was strategic.

Firstly, they sought an avenue by which trade unionists could enter into Parliament. They were frustrated by the reluctance of local Liberal associations to adopt as candidates people of working-class origin even in heavily working-class constituencies. A political career appeared to be the prerogative of the upper and middle classes with, under the established party system, the mass of the population denied the right to represent themselves. Secondly, the trade union establishment became convinced that a strong collective labour voice was now required in the House of Commons if the interests of the unions were to be adequately defended. Two developments around the turn of the century shook its earlier equanimity, one industrial, the other legal. As awareness spread of the speed with which the United States and Germany were overhauling Britain industrially, employers reacted with an offensive against the unions to hasten the introduction of new technology and work practices, particularly in the engineering industry. Craft workers whose skills and status were being rendered obsolete felt increasingly insecure whilst union officials found themselves under pressure from the drive to impose stronger managerial control. But the employers were not the only antagonists. The judiciary, wedded to individualistic common law norms and recruited overwhelmingly from the highest social echelons, had never evinced much sympathy for collective labour organization. The right to strike had not been legally recognized, and the legality of actions (strikes and so forth) which broke the employment contract – the obligation of the worker to carry out his duties as defined by the employer or 'master' – rested on protection (more technically, 'immunity') against civil damages in cases where the interruption of the contract has occurred in pursuance of a trade dispute. The famous Taff Vale House of Lords judgement of 1901 effectively removed such immunity exposing unions to legal redress if they undertook strike action. This blow (though remedied by the seminal 1906 Trade Disputes Act, passed by the new Liberal Government) convinced many union leaders that industrial action must be complemented by political representation if their basic rights were to be secured.

The original Labour Party exhibited a number of characteristics which have never been entirely lost. In contrast to continental social democratic parties, it was a party of *interest* rather than ideas. Dominated both organizationally and culturally by the unions, with their already entrenched traditions, norms and procedures, the new party did not possess the mobilizing fervour of Marxist-inspired parties. In fact, it was 'not founded on any body of doctrine at all, and has always preserved a marked anti-doctrinal and anti-theoretical bias' (Crosland, 1964: 80). It never developed a tradition of rooting policy in an analysis of social and economic trends or promulgating an overarching programme geared to achieving an elaborated vision of the good society. All political actors, however, require a body of patterning principles, a cognitive map, to structure their understanding of the complexities of social life and a set of values to lend a sense of direction and purpose. In Labour's case, these took the form of a highly eclectic belief system, a patchwork quilt of ideas derived from a multitude of sources lacking the rigour of an articulated theoretical framework. But the most influential source, in these early formative years, was undoubtedly Fabianism. The Fabian Society was originally founded in 1884 and its key figures were Beatrice and Sidney Webb, and the playwright George Bernard Shaw. They set about developing a socialist creed which – unlike, in their view, Marxism – was both 'scientific' and suited to British circumstances. They rejected the notion that society was fractured and that the driving force of change was class conflict. They preferred to view the social order as a constantly evolving organism in which change occurred not through sudden revolutionary ruptures but in slow, almost imperceptible stages: 'a gradual passing of the old order into the new, without breach of continuity or abrupt general change of the social tissues' (Webb). Whilst the working class would be its prime beneficiaries and provide much of its electoral ballast, they conceived socialism as 'the enlightened consciousness of society as a whole' which found expression 'not through the material strivings of the working class but through the rational capacity of political and administrative leaders' (Pierson, 1973: 123). They believed in what came to be known as 'the inevitability of gradualness': in their efforts to resolve social and economic problems practical politicians and administrators would be drawn ineluctably to collectivist solutions. They adduced as evidence the growth of municipally and nationally owned enterprises responsible for transport, gas and electricity; measures such as the Factory Acts in which government sought to eliminate some of capitalism's grosser abuses by use of legislative power; and the gradual assumption by public authorities of the duty to provide for welfare and educational services.

Repudiating all revolutionary theories, the Fabians insisted that radical social change must be achieved by democratic means, through Parliament. In Beatrice Webb's words: 'we don't want to pull down the existing structure – all we want is slowly and quietly to transform and add to it' (Greenleaf, 1983: 379). Whilst mistrust of the state was widespread amongst socialists, at the time the Fabian Society perceived it as the institutional expression of the public interest, staffed by a public-spirited, enlightened and capable administrative elite. Beatrice Webb's description of Fabian policies in the 1890s sums-up their general approach: 'essentially collective ownership wherever practicable; collective regulation everywhere else; collective provision according to need for the impotent and the sufferers; and collective taxation in proportion to wealth, especially surplus wealth' (Greenleaf, 1983: 374). The central Fabian organizing concept was a state-sponsored 'National Minimum'. This, the embryo of the welfare state, comprised a universal minimum standard of life embracing pensions, unemployment and sickness benefit, the legal regulation of hours of work and the public provision of health, education and housing, which would afford protection against sickness, poverty and squalor. Although it was not until the 1930s that members of the Fabian Society occupied senior positions in the Party, Fabian thinking permeated the Party from its earliest years: the commitment to gradual, strictly constitutional action; a conception of the social order as socially unified rather than fractured by irreconcilable class interests; and a definition of socialism in terms of collective (state and municipal) ownership, control and regulation of economic and social life. Both its immediate impact, and its role as an enduring source of influence, was due to the fact that it 'provided an intellectual rationale for the instinctive attitudes of leaders' (Howell, 1980: 27).

Sidney Webb, along with Arthur Henderson, one of Labour's first political heavyweights, was responsible for authoring the new Party's official statement of purpose, Clause IV Section Four of the 1918 Constitution. This read: 'To secure for the workers by hand or by brain the full fruits of their industry and the most equitable distribution thereof that may be possible upon the basis of the common ownership of the means of production, distribution and exchange, and the best obtainable system of popular administration and control of each industry or service.' Its adoption is usually interpreted as signifying the Party's formal conversion to socialism, but such a conclusion needs to be heavily qualified. A curious feature of Clause IV is that neither Webb nor Henderson actually believed that the bulk of industry, finance and the service sector should be commonly owned. Webb wrote Labour's first programme, also issued in 1918, *Labour and the New Social Order*, which was noticeably less radical in tone. It contained proposals for the eradication of waste and inefficiency, public ownership of land, coal, transport and electricity, redistributive taxation of inheritance and capital and – the heart of the programme – a commitment to the Fabian 'national minimum of civilized life'. Henderson was a shrewd politician, an organizer by bent, whose beliefs never departed much from the Liberalism of his younger day. In political terms, the senior partner of the two, it was his calculating mind that guided Webb's pen.

How can we explain the paradox of this epitome of the cautious, practical trade unionist devising Labour's radical new agenda? The clue lies in the circumstances in which it came to be written. The main organizational effect of the 1918 constitution, as we note below, was to remove the separate representation of the socialist societies from the Party executive, entrusting the politically much more 'moderate' trade unions with sole control as well as confirming their voting dominance of Conference. Clause IV was a consolation prize, intended to appease the socialists. But it was designed at a moment of peculiar fluidity in the party system. The Liberals were wracked by internal disputes, split into two rival parties and on a downward electoral slope. Labour was emerging as the main challenger to the Conservatives and required a sharper profile to mobilize a much-enlarged electorate. Finally, the year in which the new constitution was agreed was one of intense ideological ferment within European socialism, with the upsurge of revolutionary sentiment fired by that most dramatic and unique historical event, an apparently successful socialist revolution in Russia. Throughout Europe, such stalwarts of the socialist movement as the German Social Democratic Party (SPD) and the French Socialist Party (SFIO) were being torn apart by revolutionary fervour with large numbers of members soon to desert to join newly-founded Communist Parties. Dedicated constitutionalists such as Webb, Henderson, MacDonald were shocked by the Bolshevik revolution, horrified by the intolerance shown to moderate socialists and, given the highly volatile and radical temper in urban strongholds (like Glasgow), apprehensive about the challenge posed by Britain's own brand of revolutionaries. Riveting Labour to socialist objectives seemed a small price to pay to placate those who might otherwise be seduced by other philosophies.

This interpretation is consistent with Labour's behaviour in the next decade or so. From 1918 to 1931, its approach to matters of policy was set by leaders who coupled an adherence to a sentimental and insipid brand of rhetorical socialism with an immense admiration for the British constitution. They spoke an often emotive language of a future world of human fellowship, declaimed passionately about the miseries of mass unemployment and poverty under capitalism which only socialism could remedy, whilst at the same time repudiating any policies that seriously threatened the existing order (Cronin and Weiler, 1991: 54). Hence any tangible proposals for tackling unemployment – for instance as pressed by the ILP (by now moving rapidly to the left) which called for a minimum income, raising purchasing power and a programme of public works – were rejected out of hand in favour of the bland *Labour and the Nation* statement agreed in 1928 which eschewed all but a minimum of specific commitments (Howell, 1980: 37).

However, in the decade or so after the war, the rise of the new Party seemed unstoppable. Two developments helped: the war-time split in the ranks of the Liberals was never remedied and universal male suffrage was granted in 1918. In that year, Labour won 2,400,000 votes and by 1922 this had almost doubled to 4,250,000. Labour first briefly ruled, as a minority government, in 1924, and its only legislative achievement was the Wheatley Housing Act, named after the left-wing Minister of Housing. It only survived for a few months before being forced to resign. In the ensuing election, it lost seats, but not votes, with the main casualty being the Liberals whose Parliamentary contingent shrank by two-thirds and which was henceforth consigned to third-party status.

In the years immediately following the War there were numerous strikes but, as a serious recession set in, these diminished. In 1925, the Chancellor of the Exchequer, Winston Churchill, was persuaded by the Bank of England to return to the Gold Standard – in effect, a revaluation of the pound whose effect was to price many British goods out of foreign markets. The coal owners, determined to drive down costs, cut wages thereby provoking a Miners' strike. The TUC came out in solidarity, initiating the General Strike. However, most union leaders had no stomach for taking on a resolute government and the action was soon called off – leaving the Miners to fight a long and hopeless battle alone. The main consequence for the Labour Party was that the events convinced many that the only real hope for improvement in the conditions of the mass of the working class lay in political action. In the ensuing election, in 1929, Labour won almost eight and a half million votes, obtaining 287 seats which made it, for the first time, the largest party in the House of Commons. But it still lacked a majority, so once again a minority government led by MacDonald was formed and upheld by Liberal votes. Unfortunately for Labour, the period coincided with the great depression, triggered off by the Wall Street crash of 1929. The numbers out of work jumped rapidly from a little over million in 1929 to 2,800,000 in July 1931, a major blow to a party which professed to protect the interests of the working class. Whilst Labour's capacity to act effectively was to some

extent restricted by its reliance on Liberal support the real problem
was that the MacDonald government had no strategy for grappling
with the depression. Snowden, the 'iron' Chancellor of the Exchequer,
was unflinchingly committed to the canons of financial orthodoxy – a
balanced budget, free trade and a strong pound (Howell, 1980: 38).
Dissenting voices mainly on the left urged proto-Keynesian policies,
but with no effect. As the confidence of the international financial
community in the government began to ebb, it responded – in line
with the precepts of the ruling economic wisdom – by seeking to
close the budget deficit produced by the falling tax revenues and
higher benefit outlays which were the inevitable consequences of the
collapse of output and the lengthening jobless queues. MacDonald and
Snowden were backed by the bulk of the Cabinet – until they proposed
cutting unemployment benefit.

A horrified TUC denounced the move and a sizable minority of the
Cabinet, emboldened by its stance, voted against. Largely as a result,
MacDonald, Snowden and a couple of others reached an agreement
with the Conservatives and the Liberals to form a so-called 'National
Government' and Labour suddenly found itself banished into opposition.
In the subsequent general election, deserted by its best-known leaders
and facing, for the first time, united opposition, the Party was decimated
– though in seats far more than in votes. The combination of the
circumstances in which the Labour Government fell, the apostacy of
MacDonald and the electoral catastrophe that followed had an enduring
impact on Labour's psyche as the traditional respect, even adulation,
for leaders was henceforth always to be balanced by fear of another
betrayal.

The 1930s

In response, the Party swung strongly to the left. Because of the scythe
which had passed through the parliamentary party, only one former
minister of any seniority survived, the left-wing George Lansbury. He
was assisted, in a group of a mere forty-six Labour MPs, by Clement
Attlee and Sir Stafford Cripps, the former mildly left of centre, the latter
in the process of blossoming out into a radical left-winger. Gradually
as the remainder of the old leadership, with the powerful backing of

the unions, reasserted themselves, it was soon pulled back to a more mainstream course. Nevertheless considerable changes did occur. The pre-1929 diet of financial orthodoxy spiced with vague socialist oratory was replaced by efforts to develop a socialist analysis of economic decay and a coherent set of polices. The impact of the depression convinced most that the objectives of full employment, a decent living standard for the bulk of the population and social justice could only be attained by radical changes which needed to be embodied in a programme of practical socialism. Prime responsibility for formulating the programme was given to two rising politicians on Labour's right-wing, Herbert Morrison and Hugh Dalton, both heavily influenced by Fabian ideas and methods. To ensure that in future Labour was armed with carefully thought-out and well-researched proposals Dalton assembled a group of specialist advisors, some drawn from the Fabian Society, others from the 'XYZ' group of Labour-leaning economists and financial experts. These included young economists such as Hugh Gaitskell, Edwin Durbin and Douglas Jay who were later to pursue political careers and disciples of John Maynard Keynes such as James Meade and Colin Clarke (Johnman, 1991: 30). 'By the outbreak of war the Labour Party had travelled light-years in the depth and sophistication of its knowledge of British financial institutions and economic policy options since the dark days of 1931' (Durbin, 1985: 261). Via Dalton's strategic position within the policy-making machine, these specialists made a major contribution to the formulation of the Party's economic strategy in its main programmatic statements, *Socialism and Peace*, 1934 and *Labour's Immediate Programme*, 1937 (Pimlott, 1985: 224).

In 1935 Lansbury resigned the leadership, after a blistering attack on his pacifist beliefs by a major figure emerging from the ranks of the trade unions, Ernest Bevin, General Secretary of the Transport and General Workers Union (TGWU). The aged left-winger was replaced by Attlee, who consolidated his position after the 1935 general election when he beat off challenges from Arthur Greenwood and Morrison. But public office appeared as elusive as ever for although Labour regained around a hundred seats at the election, enlargening the PLP to 154, this still left the Government with a huge majority (Howell, 1980: 79). Furthermore, by-elections held in the following four years gave little promise of a swing large enough for a Labour government. Nevertheless, the Party was far better equipped with a clear and coherent programme for government by the end of the 1930s than it had been earlier in the decade.

Labour's Programme

In the first decades of its life, the main fault of capitalism was seen by Labour to be its inability to distribute equitably the fruits of economic progress. Its manifold injustices, its wastefulness and its dehumanizing effects were excoriated and most of the Party's proposals were designed to alleviate poverty and squalor. On such economic questions as the level of output, productivity, even unemployment, it had little tangible to say. The feeble performance and ignominious collapse of the 1929–31 Labour Government demonstrated the dire need for a feasible economic strategy whilst the onset of economic depression and mass unemployment seemed to offer irrefutable evidence that capitalism, disfigured by persistent mass unemployment, endemic economic instability, rampant poverty and social deprivation, was no longer capable of generating sustained economic growth. The Party's response, as it emerged in the mid and late 1930s, can be summed up as a collectivist strategy composed of four elements: public ownership, planning, Keynesian demand management and a collective system of welfare.

Public ownership

A major extension of public ownership was the centre-piece of Labour's programme. Nationalization of coal, the railways, gas, electricity, water and the Bank of England was universally supported within the Party and regarded as a condition of achieving full employment and the regeneration of industry. Public ownership had multiple goals: it was the means by which the appropriation of the economic surplus could be transferred from the shareholder to the community as a whole, hence striking at the tap-root of economic inequality; it would enable the state to manage the economy and thereby tackle unemployment and the oscillations of the business cycle; it would help replace the waste and inefficiency of competition by the orderly development of industry. There was, however, less unanimity about the form public ownership should take. Morrison, Labour's main political expert in the field, favoured the 'public corporation' model in which nationalized industries would enjoy a considerable degree of autonomy, subject to accountability to parliament. A sizeable slice of trade union opinion pressed for the right of the workforce to be represented in the running of the corporation. This was, in itself, a much diluted version of the demand for workers' control, or industrial democracy, which had been articulated by the once vocal guild socialist movement in the years before and after the First World War. However, this call was eventually rejected, on the grounds that efficiency and the public interest was best served by vesting managerial control solely in the hands of professional managers appointed by the state and responsible to Parliament. But whatever the differences, few dissented from the view that public ownership of major sectors of the economy was an essential condition of full employment and decent living conditions for the mass of the working population.

Planning

The notion of subjecting economic life to some degree of rational control can be said to be inherent in socialism. In George Bernard Shaw's words, the 'scramble for private gain' must be replaced by 'the introduction of design, contrivance, and co-ordination' if 'collective welfare' was to be promoted (Greenleaf, 1983: 366). Economic orthodoxy insisted that optimal efficiency in the deployment of economic resources required minimal interference with the free play of market forces, but to the Labour Party a system which reduced people to the status of objects of impersonal market forces was ethically unacceptable. But how the gyrations of the economy could be tamed by 'contrivance' and rational intelligence was not a matter to which a great deal of thought was given. The economic collapse following the Wall Street crash of 1929 coupled with the débâcle of the second Labour Government shook the intellectual edifice of laissez faire. The notion of economic planning leapt upon the public agenda as 'a universal idiom in which recovery plans of all kinds were framed' (Samuel, 1986: 27). It could now persuasively be argued that capitalism was doomed to reproduce a cycle of boom and slump of ever-increasing severity. The concept of planning was imprecise but politically this was one of its strengths. Many people could agree that planning was vital whilst differing over what it actually involved. It ran with the grain of the times, appealing to politicians across the political spectrum, including Liberals and progressive Tories such as

Harold Macmillan. As Durbin wrote in 1935 'it would almost be true to say that we are all planners now' (Samuel, 1986: 27). At the same time, many observers on the left were impressed by the Soviet planning experiment (or at least, their perception of it) which appeared to prove that the conscious organization of economic life constituted a more dynamic engine of economic growth than the failing market economy. For some exponents, planning was designed to construct a qualitatively different economic system in which the market's functions in capital accumulation, resource-allocation and economic co-ordination would be displaced by a central economic agency accountable to Parliament. To others, planning was meant to rectify market failings whilst preserving the price mechanism. However, there was a general agreement amongst all who contributed to Labour's economic debates that the free market was unable to generate sufficient economic activity to end mass unemployment, arrest the economic decline of whole regions and improve industrial performance.

Keynesian economics

Though Keynes was himself a Liberal, his ideas had an increasing impact upon economists sympathetic to the Labour Party from the mid-1930s onwards. The XYZ group included some of his keenest disciples and they sought to push the Party's economic thinking into a Keynesian direction. Naturally, the Party welcomed Keyne's withering onslaught on laissez faire economics, his belief in the capacity of the state to achieve full employment and his advocacy of higher levels of public spending. But it fell well short of adopting the whole Keynesian prospectus. Its most influential economic policy-makers, such as Hugh Dalton, were not convinced that demand management alone could restore full employment and end the cycle of booms and slumps, and continued to hold that supply-side policies, above all planning and nationalization, were essential to achieve Labour's aims.

Collective responsibility for welfare

The ethical core of Labour's belief system was composed of three interlinked principles: social welfare, the assumption by the state of responsibility for the well-being of all its members; social justice, the eradication of all suffering and ill-treatment imposed by social and economic arrangements; and equality, more equal access for all to life-enhancing resources like health and education, and the elimination of all disparities which did not contribute to the prosperity of the community. Practical concerns lay at the heart of Labour's creed: 'Poverty, mass unemployment, ill-health, absence of educational opportunity, these were the roots of the Labour passion for amelioration' (Addison, 1977: 16). The main instrument for the fulfilment of Labour's purposes was the state. The state would introduce the 'National Minimum', a social umbrella comprising a whole range of reforms including pensions, unemployment and sickness benefit, the legal regulation of hours of work and the public provision of health, education and housing. The extension of the role of the state in both economic and social domains became 'a central objective of the Labour Party, an essential prerequisite for the implementation of a wide range of polices designed to create a more egalitarian society' (Taylor, 1991: 22).

Power and Organization

In western and central Europe, the rise of socialism took a distinct organizational form, the social democratic mass party. Its essential features were: a highly integrated structure; mass membership and strong grass-roots organization; procedures prescribing accountability of the leadership to the membership and rank and file membership participation in policy-making; and the pre-eminence of extra-parliamentary bodies over the parliamentary party (Epstein, 1980). Constitutionally, powers were distributed according to a unitary pattern, with sovereignty vested in a congress elected by lower-level party units which, in turn, elected executive agencies with powers to direct party activities. Because of its origins as a trade union sponsored organization, the Labour Party differed from this model in a number of signal respects. Initially, Labour was a wholly confederal party but this was modified with the 1918 Constitution. A new layer of organization was established enabling individuals, for the first time, to participate by joining the Party directly rather than, as in the past, only via membership of a constituent union or socialist society. As, too, with the social democratic model, the party Conference was the sovereign body with ultimate responsibility for determining policies, strategy and internal organizational matters.

But, unlike it, the confederal principle was also entrenched: the composition of all key party bodies, including Conference and the National Executive Committee, was determined primarily by the votes of union organizations, which were wholly autonomous and not subject to the authority of the Party. In other words the direct rank and file members were neither in a position to shape – even formally – the policies of the Party or to elect or hold the leadership accountable for its actions.

The Constitution did uphold the precepts of intra-organizational democracy, but these operated indirectly. Policy was decided by Conference composed mainly of delegates representing affiliated organizations and bound by mandates received from them. Decisions of Conference were, in turn, binding on all party bodies (Minkin, 1978: 3). In the mass social democratic party, a strong grass-roots organization was vital to provide finance, recruits to organize electoral activities and campaigning, and to furnish legitimacy for the party's representational claims. 'The members are therefore the very substance of the party, the stuff of its activity. Without members, the party would be like a teacher without pupils' (Duverger, 1964: 63). In Britain, in contrast, the unions were the major source of members and funds and (in Labour's first decades) much of its campaign organization. The lesser reliance on the rank and file meant that the Party was under less pressure to take account of their views. The 1918 Constitution actually bolstered the unions' voice: whilst the NEC was divided into different sections, including one for the unions, women and the constituencies, it stipulated that all sections be elected by Conference as a whole – that is, given the preponderance of their vote, by the unions. Even after the decision in 1937 to restrict voting to the constituency section to constituencies alone, the large majority of NEC members remained reliant on union votes. This organizational form functioned, as Crossman pointed out, less to give paramountcy to the unions than to curb the activists. An active rank and file was required to staff the constituency machine but 'since they tended to be "extremists" a constitution was needed which maintained their enthusiasm by apparently creating a full party democracy whilst excluding them from effective power. Hence the concession in principle of sovereign powers to the delegates at Annual Conference, and the removal in practice of most of this sovereignty through the trade union block vote on the one hand, and the complete independence of the Parliamentary Labour Party on the other' (Crossman, 1963: 41–2).

A developmental trend within continental social democracy of major significance was the erosion of internal party democracy by the growing power of the leadership and the parliamentary representatives. In contrast, in the first two decades of Labour's history, the decentralized structure of the Party and the small size and rather poor calibre of its parliamentary representatives meant that such tendencies were weak. However, after the First World War, a hierarchy slowly emerged as the growth of the Parliamentary Labour Party (PLP) increased the influence and prestige of its leadership. Although the constitution specified that Conference should have responsibility for deciding the Party's programme, with the role of the PLP limited to matters of timing and priority, the parliamentary leadership steadily enlarged their freedom of action. This first generation of Labour leaders – men such as MacDonald, Snowden and Henderson – were highly deferential to the British parliamentary traditions and in office in 1924 and 1929–31 they observed the conventions of the British constitution with scrupulous respect (down to top hats and tail coats). Accoutred with the prestige, patronage and powers constitutionally assigned to the PM and the Cabinet, and eager to convince the political establishment of their fitness to rule, the minority Labour governments quickly barred the wider party from government decision-making (Minkin, 1978 13–14).

However, the débâcle of the MacDonald government led to a reaffirmation of the norms of intra-party democracy and collective decision-making. The sense of betrayal produced by the behaviour of MacDonald and the other defectors instilled a profound mistrust of the 'charismatic' leader. The scale of Labour's electoral defeat reduced the PLP to a rump and excluded from the House several of those best qualified to assume the mantle of leadership, such as Herbert Morrison and Hugh Dalton. Further, by quirk of chance, the few with the ability to adopt leadership roles – George Lansbury, Stafford Cripps and Clem Attlee – were, at the time, to the left of the extra-parliamentary establishment. But there were structural reasons, too, which account for the reversal of the earlier trend towards parliamentary power and autonomy and which highlight another differentiating facet of the Labour Party.

Within the social democratic mass party, the leadership's command over organizational resources and their monopoly of political skills facilitated the displacement of democracy by oligarchy which an amorphous rank and file was unable to resist (Michels, 1964). Labour's confederal character meant that the leadership was not only faced by an amorphous rank and file but by powerful union organizations over whom they had little constitutional authority. The effect was to give the extra-parliamentary party a powerful, organized voice which the parliamentary leadership could ignore only at its peril. Acting as political stabilizers, the unions were instrumental in extricating the Party from the orthodox fiscal and monetary policies of MacDonald and Snowden but, equally, blocked and reversed the lurch to the left in the aftermath of the cataclysm of 1931. Thereafter they were content for the most part to allow politicians such as Morrison and Dalton to take the initiative and they tended to restrict their efforts in internal party relations to sustaining two organizational precepts. The first was a distinctive – though never wholly unambiguous – doctrine of internal party government, majoritarian democracy. 'The Conference sets the principles; the parliamentarians applied them. The Conference took the policy decisions, the parliamentarians decided upon their timing and application. The parliamentarians were an arm of the movement; but they remained an autonomous body regulating their own affairs' (Minkin, 1978: 19). The doctrine survived for a generation because the new generation of leaders – Attlee, Morrison, Bevin and Dalton – were the first to be socialized into the norms of the Party, and were fully ready to accept the principle that when a major issue of had to be resolved, Conference was the appropriate body (Minkin, 1978: 20).

The second precept was social democratic centralism. Authority was rooted in a fair measure of consent but it was exercised in a centralist manner. A cardinal principle was that majority decisions, whether reached in the PLP or Conference, were binding on all members. This was treated as an obligation of membership, not only because it was thought right and proper that the voice of the majority prevail but as a device to maintain the unity and integrity of the movement in a largely hostile environment. Groups or individuals that refused to accept the authority of Conference and campaigned against majority decisions were eventually penalized. Thus in 1932 when the ILP (by then well to the left of Labour) refused to be bound by Conference and NEC decisions, it was left with little option but to disaffiliate; the left-wing ginger group, the Socialist League, as punishment for its refusal to buckle under, was forced in 1937 to dissolve itself; and high profile proponents of co-operation with the Communist Party (the so-called 'United Front' strategy) and, later, the Liberals too (the 'Popular Front') in an anti-Fascist alliance, were expelled from the Party when they continued to defy its edicts: such was the fate of two figures destined to be prominent members of the post-war Labour Government, Cripps and Aneurin (Nye) Bevan. The leadership were able to command the decision-making process because of a pattern of institutional interlock which bound together the main centres of power, the Parliamentary party the NEC and the majority of trade unions. This rested on the overlapping of personnel, as after 1935 senior Parliamentarians such as Attlee, the Leader, Morrison and Dalton were also the most influential members of the Executive; and on the broad similarity of overlook amongst members of all three institutions. This ruling stratum, in turn, had little difficulty commanding Conference majorities, a task eased by the developing practice of block voting, the casting of the votes of all members of a trade union delegation as a block (Minkin, 1978: 6).

Labour's position, and perhaps its fortunes, were radically transformed by the outbreak of war. It refused to join any government led by the author of the disastrous policy of appeasement of Hitler, the Conservative Prime Minister Neville Chamberlain, but with his replacement by the anti-appeasement Winston Churchill, Labour entered the wartime coalition. Ministers included Attlee (as deputy Prime Minister), Morrison, Dalton and, most powerful of all, Ernest Bevin, who moved directly from his position as leader of the TGWU to head the Ministry of Labour, a vital role as the basis of domestic mobilization was manpower planning. The impact of the war on the Party is a complex subject but for our purposes a few comments will suffice. Firstly, the involvement of Labour members of the coalition in operating the war-time economy, with its complex array of economic regulations and controls and its exploitation of Keynesian demand-management techniques, convinced them that a planned economy would work. Many of the ideas developed by left-wing economists in the 1930s, such as control over credit, capital issues and foreign exchange, were put into effect during war-time. 'The war thus instilled Labour's tentative prewar programme with new confidence and depth' (Brooke, 1989: 164). It was also able to influence the formative work being undertaken for the creation of a post-war welfare state, notably the seminal Beveridge Report (whose author, though a Liberal, was a former associate of the Webbs) on social insurance. Finally, when the next election came eventually to be fought in 1945, Labour could field a team of experienced, highly capable former ministers rather than untried opposition politicians. When Churchill resorted to the well-honed Conservative tactic of scaremongering (accusing the mouse-like Attlee of planning to establish a Gestapo) it was totally counter-productive given the legitimacy the Party had acquired in five years of loyal, unstinting service in the war-time coalition. In fact, little could have resisted the Labour tide, as the desire for jobs, better housing, health services and living conditions, fears of a return to the unemployment and distress of the 1930s, the restless radicalism of millions of conscript troops (not all of whom were able to vote, undoubtedly depressing the Party's total), and the simple but potent wish for a better world combined into an avalanche of votes. Polling 48.3 per cent of the vote, Labour won 393 seats and an overall majority of almost 150. Somewhat to his surprise, Attlee found himself the first Labour Prime Minister to command a majority in the Commons.[2]

Notes

1   The term 'social democratic' was used in the late nineteenth century to differentiate mass Marxist-inspired parties – such as the German Social Democratic Party and (on a minuscule scale) Britain's own Social Democratic Federation – from other brands of socialists.
2   This and all subsequent electoral figures are taken from Butler and Kavanagh (1992).

2 The Triumph of Labour, 1945–1951

That first sensation, tingling and triumphant, was of a new society to
be built, and we had the power to build it. We felt exalted, dedicated,
walking on air, walking with destiny . . .

(Dalton, 1962: 3)

The Attlee Government . . . was without doubt the most effective of all
Labour governments, perhaps amongst the most effective of any British
government

(Morgan, 1984: 503)

Of the three post-war Labour administrations, only one evokes within
the Party a sense of pride and accomplishment, the post war Attlee
Government. It was responsible for its most acclaimed achievement,
the National Health Service, which institutionalized the principle of
treatment according to need and not the ability to pay. It laid the
foundations of the full employment welfare state that was to endure for
a generation. It inherited massive economic problems, but made substantial progress in overcoming them. It poured resources into the rebuilding
of a war-battered country, holding down personal consumption whilst
releasing funds for a major programme of capital investment – but in
a spirit of equity and social justice which saw impressive improvements
in the quality of life of the bulk of the population.

To a greater extent than any other Labour government, the Attlee
administration entered office inspired by a driving impulse to reform

the social order. The 1945 Manifesto. *Let us Face the Future*, declared that Labour's 'ultimate purpose' was 'the establishment of the Socialist Commonwealth'. This was to be built by the public ownership of a significant proportion of the nation's productive assets, planning, an extensive housing programme, a National Health Service, full employment and social protection for the mass of the population. The mood of the whole Labour movement in the summer of 1945 was one of jubilation: not only had the Party swept to power with a huge majority which imparted it great moral authority but the new cabinet consisted mainly of seasoned veterans equipped with a degree of self-confidence in their capacity to run the country and introduce major social changes unique in Labour's history. But it inherited economic and social problems of the utmost severity. A large proportion of the (thoroughly inadequate) pre-war housing stock had been damaged or destroyed by bombing raids and hardly any building or repairs had occurred. Much of the country's plant and industrial machinery was worn out or obsolescent and a vast programme of retooling was required to reconvert wartime productive capacity to peaceful use. The economy had been strained almost to breaking point by the relentless demands of wartime mobilization. During the war Britain's national wealth had shrunk by one quarter and the bulk of overseas foreign assets, upon whose whose earnings the country had been reliant to maintain balance of payments equilibrium, had been liquidated to finance the war effort (Morgan, 1984: 144). Sterling and dollar liabilities amounted to £3,500 million and the UK was weighed down by the largest external debt in its history, with exports comprising less than 30 per cent of their pre-war volume, and with acute shortages of such vital materials as steel, timber, coal as well as of skilled manpower (Robinson, 1986: 166, 169). Markets had been lost and the country lacked the means to purchase essential imports of food and raw materials. In Keynes' succinct phrase, the incoming Labour Government faced what could be described 'without exaggeration' as a 'financial Dunkirk' (Cairncross, 1985: 10).

The British economy had been sustained since 1941 by the Lend-Lease programme by which the Americans had provided dollars to allow the UK to mobilize fully for war without worrying about its external account. Labour's new cabinet had scarcely settled into its new places before this artery was cut.[1] The new Government with all its heady ambition confronted the grim reality that vital imports could only be purchased, draconian cuts in consumption averted and the process of reconstruction begun if the US could be persuaded to help (Cairncross, 1985: 6–10). Whilst output of peace-time goods and investment had withered in Britain – and in virtually all the rest of Europe – after years of war, the American economy, already in 1939 the largest in the world, had expanded by leaps and bounds and was by far the largest supplier of industrial goods and foodstuffs, all after 1945 in desperately short supply. Finding ways of plugging the dollar gap dominated every thought, every action of the Labour Cabinet since upon this all its plans hinged.

A delegation was dispatched to Washington to negotiate an aid package, headed by the UK's most eminent economist, Lord Keynes. Initially, Keynes was optimistic,[2] but even if President Truman had been more inclined to treat the war-time partner generously, Congress (whose importance both officials and ministers in the UK constantly underrated) was full of politicians reluctant to relax their grip on America's purse-strings and deeply mistrustful of the new socialist Government with its 'wasteful' and 'extravagant' social schemes.[3] Long and painful negotiating sessions followed in which Labour ministers were forced to contemplate – as Dalton recalled – a transition:

> slowly and with a bad grace and with increasing irritation, from a free gift to an interest-free loan, and from this again to a loan bearing interest; from a larger to a smaller total of aid; and from the prospect of loose strings . . . to the most unwilling acceptance of strings so tight that they might strangle our trade and, indeed, our whole economic life. (Pimlott, 1985: 431)

The alternative to accepting the Loan, on the conditions prescribed by the Americans, appeared to be so dismal that the Cabinet concluded that it had no option but to sign. In fact, the interest rate and schedule for repayment of the loan were not unreasonable: the real hostage to fortune was American insistence that Britain returned to sterling convertibility within a year after the ratification of the loan. In a world avid for dollars to purchase American goods, a measure permitting sterling-holders to exchange British for US currency was bound to lead to massive sterling sales and a full-scale foreign exchange crisis. However, the determination of US officials to establish as rapidly as possible a liberal, multilateral world financial system, coupled with the soothing but wrong-headed assurances of UK Treasury officials, many of them sympathetic to

American goals, pushed the new Labour Government onto a most hazardous course.

The breezy self-confidence – epitomized above all by Dalton – of the first eighteen months of Labour's rule received its first major blow with the coal crisis of the winter of 1946–7. An alarming coal shortage, which the complacent Minister of Fuel, Manny Shinwell, had failed to foresee, was seriously exacerbated by one of the coldest winters of the century. With coal stocks plunging to a dangerously low level, industry began to grind to a halt and millions were for a time laid off. Unpleasant as the episode was, it was but a precursor to the financial crisis of what Dalton dubbed *annus horribilis*. Throughout 1947 the precious dollars provided by the US Loan drained away at an accelerating pace. Imports ran at a level higher than anticipated, inflation in the US pushed up the cost of imports, dollars leaked out of the sterling area and above all Britain's overseas commitments made heavy demands on hard currency. By March 1947 an increasingly anxious Dalton was telling the cabinet that 'we were racing through our United States dollar credit at a reckless and ever-accelerating speed' and warning of 'a looming shadow of catastrophe' (quoted in Cairncross, 1985: 131). However, the Chancellor's urgent pleas failed to rouse the other key figures in the Government, Attlee, Bevin and Morrison (Cairncross, 1985: 137–8). So the Government hit the rapids of convertibility and, with sterling holders free to trade British for US currency, the loss of dollars became unstoppable and convertibility was almost immediately suspended in August 1947.

The convertibility crisis 'tore the whole financial credibility of the Labour Government into shreds' (Morgan, 1984: 347). The drain of dollars only ended with Dalton's November 1947 budget which inaugurated the period of 'austerity' so much associated with his successor, Cripps. Dollar imports were cut back sharply, food subsidies frozen and purchase and profits tax raised. Reining back purchases of American goods, agreed only after 'much furious argument' in cabinet led to reductions in rations for meat, sugar and other foodstuffs (Morgan, 1984: 347) and consumer purchasing power fell significantly. Popular faith in the Attlee Government plummeted. Many people were bewildered and angered by rationing even tougher than had existed during the war – failing to appreciate the extent to which the war-time economy had survived through American largess. The self-confidence of Labour ministers themselves was badly shaken. Much of the serious deterioration in Britain's economic position in 1947, culminating in the convertibility crisis, was the result of a foreign policy 'which obviously exceeded the country's economic capacity' (Gardner 1969: 309). In early 1946, Keynes had given vent to his fears that the American Loan would be used 'to maintain our military prestige overseas and, generally speaking, to cut a dash in the world considerably above our means' (Tomlinson, 1989: 6). His fears were justified. With the American Loan shrinking at an alarming rate, Dalton volleyed the cabinet with demands to cut the overseas commitments which were eating up much of the country's vital hard currency reserves. These demands, Dalton recalled, 'often met stubborn and sometimes quite stupid resistance' (Dalton, 1962: 70). 'Given the straits to which the British economy was reduced in 1947, where it was necessary to ration even bread and potatoes, an outflow of capital equal to about 8 per cent of net national income and nearly equal to total net domestic capital formation (including stock-building) is a very extraordinary event. It was certainly not the purpose for which the American and Canadian loans were procured' (Cairncross, 1985: 153).

The official defence was that if Britain had cut back its international commitments, a vacuum would have been left into which the Soviets would have poured. Bevin was 'bombarded from the Foreign Office with pessimistic diagnoses of the long-term ideological roots and urge for world expansion of the Soviet leaders, inherent in their Marxist-Leninist philosophy' (Morgan, 1984: 244). His officials had little need to persuade, since Bevin was only too ready to adopt this simplistic view. But the thesis that the USSR was bent on world conquest – denied by critics on the left at the time – is not one that is now given much credence, not least because the crippling losses Russia had suffered during the war, infinitely greater than its chief adversary, the United States, rendered it quite incapable of such a move.[4] The decisive consideration was Labour's insistence on upholding Britain's status as a world power rather than fear of Soviet expansionism. It was for this reason that the cabinet majority – ignoring objections from Dalton and Bevin – were convinced of the need to maintain a large military establishment, a ring of overseas military bases dotted throughout the world and a strong naval presence (Morgan, 1984: 279). Dalton himself was soon to resign, for a reason (a minor budget leak) which by today's standards of ministerial conduct seems idiosyncratic. In truth, his personal authority had been battered because of the crisis and he may well have felt relieved to quit. Eventually it was to be the provision of Marshall Aid – the highly imaginative act of enlightened self-interest by which the US pumped millions of dollars in grants in aid into the ailing economies of western Europe – which furnished the dollars that, as a senior economic advisor later recalled, saved the country 'in the nick of time' (Robinson, 1986: 173).

Socialism and Public Ownership

In 1946, speaking as the first prime minister to preside over a Labour majority, Attlee assured Party conference that the new government was 'resolved to carry out as rapidly and energetically as we can the distinctive side of Labour's programme: our socialist policy, our policy of nationalisation' (quoted in Beer, 1965: 134). The interim report *The Old World and the New Society* had argued that 'we have learnt in the war that the anarchy of private consumption must give way to ordered planning under national control. That lesson is no less applicable to peace. The Labour Party therefore urges that the nation must own and operate the essential instruments of production, their power over our lives is too great for them to be left in private hands' (Taylor 1991: 8). By 1951 an extensive portion of industry had been brought into public ownership, including coal, the railways, cable and wireless, much of road haulage, civil aviation, gas, electricity and iron and steel, employing over 2,300,000 people and responsible for a very sizeable percentage of overall investment (Cairncross, 1985: 466).

The anticipated gains of nationalization included the redistribution of wealth, full employment, an effective system of economic planning, improved status and conditions for the workforce and greater efficiency. It had long been a basic socialist tenet that the private ownership of productive resources, by allowing a narrow stratum of property-holders to profit from dividends and the appreciation of capital values, lay at the root of massive disparities of wealth. However, public ownership would only transfer capital wealth to the community if two conditions were met: the industries nationalized were profitable and compensation was strictly limited – but neither were. Leaving aside the utilities (already in part publicly owned through the municipalities) nationalization was mainly confined to the least profitable industries whilst compensation was granted on terms 'which, in retrospect, seems almost inconceivably generous' (Morgan, 1984: 109). Provisions for the railways afforded a 'bonanza for the stock exchange' (Nigel Davenport, a City columnist, quoted in Morgan, 1984:136), shareholders in the Bank of England were treated 'particularly generously', whilst the coal owners received ample reward for years of incompetent management (Leruez, 1975: 42; Morgan, 1984: 109).

Proponents of public ownership hoped that established workplace hierarchies would be challenged and more participative forms of organization introduced. However, few changes were made, as Morrison insisted on traditional forms of management. The new public corporations were bureaucratically-structured, with traditional status divisions between management and workforce perpetuated. Existing internal-decision making were left largely intact with about 75 per cent of the members of the new boards of the nationalized industries and all but one of the chairmen drawn from the private sector (Addison, 1977: 51; Leruez, 1975: 66).

In his influential interpretation of the Attlee Government, Beer argues that the 'principal case' for public ownership was public control over the economy and that 'nationalisation and economic planning were logically interdependent in socialist thought' (Beer, 1965: 190). Attlee himself declared in 1945 that 'fundamentally nationalisation had got to go ahead because it fell in with the planning, the essential planning of the country' (Beer, 1965: 190). In practice, nationalization was 'not closely linked at any stage with the idea of economic planning' (Cairncross, 1985: 464). Morrison's insistence upon the autonomy and managerial independence of the new public corporations rendered the notion of nationalization as means of planning a 'chimera' (Tomlinson, 1992: 161). Indeed 'Labour failed to see the possibilities of using the new public sector as a way of steering the whole economy in the direction they desired. They behaved as if, while carrying through their plans for nationalization, they had no understanding of the real meaning of what they had done. Ownership had changed; power did not' (Leruez, 1975: 75). For an institution intended to be the centre-piece of a socialist economic system, astonishing little thought had been given as to how precisely the public corporation would operate. 'The details of organizational structure, finance, the compensation of private stockholders, pricing policy, the system of consultation with the workers, the relation to the consumer – all were left studiously vague' (Morgan, 1984: 97). Far from being an act of political boldness the nationalization programme was introduced by 'a set of rather conservative politicians whose main anxiety was to secure efficient management and give it a fairly free hand provided it followed commercial precedents' (Cairncross, 1985: 494).

The strategic weakness of the public ownership programme was part caused and part reflected the ad hoc fashion in which the list of industries due to be nationalized was compiled – mostly as a result of pressure from the industry's union or in response to particular problems in the industries themselves. Most suffered from inadequate investment, incompetent management and monopoly control – and in virtually all cases official commissions of enquiry had at some time recommended nationalization. The one major exception was iron and steel. Morrison had opposed its incorporation into the 1945 manifesto and conducted a stubborn rear-guard effort for it to be dropped. The more leftist ministers were joined by Dalton, but the grounds upon which Dalton and, eventually Attlee, backed nationalization were never very clear though there was, in fact, a solid economic case for the measure (Morgan, 1984: 111–12, 120). In the final analysis, it seems that political factors (the balance of opinion within the cabinet and the desire to maintain cohesion within the party) were probably decisive. But steel was *sui generis*: it neither featured as part of a broader economic strategy nor did it presage a further advance into the profitable sectors of manufacturing industry.[5]

The bureaucratic model of nationalization both at the time and subsequently was widely criticized for its failure to develop more democratic forms of organization, its insensitivity to consumer demand and the inefficiency of monopoly forms of organization. Gaitskell at the time worried that the new public corporations would be 'slow, cumbersome, impersonal and probably slightly conservative' (quoted in Chick, 1991: 65). He and others called for a more decentralized and flexible structure with, where suitable, a measure of competition within nationalized industries. This was blocked by Morrison who strongly favoured a centralized structure, because it appealed to his sense of bureaucratic neatness and it eased the transfer of assets on vesting day (Chick, 1991: 65–6). All this was to store up trouble for the future. However, the flaws of the new corporations should not be exaggerated. Their performance stood comparison with either their privately-owned counterparts in other economies or with the private sector in Britain. 'In terms of efficiency, the gas and electricity supply industries were both to emerge as impressive models of public enterprise' whilst by 1952 the National Coal Board was profitable *and* working conditions had vastly improved (Morgan, 1984: 138, 139).

Planning

Herbert Morrison, the responsible minister, claimed that Britain 'was the first great nation to attempt to combine large-scale social and economic planning with a full measure of individual rights and liberties. Planning as it is taking shape in this country under our eyes, is something new and constructively revolutionary' and a 'vital' contribution to civilization (quoted in Donoughue and Jones, 1973: 353).[6] Labour inherited from the war-time economy a formidable apparatus of direct controls. During the war years, the ambit of the state had vastly increased as in the drive to mobilize the nation's resources ' a comprehensive set of controls, covering investment, consumption, and prices, manpower, trade and foreign exchange' was installed (Tomlinson, 1992: 159). To Labour the success of the war-time economy proved the effectiveness of government direction of the economy.

The defining characteristic of economic planning, Tomlinson has suggested, is the attempt by state agencies 'to determine the composition of output (and hence of investment) according to some strategic goal related to the long-run growth of the economy' (Tomlinson, 1989: 14). In the 1930s the view that the market was inherently defective and exploitative had become a canon of socialist belief. But whilst Labour's notion of planning in 1945 did indeed 'embrace the idea of substantial state allocation of resources', war-time controls were retained primarily to cope with shortages of goods and sparse supplies of hard currency (Tomlinson, 1992: 159; Tomlinson, 1989: 14). Morrison was content to use the tested war-time machinery to tackle the acute problems bequeathed by the war and displayed little interest in the use of planning to foster economic modernization (Leruez, 1975: 38, 43–4). The author of the most exhaustive analysis of the Attlee Administration concluded that 'planning, in any meaningful sense, played no prominent part in the government's economic strategy either in the cheap money period of Dalton or the corporate partnership of the Cripps era from late 1947' (Morgan, 1984: 492; see also Cunningham, 1993: 13).

The crises of 1947 prompted major doubts about the effectiveness of the economic policy-making process and led to a radical shake-up of the planning machinery as well as, in due course, to a reorientation of economic strategy. Three new planning institutions were created: the Central Economic Planning Staff (CEPS), the Economic Planning Board (EPB) and a new Ministry of Economic Affairs, headed by Stafford Cripps, with the task of overseeing economic planning. Shortly after, Dalton resigned and was replaced as Chancellor by Cripps who, combining the two posts, emerged as the acknowledged economic supremo, equipped with the powers – denied to Morrison and Dalton – to direct overall economic policy. CEPS was led by Sir Edwin Plowden as Chief Planning Officer. According to Attlee, henceforth planning would seek 'to enable decisions to be reached as to the best allocation of available man-power, materials, services and manufacturing capacity' and the primary task of CEPS was to 'develop the long-term plan for the use of the country's man-power and resources' (Cairncross, 1985: 325–6). In fact, CEPS operated primarily as a co-ordinating mechanism and source of expertise and advice on current economic policy (Leruez, 1975: 49). The Economic Planning Board was charged with helping in the preparation of a long-term economic plan (Plowden, 1989: 12). In form it was a quasi-corporatist body. Composed of representatives from the TUC, employers, senior civil servants and members of CEPS, it sought to involve both sides of industry, in an advisory capacity, in economic policy-making (Leruez, 1975: 49). In practice it developed into a talking-shop, seldom took policy initiatives, attracted little interest from ministers, and met less and less frequently, with an ever smaller attendance (Plowden, 1989: 23). Much of the work of CEPS in its first year consisting of the drawing up of a long-term plan.[7] This was completed in September 1948 but its aspirations were modest. A plan at the very least must operate as a frame of reference for ministers and their advisors, setting the parameters for economic policy-formation. The *Long Term Programme* never even performed this function (Leruez, 1975: 59).

The reorganization of 1947 in fact marked a retreat from planning. As a top government adviser recalled, after 1947 'we turned more and more to demand-management rather than direct intervention in the allocation of resources' whilst planning such as it was 'came increasingly to be expressed in terms of the management of demand in a Keynesian macroeconomic manner in order to counterbalance the natural cyclical behaviour of the economy' (Plowden, 1989: 51, 168). Yet during this period, France and Japan in their different ways harnessed the power of the state to promote industrial modernization – in both cases coming in due course to enjoy more success than Britain. They recognized that the key to an effective state-led industrial strategy was not the ownership of 'basic' – in practice, careworn – industries like coal but control over the flow of credit and investment (Zysman, 1983: 77, 80–1). Initially, Labour appeared to understand this too. *Let Us face the Future* proposed the establishment of a National Investment Board to enable it to 'determine social priorities and promote better timing in private investment' (Craig, 1975: 126). It would be armed with the powers to 'license and direct investment into specific concerns and mobilize available financial resources' as well as to co-ordinate all public capital expenditure. 'Effectively, the Board would be the focal point of the state-managed economy' (Taylor, 1993: 15). This idea had been much discussed by socialist economists in the 1930s, and Dalton, in his book *Practical Socialism* described the National Investment Board as 'one of the most effective instruments of Socialist planning and national development' (Pimlott, 1985: 218).

Dalton had rejected the nationalization of the banking system on the grounds that public ownership of the Bank of England would suffice to secure control over the financial system (Pimlott, 1985: 458). In fact very little came of this. A rare Labour sympathizer in the City later wrote: 'We had found Labour politicians talking of how they would seize "the commanding heights of the economy" . . . We had tried to explain to them that "the commanding heights of the economy" were all to be found within the square mile of the City clustered around and about the Bank of England . . . But what Dalton did was a great nonevent' (quoted in Hennessy, 1993: 203–4). There was virtually no change in the board of governors of the Bank and the Governor, the highly conservative Lord Catto, was simply reappointed. No attempt was made to alter the composition or functioning of the Bank, or to use its power to gain greater control over the City or capital movements. Nationalization of the Bank amounted to 'a nominal shift of power to the state; in practice, business-as-usual' (Hennessy, 1993: 204).

Not surprisingly, there was hardly a murmur of dissent from the Conservatives: 'nothing of consequence changed, and neither the City nor the Stock Exchange was unduly worried, for it was obvious that the financial community would continue to operate much as it had done in the past' (Leruez, 1975: 42). Although a National Investment Council and a Capital Issues Committee were established in 1946 to co-ordinate private sector investment and savings policy they were staffed almost entirely by members of the financial establishment. The Attlee Government's policy 'in this crucially important area' was 'timid' and 'a major asset in creating effective planning was virtually thrown away' (Leruez, 1975: 43).

How can we account for the Labour Cabinet's failure to use state power more effectively? One problem faced by exponents of planning was that 'interventionist policies ran against the training and traditions of the bureaucracy' (Zysman, 1983: 202). In December 1945 an official paper entitled *A Central Economic Planning Staff* explained that 'The Whitehall machine is naturally enough ill-suited in many respects to handle the type of central integration demanded by this new function [of planning]. The spirit in which the job must be tackled is quite new and antipathetic to the civil service.' This was particularly the case in the Treasury, at the very heart of policy-formation, whose historic role, the control of public expenditure, bred an innate preference for limited government. Some senior officials were described as having 'a clear and deep-seated instinct to minimise economic intervention and to balance the Budget, which is the abnegation of positive economic control' (Barker, 1986: 478). The decision to appoint as the Government's Chief Planning Officer Sir Edwin Plowden (an industrialist) reflected Labour's reluctance to disturb established economic institutions. He stated frankly that 'to me the idea of planning and control for its own sake was unrealistic, both politically and economically. It was our job to plan so that we might return the economy to a more normal state of affairs where consumer sovereignty would be re-established. Planning was a means by which we could overcome the enormous effects of the war on our nation' (Plowden, 1989: 46). Robert Hall, the Director of the Cabinet's Economic Section and chief economic adviser who worked very closely with Plowden shared his view. Indeed he 'seemed to have seen their role as being to deflect the Government from its excessive attachment to *dirigiste* policies' (Tomlinson, 1993a: 13).[8]

The views of senior officials were important because the policy system in Britain was (until recently) unique amongst western countries in the degree to which it affords the largely self-regulating civil service a virtual monopoly in the provision of expertise and advice. The Cabinet demonstrated the utmost conservatism in its approach to institutional questions. Thus it refrained from any reforms which might have augmented the capacity of the state to act as a source of innovative economic ideas, such as the introduction of outside experts, French-style ministerial *cabinets* or new forms of training civil servants (along the lines, for example, of the *Ecole Nationale d'Administration* established by the de Gaulle government in the aftermath of the War). It failed to recognize that more interventionist purposes could not simply be tacked on to the existing state structure. Whatever its strengths, 'it wasn't a "can do" organization like its French equivalent, highly trained and motivated thanks to the *grandes écoles*, especially the new post-war one, custom-built for the purpose, the *Ecole Nationale d'Administration*' (Hennessy, 1993: 380). Why did the Government display such little interest in reform? One reason was that the state machine's effective war-time performance, which most senior ministers had witnessed as members of the coalition government, persuaded them that little needed to be changed. 'They knew the wartime machine personally and liked what they saw' (Hennessy, 1989: 137). This experience confirmed their instincts since Labour's ascendant right generally shared the admiration that the Webbs had felt for the British political system. Furthermore, Labour's leaders were practical people looking for practical solutions: if the machine worked, why tamper with it?

An additional constraining factor was the animosity of business to interventionist strategies. The assumption that a substantial developmental role for the state was not compatible with a market economy and private entrepreneurial activity came naturally to a business culture imbued with nineteenth-century liberal assumptions. This is illustrated by the response to the efforts that were made by the Government – notably by Cripps at the Board of Trade from 1945 to 1947 – to tackle the serious problems of low productivity and lack of innovation in industry. Various bodies designed to enhance corporate efficiency were established but although industrialists served on them – Cripps himself stated that 'to do things by compulsion is far less effective than to do them by agreement' – business reacted with considerable suspicion (Leruez,

1975: 68; Morgan, 1984: 128). Government policy was denounced by the main employers' organization, the Federation of British Industry, as an unacceptable abridgement of managerial prerogatives. As a result, little was achieved and 'the whole episode represented a complete defeat for the government at the hands of private industry' (Mercer, 1993: 81–3). Furthermore, the extensive range of physical controls inherited from war-time were less impressive as a means of inducing industry to co-operate than they appeared on the surface since the control system was largely administered by trade associations and staffed by personnel from the private sector. The reliance upon the private sector extended to the government machine itself: for example the Principal Adviser to the Board of Trade was chairman of the Rayon Federation and the Ministry of Food was full of commodity company directors (Saville, 1993: 46). Morgan concluded that 'the degree of control exercised by the government over private industry, including such vital areas as the direction of exports, the level of wages and profits, vital aspects of long-term investment, was very limited' (Morgan, 1984: 129).

The conciliatory stance by economics ministers towards industry also reflected their own beliefs. Labour's right, which dominated the Attlee Government, adhered to an essentially consensual view of society that bred a preference for co-operative solutions. 'As one dedicated to the values of the mixed economy, with all the zeal of a convert, Cripps sought above all to collaborate with private industry rather than to coerce or threaten' (Morgan, 1987: 170). This inhibited any firm action to restructure industry (Tomlinson, 1989: 21). Indeed Cripps' main objective 'was to restore confidence in industry by partnership rather than by planned direction' (Morgan, 1984: 367). During the 1930s, Labour's leaders had toyed with more radical economic policies because it seemed then that only public ownership and planning could eradicate mass unemployment and poverty. If Keynesian fiscal policy could, by sustaining high levels of demand, secure full employment and steady output growth, then a more collectivist approach seemed redundant. As a result, as the former Chief Planning Officer commented, 'the unthought-out and nebulous concept of "democratic planning", with its implication of detailed intervention which Labour had propounded in 1945, fell by the wayside' (Plowden, 1989: 168). 'Demand management, rather than intervention to control the use of resources directly or improve their efficiency was the order of the day' (Cairncross, 1985: 328).

Austerity

The lean and ascetic Stafford Cripps, who replaced the ebullient Dalton as Chancellor in November 1947, was determined to bring public expenditure under tighter control and to hold back personal consumption in the drive to boost production and exports (Morgan, 1984: 363). The claim that 'Old Labour' neglected the needs of the productive economy is particularly wide of the mark when applied to the Attlee Government. Personal consumption was remorselessly squeezed and imports rigorously controlled to enable resources to be poured into exports and capital investment in industry (Plowden, 1989: 35–6). Controls were used at home to direct resources into investment and industries with a high export potential and abroad to concentrate limited hard currency on food and raw materials, at the expense of consumer goods. By 1948 these efforts appeared to be bearing fruit as production and exports forged ahead and the overall balance of payments moved into surplus. By 1949, with the invaluable help of funds from the Marshall aid programme, impressive progress had been made. 'Exports (by volume) had risen from 50% below the prewar level to nearly 55% above, and paid for 85% of exports instead of one-third . . . Industrial production by volume in the first half of 1949 was 30% above 1938, and output per man-hour had since the war increased faster than in the United States' (Williams, 1982: 142).

But life is never smooth, even for the virtuous. Later that year, the US economy slipped into recession, shrinking the market for British exports and straining the dollar reserves. Sterling weakened dangerously and with senior officials in Washington intimating it was over-valued an avalanche of selling with distracting speed brought it to its knees (Plowden, 1989: 54). In consternation the Cabinet was forced to consider devaluation. This was deemed not to be simply a technical matter, for the integrity of sterling had been the pillar of the British imperial order, of the UK's prestige as a major international power and of the City's role as a world financial centre. With Cripps extremely ill, Bevin also ailing, Morrison at sea over economic matters, and Attlee offering little leadership, a prominent part was played, most unusually, by more junior ministers: Hugh Gaitskell (Cripps's deputy, though not even in the Cabinet), Harold Wilson, the President of the Board of Trade, and Douglas Jay (another junior Treasury minister). Though

Wilson wobbled, Gaitskell and Jay became convinced that devaluation was inevitable and eventually persuaded Attlee. There then followed a period of protracted discussions over the type of measures needed to be taken to ensure that devaluation worked.

Senior officials within the Treasury and the Bank of England, and the Government's top economic advisers, all repeatedly urged that devaluation be coupled with (in Hall's words) 'a stiff dose of disinflation' – substantial reductions in public spending and a tighter monetary stance (Cairncross, 1985: 189–93). According to the Bank of England, 'Britain's financial credibility and stability could be restored only by drastic action to cut public expenditure, particularly on food subsidies and the National Health Service, and a deferment of further nationalization plans' (Plowden, 1989: 57). Significantly, the Attlee Government – unlike its successors – adamantly resisted measures that would have seriously curtailed its welfare programmes and endangered jobs. Gaitskell and Jay resented the 'very heavy [pressure] from all official quarters "to do something else" as well as devaluation . . . What they all want is a slash in public expenditure on social services' (Gaitskell Diary, quoted in Williams, 1982: 146). Dalton, by then back in the Cabinet, complained: 'in spite of all our Cabinet discussions and decisions, the officials . . . put up a brief for ministers, immediately before they were due to leave for Washington, with all the old stuff about the "need to restore confidence" and hence to make large reductions, including changes of policy, in public expenditure . . . HG [Gaitskell] and DJ [Jay] fought this out . . . ' (quoted in Williams, 1982: 147). After a meeting of the Economic Policy Committee in July 1949 officials were asked to leave the room and Cripps then proceeded to tell his ministerial colleagues that he did not trust his own officials and advisers in the Treasury who adhered strongly to notions of the 'free economy' (Cairncross, 1985: 189). In November, Hall wrote in his diary that Cripps had told Plowden that 'he felt suspicious of all his advisers and had to read all their stuff to see that they did not slip anything over on him that was flatly against his party beliefs' (Cairncross, 1989: 63–4). Attlee, similarly, complained to Dalton that he was being 'served up from the Treasury and the Bank arguments which he thinks are fallacious on the evil effects of our public expenditure' (quoted in Cairncross, 1985: 189). To Labour ministers, even those who saw merit in its analysis, the Treasury seemed unduly keen to scythe through social programmes. 'There has, indeed, seldom been a time when ministers have been more suspicious of their civil servants' (Pimlott, 1992: 146–7).

Eventually ministers reluctantly assented to a (modest) package of cuts but this fell considerably short of what their advisers wanted.[9] However, though 'no fresh measures were taken . . . by the end of the year the gold reserves had recovered strongly and the gold and dollar deficit had virtually ceased'. Despite the heavier cost of imports, the rise in prices was modest (Cairncross, 1985: 196, 199). As one of the main players acknowledged, a little grudgingly, although the financial measures accompanying devaluation 'were by no means as wide-ranging as they should have been, its results were satisfactory in terms of both the short and longer term' and 'fears of a wage-price spiral's eroding the benefits of a lower exchange rate proved unfounded' (Plowden, 1989: 68, 67). The consequences which officials predicted if a tighter fiscal stance was not enforced did not, in short, materialize. To the contrary, as Cairncross concludes in his definitive account, the much-need shift in exports to dollar markets occurred without clamping down on domestic demand; inflation did not increase and the politicians 'had largely avoided the cuts in public expenditure that their advisors kept insisting were indispensable'. Devaluation achieved its objectives of stopping the dollar drain and the advantages that accrued to Britain's competitive position outlasted the crisis of the Korean War (Cairncross, 1985: 207, 211; Morgan, 1984: 386–7; Plowden, 1989: 69–70).

The episode exhibited some notable features of the Attlee Government: the determination with which they adhered to their two main goals of full employment and enhanced social welfare; the self-confidence with which they resisted official advice, and their willingness to challenge the postulates upon which that advice was founded. Hence they constantly queried the Treasury's insistence that inflationary pressures were the chief threat to economic stability and growth, and its calls for major cuts in public spending (Cairncross, 1985: 411). In these respects, the post-war Government exhibited a radicalism and strength of purpose that were not to be emulated by its successors. Nevertheless, the role of sterling as the emblem of British power and prestige meant that devaluation was treated as a national humiliation – despite the fact that its economic effects were almost wholly positive. The opposition was appalled, the City professed horror at this stain on the country's reputation inflicted by a feckless socialist administration and the government was left feeling guilty of a culpable act.

The Government and the Unions

Throughout the Attlee Government, relations with the unions were amicable and the frictions that inevitably arose never – as happened with its two successors – deteriorated into serious clashes. The main problem was over inflationary pressures with the Government constantly exhorting the unions to temper their wage claims, especially after the crises of 1947. Treasury officials proposed the imposition of a statutory wage freeze but were unable to persuade ministers. In February a White Paper, a *Statement on Personal Incomes, Costs and Prices*, was issued. It recommended a voluntary freeze of wage rates and incomes from profit and rent, though allowing flexibility in cases of labour shortages and productivity gains. Initially, the unions had been strongly opposed to any form of wage regulation, but Arthur Deakin, the powerful leader of the TGWU shifted his view in 1947 because of growing concern with inflation. Hence the White Paper aroused less antagonism than might have been expected, given that 'artificial curbs on wage negotiations went against the entire thrust of collective bargaining as the trade unions . . . had understood it for generations' (Plowden, 1989: 37–8; Morgan, 1984: 373). Though union leaders resented the Government's failure to consult them they arranged a special conference which voted to accept the freeze. To signal that all were expected to make sacrifices Cripps announced a capital levy on investment income. Labour MPs wanted this to become permanent but Treasury officials were perturbed about its impact on industrial confidence and Plowden eventually managed to convince Cripps that the levy should be a 'once and for all' measure and should be scaled down 'to a level more acceptable to City and industrial opinion' (Plowden, 1989: 38). Workers, however, shouldered their share of the sacrifices: between 1947 and 1950 the index of wages moved from 100 to 110, that of retail prices from 100 to 113 and that of food prices from 100 to 121.3 (Coates, 1991: 162). In the eighteen months between the issue of the White Paper and devaluation wages rose only by only 3 per cent per annum and the following year by a mere 1.4 per cent (Plowden, 1989: 38, 69). Gradually, rank and file resistance mounted and the policy buckled in 1950 as costs rose faster due to the Korean war. But there was no flood of pay claims and to the end of the Government 'a broad policy of restraint in the pursuit of wage increases was followed by major unions . . . In effect, the wage freeze . . . was continued with trade-union blessing for three vital years' (Morgan, 1984: 373). Despite a rash of unofficial action, harmony generally prevailed on the industrial front. Not only were the unions amenable over pay restraint they also co-operated, as far as membership feeling allowed them to, in the Government's drive to increase production and productivity 'with remarkable results' (Tomlinson, 1993b: 94–5). The main organized opposition to Government policies came from Communists and the Cold War atmosphere then taking hold enabled the union leadership to isolate them.

The degree of loyalty exhibited by the unions derived from a range of sources: they were largely headed by people who shared the same outlook and priorities as the Government; they perceived Party and unions as the 'industrial and political wings of the movement', partners engaged in a common enterprise – a conviction affirmed by the Government's commitment to 'fair shares' and the many other efforts it made to improve the level and quality of living conditions for the working class; and the solidity of the links were fortified by the maintenance of close personal and institutional relations binding them together. Finally, union leaders could feel confident that their rank and file stood behind them, reflecting the widespread sentiments of class solidarity and the sense of allegiance to 'our Labour Government'.

The Welfare State

The most significant achievement of the Attlee Government was the creation of the welfare state. Despite the tenuous finances of the country, despite the huge and multiple pressure for funds, despite indeed the criticism of many economists that heavy public spending was stoking-up inflation and endangering recovery, the Labour Cabinet persevered in the task of erecting a fabric of social protection that, for years, was regarded as one of social democracy's finest accomplishments. 'From 1945–51 onwards, Labour's central political faith, its prime claim to be the unique custodian of the progressive idea, lay with its inextricable identification with the rise and decline of the welfare state' (Morgan, 1984: 187). The jewel in the crown was the National Health Service. It was one of the Government's 'outstanding triumphs, admired throughout the world, an immense landmark in the building of the welfare state' (Morgan, 1984: 162). The Minister of Health responsible for steering the reform through was the controversial and mercurial left-winger, Aneurin Bevan: 'no other politician's name [became] so uniquely or firmly attached to a great British institution' (Hennessy 1992: 133). The establishment of a universal, free health service where treatment would be determined by need rather than ability to pay enshrined fundamental socialist values. It was difficult to believe that a Conservative government would have mustered the determination – borne out of his deep, philosophical commitment to the idea – displayed by Bevan to overcome the vehement objections of much of the medical profession.

Throughout long and complex negotiations, the British Medical Association (BMA) was stubborn and un-cooperative, castigating the Minister's scheme as a threat to the professional freedom and integrity of GPs. Bevan strove to accommodate the BMA as much as possible, for instance by agreeing to abandon Labour's plan for a full-time salaried medical service but the BMA was unrelenting and in ballots of GPs organized by the Association in December 1946 and February 1948 large majorities of doctors indicated their unwillingness to participate in the National Health Service (Morgan, 1984: 156–60). The BMA tended to reflect the views of the wealthier members of the profession and there were always doubts as to how representative it was of the average doctor. But Bevan felt he had no option, if he was to circumvent its opposition, but to strike up an alliance with the consultants, the established elite within the profession. But the price was high: special status was granted to top teaching hospitals, where many senior consultants worked. Pay beds, or private practice within hospitals, was permitted, and consultants were allowed to award themselves 'merit awards' which gave a very considerable boost to their income (Lowe, 1993: 172). In Bevan's own graphic metaphor, he secured the support of consultants by 'stuffing their mouths with gold' (Hill, 1993: 33). Not only was their income and status enhanced, but as a result of their privileged position in the new NHS they were able, in the name of 'professional judgment' and 'clinical objectivity', to advance their professional self-interest. 'From the outset the National Health Service was exceptionally deferential to medical interests and could only be implemented by a further concession to medical power' (Hill, 1993: 35). In consequence, Labour's hopes of giving much higher priority to preventative health services were never realized (Lowe, 1993: 174). However, on some issues, Bevan stood firm. He succeeded in eliminating most of the commercial aspects of health care, such as the sale of practices and also in abolishing the system of contributory health insurance which, although it was less cost-effective, was retained by all other western countries.

The construction of the National Health service by no means ended Bevan's struggles. Its finances proved hard to control and very soon the Minister was under powerful pressure from the Treasury and other Cabinet members to clamp down on spending. The main problem – aside from the paucity of resources available – was the quite unrealistic expectations of many in the Government and the Treasury about the appropriate level of health expenditure, especially since so much ground needed to be made up. Bevan proved himself a doughty champion of the health budget, but it was this issue that was finally to terminate his career as a minister.

Bevan was also responsible for housing and here he encountered even more intractable problems. Labour's manifesto gave housing a very high priority not least because the heritage of poor, overcrowded living conditions for much of the working class was compounded by massive war-time damage to the housing stock. The speed at which houses could be built depended on the availability of materials but many of the building materials required could only be obtained by scarce dollar purchases, and precedence was often given to factories in the drive to maximize exports. Furthermore, there was a shortage of labour in the construction trades, in part because of the Government's insistence on maintaining a large military establishment. Bevan's knuckles were rapped by the Conservatives and the press for two choices he made. He insisted, firstly, that priority be given to the building of council houses and secondly – in his desire to narrow social class distinctions and prevent council houses being regarded as an inferior sort of accommodation for the 'lower orders' – that such housing be built to a high standard. 'For all that, the rehousing of several million people in new or renovated houses, at a time of extreme social and economic dislocation, was a considerable achievement' (Morgan, 1984: 170). The Conservatives, in their popular pledge to accelerate the housing programme whilst holding down costs, reduced the quality barrier, as did – for similar reasons – the Wilson Government of 1964–70 with its enthusiasm for high-rise flats. Not the least of history's ironies was the respective fate of much of the stock built by the two Labour administrations. Many high-rise flats have either been pulled down or become pools of squalor and deprivation as bad as the habitations they replaced. In contrast, much of the council accommodation built in the 1940s is now owner-occupied, bought by eager tenants under the Thatcher Government's sales of council house policy.

The other main element in the new welfare system aroused much less controversy than health or housing. With the National Insurance Act of 1946, Labour laid the basis of a system of comprehensive income support for those who, through unemployment or sickness, were deprived of an income. The legislation closely followed the seminal Beveridge Report which had been accepted by the war-time coalition. A minimum number of contributions had to be made before a recipient could qualify and a flat rate of benefit was payable. The provisions were a little more generous than those proposed by Beveridge though contributions were also slightly higher (Hill, 1993: 28–9). For those who were not eligible for insurance benefit, benefits could be drawn, as of right, under the National Assistance Act of 1948, which swept away the last vestiges of the hated Poor Laws. The reforms assumed the continuation of full employment, rising wage levels and the nuclear family where the male was the major bread winner. When these conditions ceased to hold, cracks in the system appeared though it was not until the mid-1970s that the legitimacy and viability of the welfare state came under sustained assault.

'Fair shares' was the guiding precept in other aspects of policy with the Government taking a number of steps to alleviate the burden of post-war austerity and reconstruction on those least capable of bearing it. Council house rents were kept low by government financial help whilst food subsidies were specifically designed to cut costs for the poorer section of the community. Though much misrepresented, then and later, the Government's retention of rationing also reflected its 'fair shares' ethos. The Government came under insistent pressure from the press, most economists and many of its own advisers to act more firmly against pent up inflationary forces by tightening fiscal policy (depressing demand by heavier personal taxation or cuts in public expenditure) and by freeing prices, allowing them to rise to soak up excess demand. However, ministers firmly resisted this advice because they were not prepared to price many goods out of the reach of lower income groups, regarding rationing as a more equitable way of distributing goods in short supply; nor were they willing to pursue an anti-inflationary strategy that endangered their programme of domestic social reform and risked a relapse into a recession and unemployment.

Rearmament

The early months of 1950 augured well. Devaluation had boosted the economy, exports and industrial production were rising steadily and the balance of payments had moved strongly into surplus. 'The economic news is uniformly good these days' pronounced *The Economist* in the summer of 1950. Labour's success in holding two highly marginal seats suggested that its electoral prospects were equally encouraging (Morgan, 1984: 411–12). But the storm clouds were massing. At dawn, on 25 June 1950, North Korean tanks crossed the 38th parallel, the border with South Korea, precipitating four years of war. Under the auspices of the United Nations Security Council (which Stalin was boycotting at the time) American troops, with a British contingent, were sent to repel the invasion. The Government's support for the American-sponsored action was almost universally backed within the Party. As fears of the spread of war mounted, Britain came under stiff pressure from the US to launch a major programme of rearmament. A programme costing £3,400 million (soon augmented to £3,600 million) was agreed by the Cabinet, though with growing disquiet within the Party, and, indeed, amongst some ministers. But the Truman Administration (engaged in a massive rearmament programme itself) insisted that the UK response was inadequate and promised generous assistance if the British military build-up was intensified. A mission was sent to Washington headed by Plowden. However, it soon became evident that, as Plowden recalled, assumptions made in Britain about the scale of American assistance were 'wildly optimistic' and only a particle of their requests would be met (Plowden, 1989: 97, 101).

Notwithstanding, the Treasury, which since devaluation had been pressing very hard for reductions in social spending, was able to convince the new Chancellor, Hugh Gaitskell, that an infinitely greater upsurge in expenditure, a massive defence budget of £4,700 million – a doubling of the pre-Korean level, amounting to no less than 14 per cent of GDP – was affordable (Plowden, 1989: 111). The problem was how to finance it. Gaitskell proposed a combination of cuts in personal consumption and public programmes, most controversially, the imposition of National Health Service charges. Bevan had recently been moved to the Ministry of Labour, greatly aggrieved that the Chancellorship had, after Cripps's resignation, been given to Gaitskell, a much more junior figure, rather than himself.[10] Disliking the new Chancellor – whom he dubbed 'a dessicated calculating machine' – he was furious when he insisted upon NHS charges. When Attlee indicated his backing for Gaitskell, Bevan shook the political world by resigning from the Government, along with another Cabinet member, Harold Wilson and a junior minister, John Freeman. The bitter Gaitskell–Bevan clash – which soon exploded into the most serious left–right split in the Party since the 1930s – was about far more than charges for dentures and spectacles. Much earlier, Bevan had expressed serious misgivings about the scale of rearmament (Plowden, 1989: 98). He argued in his resignation speech that the £4,700 million programme could not be achieved 'without irreparable damage' to the economy, indeed that, in view of shortages of materials, it was physically unattainable (Shaw, 1974: 215–16) points which Wilson, as former President of the Board of Trade, amplified with a wealth of data.

The Bevan–Gaitskell clash has been explored in immense detail (see especially, Williams, 1982; Foot, 1962) but, as Morgan comments, 'it cannot reasonably be disputed now that on the main issue Bevan and Wilson were right, and Gaitskell was wrong. The Budget of April 1951 may fairly be considered a political and economic disaster . . . ' (Morgan, 1984: 457). The programme was later wound down by the Churchill Government. The military build-up had dire economic and political consequences. 'The entire financial basis of the defence programme was quite misconceived' not least because the US-envisaged contribution never materialized. It amounted to a 'major assault' on the productive investment capacity of industry (Morgan, 1984: 458). 'It was precisely in these years,' a leading economic historian has observed, 'that other countries, above all Germany and Japan, could begin to build up a technical lead . . . While we built tanks and planes, they built machinery with which to achieve their later success' (quoted in Hennessy, 1992:

416–7). Rank and file dissent within the unions caused by rising prices forced the end of wage restraint, whilst the balance of payments slumped into a £369 million deficit, a massive swing of some £700 million over the previous year (Plowden, 1989: 113). Rationing was tightened and taxes raised, inflicting major blows upon Labour's electoral standing.

According to one lengthy analysis, 'it seems almost unbelievable that intelligent men in responsible governments should make such impossible plans' (Mitchell, 1963: 62). And the issue that finally provoked the resignations, 'the £13 million notionally collected from the Health Service charges seemed pathetically small' in the context of the total military outlay (Morgan, 1984: 458). Yet, as a major protagonist of the £4, 700 million programme stated, 'one thing is certain. The resignations of Bevan and Wilson which it helped to bring about split the Labour Party for many years and contributed greatly to the downfall of the Attlee Government six moths later. They further weakened and undermined the confidence of an aging administration which was already weary and beleagured . . . ' (Plowden, 1989: 120). How, then, could a decision with such prodigiously harmful consequences have been made?

On a personal level, Gaitskell, with all his qualities, was, on what he considered to be major matters of principle, quite unyielding. However, his attachment to the £4,700 million budget was in no way idiosyncratic, since it was eagerly endorsed by the Treasury. The Chancellor's Permanent Secretary, Sir Edward Bridges, told him ' I want you to know that . . . all those in the Treasury who know about it tremendously admire the stand you have made . . . It's the best day we have had in the Treasury for ten years.' 'I was so overcome with emotion,' Gaitskell confided to his diary 'that I could not say a word' (quoted in Hennessy, 1992: 417). But whatever their enthusiasm for beating plowshares into swords and pruning-hooks into spears, Bridges, Plowden and the Treasury had not lost their sense of thrift. They were convinced that the finances of the National Health Service were out of control 'and that a stand had to be taken in order to prevent a continued rise in government expenditure in an inopportune moment' (Plowden, 1989: 118).[11] The decision of the Treasury hierarchy to urge a course of action which they must have known to be economically deleterious derived from two – highly contestable and far-fetched – assumptions: that the Americans had to be persuaded of the willingness of the UK to make real sacrifices to defend itself to keep their forces in Europe; and that without the programme and its influence in persuading the US Congress to engage in a massive arms build-up 'Western Europe might have been overrun' (Plowden, 1989: 119–20).

The Politics of Grandeur

The majority of the Cabinet shared this analysis but the decisions it made were, at a deeper level, only explicable in terms of its overall approach to external affairs. Since 1945, it had sought to invoke American assistance not only to repel the assumed danger of Soviet military aggression but to sustain the UK's faltering world role. The willingness to pour resources into the defence budget was not simply a response to an emergency but the reflex action of ministers to whom upholding Britain's status as a Great Power was a national imperative, a paramount object of policy to which considerations of domestic economic management were consistently routinely subordinated (Tomlinson, 1989: 20).[12] To a greater extent than is generally understood, Labour's mentality had been stamped from its inception by values and beliefs derived from the established national culture.[13] Its reformism was largely confined to matters of social and economic organization whilst its conception of the interests of the British state and of its role in the world were heavily traditional. 'What would Lord Curzon do if he were in my shoes' was a query the Foreign Secretary often put to his officials (quoted in Shaw, 1974: 252). The belief, in Bevin's words, that 'we regard ourselves as one of the Powers most vital to the peace of the world and we still have our historic role to play' (Shlaim, 1978: 101) formed a mind-set which coloured the thinking of most Cabinet ministers. Bevin, Lord Listowel, the Secretary for India commented, 'was at heart an old-fashioned imperialist, keener to expand than to contract the Empire' (Hennessy, 1993: 233). Whilst at home the Government strove to build a new society, abroad it remained entrapped in the dreams of imperial splendour which had, for generations, seduced statesmen of a more traditional caste. Thus the underlying cause of the financial crisis of 1947 was the burden of a global role 'which obviously exceeded the country's economic capacity. Despite its impoverishment Britain was still trying to bear its accustomed responsibilities as a great world power' (Gardner, 1969: 309). Dalton's pleas for a reduction in overseas spending 'often met stubborn and sometimes quite stupid resistance' (Dalton, 1962: 70) for Bevin 'took as axiomatic the preservation of the British influence in south-east Europe and the eastern Mediterranean. He was also instinctively committed . . . to a permanent military and economic involvement in the Middle East . . . ' (Morgan, 1984: 235). So though hard currency reserves were relentlessly dribbling away, and notwithstanding the violent hostility of both Arabs and Jews, Bevin insisted – till brute reality (and American pressure) forced him to desist – that a continued presence in the Middle East was absolutely crucial to Britain's international position (Tomlinson, 1991: 54).[14] And to the end the Foreign Secretary, and his successor, Morrison, had sufficient support amongst his colleagues to ignore considerations of cost and ensure that Britain continued to maintain armed forces numbering well over a million, guard sea-lanes and protect far-flung dependencies, commitments which soaked up large amounts of scarce hard currency and skilled manpower.[15]

No better example exists of the willingness to give priority in the allocation of scanty resources to maintaining the world role over the needs of the economy than the decision to equip the UK with its own nuclear forces. The added weight this imposed on the fragile British economy provoked, at a crucial meeting in 1946 called to consider the matter, strident opposition from Dalton and Cripps – both of whom were subsequently excluded from the highly secret Cabinet committee established to explore the matter further (Morgan, 1984: 282). The main motivation was not, as was often claimed, to act as a reassurance policy against Soviet military aggression if, for some reason, the American nuclear shield was withdrawn – indeed the files recording the decision to manufacture the bomb made no mention of the Soviet Union (Hennessy, 1993: 268) – but to uphold the UK's global status. Bevin told the Cabinet sub-committee established to discuss the matter that Britain 'could not afford to acquiesce in an American monopoly of this new development'. To the objection from Dalton and Cripps that the project was too costly, Bevin riposted: 'We've got to have this thing over here, whatever it costs . . . We've got to have a bloody Union Jack flying on top of it' (Hennessy, 1993: 270, 268). In Sir Solly Zuckerman's stark words, the decision to develop an atomic bomb was taken 'solely to bolster the nation's political power, and with no knowledge of the military or scientific consequences' (Morgan, 1984: 284). Sir Henry Tizard, Chief Scientific Adviser to the Ministry of Defence, warned that 'we persist in regarding ourselves as a Great Power, capable of everything and only temporarily handicapped by economic difficulties. We are not a Great Power and never will be again.' These words met, Margaret Gowing, the historian of Britain's nuclear armoury, observed, 'with the kind of horror one would expect if one had made a disrespectful remark about the King' (Hennessy, 1989: 155).

Conclusion

Whatever its mistakes and defects, the accomplishments of the post-war Labour Government were formidable and neither of its two successors measured up to it. Although its most celebrated achievements lay in the social realm, economically it laid the foundation for post-war prosperity: Cripps was 'the real architect of the rapidly improving economic picture and growing affluence from 1952 onwards' (Morgan, 1984: 408). Industrial investment grew at a rapid rate, exports leapt ahead (admittedly in propitious circumstances) and inflation was low. Although its main monument was the welfare state, Labour had not neglected industrial modernization, science and technology. When it departed office, Britain 'had a strong aerospace industry and a flourishing chemical industry, and was represented across the range of high technology manufacture' (Hutton, 1995: 130). The increased range, amount and availability of benefits did much to reduce acute social deprivation and hence improve the quality of their lives for millions of people as well as making a significant contribution towards a more equal distribution of income (Morgan, 1984: 186). The Government staunchly resisted pressure from the Treasury and the City, notably during the devaluation crisis of 1949, to cut back heavily on social spending. Despite the allegations of economists and Treasury officials that rationing and controls were distorting the balance between supply and demand, there is little evidence that these had any really negative economic effects. On the other hand, all the available indicators 'suggest that the standard of health and of robust physique steadily improved during the entire 1945–51 period, from infants, whose survival rates continued to improve, to old people, whose expectation of a long and happy retirement steadily lengthened' (Morgan, 1984: 370). It is worth noting that such measures of social well-being, so vital to the actual lives of human beings, are never incorporated in indices such as GNP commonly used by economists and politicians as measures of national success. However, class divisions remained obtrusive. The major sources of structural inequality, such as the distribution of wealth, the system of private education and private insurance schemes were hardly affected. 'No real effort was made to eliminate, or even partially modify, the maldistribution of wealth and property which remained very pronounced in Britain after six years of supposedly socialist government' (Morgan, 1984: 493). Notwithstanding the progress made, access to life-enhancing resources and therefore the prospects for self-development were still distributed in a highly unequal manner.

For a later generation of 'New Labour' modernizers, 'Old Labour' was charged with being 'too preoccupied with state ownership' (Tony Blair quoted in the *Observer*, 16 July 1995). But what is striking about the post-war Government was the modesty of its nationalization programme, and the failure to use the public sector either as a vehicle for the redistribution of power, wealth and status or as an instrument of economic modernization. By the same token, despite all the rhetoric, little by the way of planning or strategic industrial intervention took place. Indeed, the leading analyst of post-war economic policy (who was also a departmental economic adviser at the time) wondered whether, in practice, economics ministers 'meant no more by planning than introducing foresight and consistency into the framing of economic policy' (Cairncross, 1985: 303). As the economy revived in 1948 with a steady improvement in the balance of payments and the abatement of shortages, the government began to remove controls. The Government accepted the view of most of its advisers that the utility of physical controls was confined to the orderly transition from the war-time to a predominantly market economy. 'Despite the rhetoric about economic planning of the 1945 Labour Government, the state was actually dismantling the institutions that might have allowed it to reorganise industry' (Hall, 1986: 73). As Schumpeter commented in 1950: most of the planning 'that has actually been done or suggested has nothing specifically socialist about it unless we adopt a definition of socialism that is much too wide to be of any analytical use' (quoted in Coates, 1975: 59).

Yet with the advantage of hindsight, the scale of its achievement is more impressive than it might have seemed fifteen or so years ago: the economy recovered from war-time dislocation, industrial output, productivity and investment all rose substantially, equilibrium in the external account was reached (until rearmament), inflation was well under control, a welfare state was created and, above all, for the first time, full employment was secured. All this was achieved by a Government presiding over an economy financially prostrate over years of total war. 'Whether one tries to look forward from 1945 or backwards from forty years later,' an eminent economist who served governments of both stripes for a well over a generation concluded, 'those years appear in retrospect, and rightly so, as years when the government knew where it wanted to go and led the country with an understanding of what was at stake' (Cairncross, 1985: 509).

Notes

1 Under US legislation Lend-Lease, which had financed the UK's balance of payments deficit, had to cease with the end of the war. President Truman rather peremptorily terminated the aid as soon as Japan surrendered – much earlier than the British Government had expected – after the dropping of Atomic bombs.

2 This rhyme, circulated at the time:

> In Washington, Lord Halifax
> Once whispered to Lord Keynes:
> It's true *they* have the money bags
> But *we* have all the brains.

(Gardner, 1969)

3 The Administration was eventually only able to secure passage of the Loan agreement, as it finally emerged, by emphasizing Britain's importance as a bulwark against (the considerably exaggerated possibility of) Soviet aggression (Gardner, 1969).

4 In addition, until the late 1940s, the US had an atomic monopoly.

5 Nationalization of the Bank of England is discussed below.

6 The Economic plan, as developed by Morrison and his officials, involved forecasting the demand and output for labour and materials of the varying branches of industry and the economy as a whole. An Economic Survey collected the data and then gathered information from the various government departments about their particular needs and plans. A Steering Group, serviced by working parties on manpower, investment and import and export trends, then collated all data accumulated into 'a national balance sheet of manpower, national income and expenditure, and overseas payments

and receipts' which was intended to identify the gap between demand and resources. Morrison's Lord President's Committee, after assessing the cases presented by private and departmental bidders, then allocated the raw materials accordingly (Donoughue and Jones, 1973: 352–3).

7   Here it was responding to the requirement of the Organization for European Economic Co-operation (OEEC, precursor of OECD and the body responsible for distributing Marshall Aid) that all countries receiving Marshall Aid should submit reports indicating how they proposed to achieve external balance by 1952.

8   Plowden enjoyed Cripps's confidence and greatly influenced his thinking (Cairncross, 1985: 326) whilst Hall played a key role in shaping the development of economic policy (Plowden, 1989: 25).

9   As Plowden later recalled, Hall and I certainly would have liked firmer action but were 'forced to recognise the political realities of the situation.' (Plowden, 1989: 66; Cairncross, 1985: 190).

10   He was further angered when, again, he was overlooked and Morrison, a man with no knowledge of international affairs, was appointed Foreign Secretary.

11   'Given the tightening of the housing, education and national insurance budgets, we saw no reason why the NHS should be an exception' (Plowden, 1989: 118). Morgan suggests that Gaitskell might have been unduly influenced by praise from Bridges, Plowden and other leading officials (Morgan, 1984: 457).

12   But it was by no means universally shared within the Party. 'Realism,' the noted Party theorist G. D. H. Cole observed, 'means accepting the waning of British power' coming to terms with its shrunken status in the world (quoted in Shaw, 1974: 126). 'Perhaps the greatest failure of the Labour Government,' the *New Statesman* claimed in 1948, was 'its misjudgment of Britain's comparative strength' (*New Statesman*, 30 October 1948; quoted in Shaw, 1974: 124).

13   A perceptive German observer, Egon Wertheimer, commented in 1929 that 'separated by no class barriers from the mental and spiritual concepts of capitalism . . . the Labour Party has never been able to make a clean breakaway from capitalist culture' (quoted in Shaw, 1974: 272).

14   Attlee, in contrast, privately argued that Britain lacked sufficient resources to remain in the Middle East and saw the attachment to the area as 'sentimental'. Eventually he climbed down, mainly because of a threat by Chiefs of Staff to resign (Tomlinson, 1991: 55).

15   All the while they never stopped to ask 'whether there [was] anyone left at the other end of the lifeline whose life depended on rapid aid from Britain' (Shonfield, 1959: 99).

3 The Rise of Keynesian Social Democracy

Whatever the modes of economic production, economic power will, in fact, belong to the owners of political power.

(Crosland, 1964: 10)

The price mechanism is now a reasonably satisfactory method of distributing the great bulk of consumer-goods and industrial capital-goods.

(Crosland, 1964: 346)

Labour in Opposition

The programme of action outlined in the 1945 manifesto had been more or less completed by the end of the decade. What should the Party seek to do next? This raised fundamental questions about the Party's role and purposes. The majority supported Herbert Morrison's call for a period of 'consolidation', digesting the accomplishments of the post-war administration and concentrating on administering the new welfare state. A left-wing minority, spearheaded by Bevan, called, in contrast, for pressing ahead with fresh extensions of the public sector. The dispute rumbled on for a number of years, with differences from time to time patched up but with no resolution of the issue. Although it had lost office in 1951, Labour had in fact gained more votes than the Conservatives – indeed more than it had ever won, before or since – so a further election setback in 1955 came as a shock. On a lower turnout,

Labour lost almost one and a half million votes, its percentage of the poll fell from 48.8 per cent to 46.4 per cent and it lost twenty seats whilst the Conservatives were returned with a comfortable majority of 60. In fact, the Tory victory was not unexpected: belying Labour's admonitions in 1951, there was no return to depression and mass unemployment but years of solid gains in personal living standards – the beginnings of 'the affluent society'. The septuagenarian Attlee held on as leader, mainly to destroy the prospects of his long-time rival Morrison – only a few years younger – from succeeding him. Shortly after the election, he resigned and three candidates entered the fray, Morrison, Bevan and Gaitskell. Gaitskell had augmented the reputation he had first won as a capable Chancellor of the Exchequer, winning the admiration of the unions by his tough-minded attitude to the Bevanites and his fellow members of the PLP by his obvious ability. He saw off both his rivals with little difficulty. He believed it vital that the Party be educated in the new realities of post-war Britain and that its programme should accordingly be renewed (Howell, 1980: 205). With his accession, a third political tendency gained ascendancy, the revisionists. Headed by the new leader, they rapidly secured an ideological hegemony with the publication in 1956 of the most important work of post-war British social democracy, *The Future of Socialism*, written by Gaitskell's close friend and ally, Tony Crosland. Revisionism was a frontal assault on traditional socialism as it had been understood prior to the war. The theses that socialism entailed the public ownership of productive resources and the replacement of the market economy were subjected to withering intellectual fire. They were rooted in an outdated analysis of the economic and social order and reflected a confusion between means and ends. Socialism was about values, above all equality and social justice. With the achievement of the post-war settlement – the mixed economy, the welfare state and full employment – the social revolution had been completed and socialists could now confine their efforts to further improvements within these structures. In a series of policy statement issued by the NEC over the following years, most notably *Industry and Society* (1957), revisionism came to be adopted as Labour's ruling discourse.

The Critique of Traditional Socialism

Traditional socialism had viewed capitalism as an endemically unstable system, impelled to oscillate between booms and slumps, generating poverty, waste, mass unemployment and gross inequalities. The only remedy was a planned economy with a large public sector. To revisionists, in contrast, Keynesianism had rendered the economic case for public ownership obsolete. Using Keynesian fiscal and monetary policies, a government could now fix the level of demand at a level sufficient to maintain steady growth, full employment and rising living standards. By managing the level of demand it could counter the sharp swings of the business cycle and thereby avoid depressions and mass unemployment. The egalitarian case for nationalization was no more compelling. Given the decision to pay compensation, and given too the only very gradual redistributory effects nationalization would have, it was a far less effective method for promoting equality than fiscal methods, such as a steeply progressive income tax, the taxation of wealth and unearned income, and the expansion of the social services (Gaitskell, 1956). Many of the other claims made for public ownership – for instance, that it would promote the more efficient organization of production and more harmonious labour relations – had not so far been validated by the performance of the new public corporations. Indeed, the nationalization of whole industries on a public monopoly basis had tended to lead to over-centralization and restrictions on choice (Crosland, 1964: 323). Further, public ownership was only justified when firms were found, after 'thorough enquiry', to be 'failing the nation' but for the most part, according to *Industry and Society*, private sector firms were efficiently managed (Loewenburg, 1959: 254).

The proposition that social needs were trampled upon by the uncompromising pursuit of profits was equally unconvincing. The role of the profit motive had diminished because of the profound change in industrial organization caused by the separation between ownership and control. The owners – whether individuals or other institutions – were merely the passive recipients of dividends with industry now effectively run by a new stratum of professional managers. Its interests lay in corporate efficiency and growth rather than in pure profit maximization and higher dividend. Lacking a material interest in maximizing profits, managers were as likely to be motivated by the desire for social recognition and prestige (Crosland, 1964: 15, 16). Britain, as a whole, was now a markedly less competitive society as an 'uncompromising faith in individualism and self-help' had given way to a belief in 'collective responsibility for social welfare' (Crosland, 1964: 69). Much of the revisionist case anticipated what self-styled 'modernizers' a generation later were to copyright as their contribution to updating Labour's thinking. Thus it adopted a much more positive view of profits, dismissing out of hand the traditional socialist view that production for profit was incompatible with production for need. 'What is profitable is what the consumer finds useful; and the firm and the consumer desire broadly the same allocation of resources' (Crosland, 1964: 347). Further profits were essential to any economic system, since funds had to be set aside to invest in new plant and machinery. Squeezing profits was self-defeating since it would reduce the capital available for investment, thereby retarding growth and reducing the capacity of the economy to produce jobs. 'So long as we maintain a substantial private sector . . . socialists must logically applaud the accumulation of private profit' (Crosland, 1964: 300). Major disparities in income and wealth remained but these could be most effectively remedied by fiscal policy, through increasing expenditure on public services, raising social benefits and a more progressive tax regime. By the same token, competition had much greater strengths than previously appreciated by socialists. It encouraged energy and initiative, allowed choice in the selection of goods, suppliers and employers, and increased consumer welfare (Crosland, 1964: 319–20). Nationalization on the Morrisonian model could actually be detrimental by replacing competition by monopoly, and entrepreneurial initiative by centralized forms of control. The experience of the post-war Labour Government demonstrated there was no feasible alternative to the market (Crosland, 1964: 348–9).

The tap-root of power, traditional socialism had contended, lay in the ownership of productive resources so that as long as the economy remained largely in private hands business would retain the capacity to thwart the will of a democratically-elected government. Revisionism rejected this reasoning. The evidence from history demonstrated that 'whatever the modes of economic production, economic power will, in fact, belong to the owners of political power' (Crosland, 1964: 10). In the western democratic state, effective control of power ultimately belonged to governments, sanctioned by popular election. Furthermore, this control had been formidably extended by the Keynesian revolution. "Acting mainly through the budget . . . the government . . . can exert any influence it likes on income-distribution, and it can also determine within broad limits the division of total output between consumption, investment, exports and social expenditure." Fiscal, monetary, legislative and physical controls enabled it to 'severely limit . . . the autonomy of business decisions' (Crosland, 1964: 8). Above all, full employment constituted 'a basic cause of the shift of economic power away from the business class' and one which had profoundly altered the nature of labour relations, to the extent that 'whoever governs at Westminster, the organised workers will remain the effective power in industry' (Crosland, 1964: 28). The new balance of power constituted a permanent fixture of post-war society since any government which 'tampered seriously with the basic structure of the full employment Welfare State would meet with a sharp reverse at the polls' (Crosland, 1964: 28). In short, business no longer had the capacity to frustrate a Labour Government and the Party could safely continue its pursuit of equality and social justice within the framework of a mainly privately-owned, market economy.

Revisionist Socialism

To the revisionists, socialism was a philosophy of distributional justice whose main objectives were greater equality, social justice and the preservation of full employment. The belief in social equality was 'the most characteristic feature of socialist thought' (Crosland, 1964: 77). Although revisionists repudiated theories of class conflict, they accepted that Britain remained a class-bound society, characterized by deep, cumulative and reinforcing social disparities, where 'the hierarchies of education, occupational prestige, and style of life all show pronounced and visible breaks; and these breaks broadly coincide' (Crosland, 1964: 119). 'We regard as unjust,' Gaitskell stated, 'a class structure, in which a person's income, way of living, education, status and opportunities in life depend upon the class into which he is born' (Gaitskell, 1956: 3). Social justice was a socialist imperative because large numbers of people suffered from deprivation and squalor through no fault of their own. Crosland indeed identified a socialist 'as one who wishes to give this an exceptional priority over other claims on resources' (Crosland,

1964: 76–7). The third aim was full employment (Gaitskell, 1956: 4–5). A job gave a person a sense of dignity, of purpose and status in the national community whilst depriving people of the ability to work was both materially and morally destructive.

How were these values to be realized? It was assumed that full employment, to which the Conservatives seemed equally committed, had ceased to be a major problem with the advent of the Keynesian revolution. An expanded welfare state – a more egalitarian educational system, improved health and housing services and more adequate social benefits – were the chief instruments for fostering equality and social justice. A major source of inequality lay in the distribution of property and Gaitskell argued in 1957 that a higher proportion of the total tax yield should be drawn from those who profited from capital gains and inherited wealth (Ellison, 1994: 88). Thus the 1959 Manifesto proposed taxation of 'the huge capital gains made on the Stock Exchange and elsewhere', and the blocking of loopholes and share purchases by public investment agencies to ensure that the community 'enjoys some of the profits and capital gains now going to private industry' (Craig, 1975: 227). Heavier progressive taxation of income could also generate additional revenue but revisionists were wary about any redistributive measures which involved direct losses to any social group claiming that this would raise social and political tensions. Sustained and measurable progress towards greater equality and social justice was most effectively secured by redistributing the fruits of economic growth.

Revisionism – or, as we shall henceforth call it, Keynesian social democracy – signalled a rapprochement between the egalitarian and welfare aspirations of socialism and the capitalist mixed economy. Henceforth Labour defined its mission in terms of the fairer distribution of income, wealth and power within the framework of the managed market economy. The prime areas for pursuing its goals lay in the sphere of social policy – education, health, housing, pensions and so forth – but the viability of the whole scheme rested crucially on the Keynesian economic foundation. Keynesianism performed multiple functions: by ensuring high levels of aggregate demand in the economy and hence an expanding market, government could both encourage the process of domestic capital formation and full employment; given that the lower income groups had a greater marginal tendency to consume than the wealthy, distributional justice meshed neatly with the maintenance of aggregate demand. Keynesian social democracy transformed the distributional game into a positive-sum one, where all players were winners. Its fate was 'inextricably bound to the promise of the successful management of the capitalist economy' (Scharpf, 1991: 24–5). It was upon the ability of Keynesianism to foster economic growth – and, indeed, to maintain full employment – that the viability of revisionist social democracy therefore ultimately rested.

But Keynesian social democracy was no votary of the market. It denied the market liberal claims that state intervention, higher public expenditure and redistributory politics endangered liberty and that the free play of market forces maximized economic welfare. Fundamental to its thinking was the conviction that the good of the public could never be equated with that of self-interested market actors, that there existed social needs and public purposes that could only be served by deliberate collective action. In Keynes' own words: 'The world is *not* so governed that private and social interest always coincide. It is *not* a correct deduction from the Principles of Economics that enlightened self-interest always operates in the public interest. Nor is it true that self-interest generally *is* enlightened' (Robinson, 1962: 81, emphasis in the original).

Though revisionists constantly berated the left for failing to appreciate how much society had altered, their own analysis was curiously static as they assumed the permanence of this new stage of development. Revisionists were unduly sanguine about the benevolence of business, underrating the extent to which the new humane capitalism was a response to the rise of union power, in turn largely contingent upon full employment. They were tempted to forget that 'capitalism was a dangerous and untamable beast that needed to be handled with the utmost caution' (Scharpf, 1991: 24). For Crosland the economic power of the capital markets and the financial institutions had been so attenuated that they no longer posed a serious problem for socialists (Crosland, 1964: 16, 21). In reality, their power was rapidly reviving and the Bank of England, despite its nationalization, remained a crucial conduit for the projection of their influence. John Strachey, a leading pre-war Marxist but later a convert to Keynesianism and a minister in the Attlee Government, was in broad agreement with the revisionists. But he was notably was less sanguine about the power of finance. He believed that a flight of capital could threaten the implementation of a programme of domestic reform and was emphatic about the need for a strict system of controls over currency and capital movements and trade. In a draft chapter for *Contemporary Capitalism* (his major work) he criticized the revisionist view 'that it will somehow be possible to "creep up" upon the capitalist system and transform it out of existence without anyone noticing'. He argued that within capitalism there existed 'a sort of "social ejection mechanism" which, unless its operation is foreseen and neutralized, will ruin governments of the left. In Britain this mechanism usually takes the specific form of a tendency to recurrent balance of payments crisis.' Unless a Labour government took control of the balance of payments from the outset 'they will be quickly bankrupted by the efflux of liquid capital seeking what it considers the most attractive conditions' (Newman, 1989: 149).[1] Labour's failure, during its years in opposition, to give any sustained thought to the role of sterling, exchange rate policies and how it would react to the type of speculative pressure that had overwhelmed left-wing governments in Britain and elsewhere in the 1930s, was to cost it dear (Woodward, 1993: 79).

But all this was for the future. By the end of the 1950s, Keynesian social democracy dominated Labour thinking and its maxims governed the choice of policy. It did not amount to a rupture with the past. 'There was much within the revisionist perspective that bore the hallmark of traditional moderate Labour policy. The belief that existing administrative institutions were politically neutral, the readiness to seek consensus, the commitment to incremental change' (Howell, 1980: 194). Yet the change was real enough as the Party was now explicitly committed to working within the confines of a predominantly privately-owned and market-regulated mixed economy. The adoption of Keynesian social democracy filled the ideological vacuum which had appeared in the late 1940s. Policies of public ownership and planning had been developed to remedy depression, under-consumption and mass unemployment, but the problems which the Labour Cabinet encountered – external account deficits, insufficient output, low productivity, inflation – were radically different. Keynesian social democracy furnished a body of thought which could articulate in an intellectually satisfying and persuasive manner the lessons that those who had served in ministerial positions had instinctively drawn. It provided skilfully marshalled arguments to justify the abandonment of policy-orientations and aspirations which had already lost their attraction for Labour's governing stratum. Much of Labour's inter-war programme had been carried out by the post-war government leaving the Party somewhat adrift, unsure whether the post-war measures represented the first instalment of the transition to socialism or whether to consolidate what had been achieved. By coupling Keynesian economics to the pursuit of distributional justice, Keynesian social democracy offered the Party a clear set of objectives, policy instruments to attain them and a solid theoretical underpinning.

The revisionists met considerable political, but weak ideological resistance. The Party establishment was seriously shaken by the Bevanite challenge in the early 1950s, with the toppling of the elder statesmen, Morrison and Dalton, at the raucous Morecambe Conference of 1952. However, despite the fact that Bevanism was spearheaded by a remarkably talented team – Crossman, Foot, Mikardo, Barbara Castle, Wilson, and Bevan himself, impulsive and emotional but a great imaginative thinker and the architect of Labour's most admired creation, the National Health Service – they signally failed to provide any sustained fresh political thinking and mount a serious ideological challenge to revisionism. Precisely why must remain a puzzle. They never operated as an effective team, they lacked access to research resources and 'think-tanks' and much of their attention was given over to questions of foreign policy. Bevan himself was not a natural team player, easily bored by detail and reluctant to engage in the hard grind – in which a generation later Mrs Thatcher excelled – of relating broad principles to tangible policies. Politically, too, the left suffered from the fact that their political base was primarily within the constituencies. Only at the turn of the decade did a powerful indigenous Labour left emerge in the form of the TGWU.[2] By then Bevan's break with the group over the future of the British Bomb and his rapprochement with Gaitskell had demoralized the left, depriving it of its charismatic leader at precisely the time when the revisionist offensive was in full flood.

The Internal Politics of Labour

Labour is, in constitutional terms a highly pluralist party, with decision-making rights distributed amongst a variety of institutions – Conference, the National Executive Committee (NEC) affiliated trade unions, constituency parties (CLPs) the Parliamentary Labour Party (PLP) the

Shadow Cabinet (or Cabinet when Labour is in power: often also referred to as the frontbench) and the Leader. As we have seen, conceptions of the precise relationship between the Parliamentary and extra-parliamentary wings of the Party have varied over time and the question of the ultimate location of authority was one which had never been definitively resolved. As a result, endemic tensions frequently enveloped the manner in which Labour made its policy as well as its content.

During the Attlee Government right-wing control over all key institutions – the Cabinet, the NEC, the bulk of the unions and the Conference – dispelled any prospect of success for a serious challenge to the leadership. The NEC operated, in effect, as the extra-parliamentary arm of the Cabinet, never questioning its leadership role. The fact that Attlee, Morrison and Dalton were all Executive members, along with other ministers, helped ensure the absence of institutional friction between the two bodies. The relationship between the Government and the top echelons of the trade union movement was particularly close: 'in the control of Transport House, in the command over the National Executive, and in the loyalty or docility of the annual party conference, and the grass-roots constituency parties whose voice it was, an essential ingredient for the party leadership was the firm support of the Trade Union Congress' (Morgan, 1984: 75–6). However, the Cabinet accepted that its role was bounded by the Party Constitution. A distinction was made between major policy principles and objectives, which were laid down by the 1945 manifesto, on the one hand, and matters of timing, implementation and contingencies which were, on the other, left in the main to the Cabinet. The Executive took little part in policy discussions, concentrating its efforts on mobilizing support within the Party for whatever was decided by the Cabinet. However, it resumed an influential role when the time came for framing the next manifesto. The source material was the Party's programme which consisted of resolutions and NEC statements adopted by Conference by a two-thirds majority on a card vote. A joint meeting of the Parliamentary Committee (the Cabinet when in office) and the NEC – the so-called Clause V meeting named after the relevant section of the constitution – decided which items of the programme would be included in the manifesto. The formulation of the 1950 and 1951 manifestos both followed this pattern quite closely.

During the years of opposition from 1951 to 1964 the NEC was the major forum of policy deliberation. It set up the study groups charged with the detailed development of policy, considered (via its Home Policy and International sub-committees) the various drafts and made the final recommendations to Conference which were almost invariably approved. However, in this period it would be misleading to counterpose the power or influence of the Parliamentary leadership (or the Leader) to that of the NEC. Both worked in tandem or, rather, it was through the vehicle of the Executive and its committee structure that the Leader and his frontbench colleagues pursued their policy objectives. It was very rare for the two to differ over any matters of substance. And in combination, they determined the policy agenda: which issues received attention; which policy options were given serious consideration - and which were screened out. Close co-operation between the two institutions was facilitated by an overlap of personnel and – above all – by the similarity of political composition: in both the right commanded an overwhelming majority and constituted Labour's dominant current.

The critical axis in this coalition was the alliance between the political and the trade union right. Thus whilst in theory final authority rested with Conference the ready availability of a solid phalanx of right-wing trade unions marshalled in the block vote ensured that left-wing challenges to the leadership during these years would easily be quelled. Such was the fate of the Bevanite revolt. The clash over rearmament in 1951 inaugurated a decade of strife as dissension spread to issues such as public ownership, German rearmament and nuclear weapons. The left – soon dubbed the Bevanites – initially took the offensive. The left-wing weekly, *Tribune*, edited by Bevan's close friend Michael Foot, issued a series of pamphlets criticizing the Party's leadership over rearmament and its timidity over domestic policy. A Bevanite group of MPs was formed and Bevanite 'Brains Trusts' (that is, collections of speakers answering questions from the audience on the model of a popular television and radio programme) mobilized support within the constituencies. Bevanite rebellions in the House of Commons immediately provoked demands from the right for tough disciplinary action (for a full account, see Shaw, 1988: 31–50).

The conflict burst into the open at the 1952 Party Conference, held in Morecambe. After years of docile Conferences, Morecambe came as a shock: 'rowdy, convulsive, vulgar; splenetic; threatening at moments to collapse into an irretrievable brawl' (Foot, 1975: 376). Debates were ill-tempered and heated and when a left-wing constituency delegate interrupted Will Lawler, chief of the National Union of Miners, he bawled out: 'shut your gob' (Foot, 1975: 377). Then came the results of the NEC elections: the Party establishment was outraged when it was announced that two senior and long-serving members of the NEC, Morrison and Dalton, had been ousted by the Bevanites Richard Crossman and Harold Wilson, with many MPs regarding it as 'a mortal blow at the Party' (Jay, 1980: 225). Right-wingers were appalled by the mutinous temper of constituency delegates – Douglas Jay complained of 'an apparently organised claque of extremists yell[ing] from the gallery in a chorus of combined hysteria and hatred' (Jay, 1980: 223). A combative Arthur Deakin, head of the TGWU – bringing fraternal greetings from the TUC – lumbered onto the platform to launch a biting attack on the left whilst shortly after Hugh Gaitskell delivered an equally powerful broadside in a speech at Stalybridge.

Brushing aside Attlee's efforts to lower the temperature, the right clamped down on the rebels. Although the 'conscience clause' of PLP Standing Orders gave a (restricted) right to dissent from majority decisions, conscience was expected to speak in a still, small voice, not loudly in a public forum: the plural of conscience – as one favoured maxim had it – was conspiracy. In 1952 organized groups within the PLP were formally banned and failure to follow the whip was treated as a serious offence (for a detailed account, see Shaw, 1988). Equally distempered were the trio of powerful trade union leaders, Deakin, Lawler and Bill Williamson of the General and Municipal Workers Union (GMWU) who determined to take the Party in hand. Consolidation suited the bulk of the unions: they shared the ideological outlook of the Morrison wing of the Party, felt reassured by the conciliatory stance of the new Conservative Government, and were satisfied by their new role, as an acknowledged state of the realm, in the mixed economy welfare state. They regarded the Bevanites as irresponsible and disruptive and when in 1954 the left-wing weekly *Tribune* had the temerity to criticize their conduct of industrial disputes in fury they sought to silence it. However, on this occasion the NEC had overstepped the mark and backed down. The following year they moved in for the kill when Bevan, needlessly and provocatively embarrassed Attlee. This was the moment that the trade union right, Gaitskell and others in the PLP had been awaiting. Bevan only escaped expulsion by the narrowest of margins because of a combination of luck, Attlee's support and the ineptitude of his opponents who were never able to rally together at one time the majority within the NEC who wanted the Welshman out of the Party.

The tussle between left and right then receded with Bevan's reconciliation with Gaitskell and his entry into the Shadow Cabinet. At the 1957 Party Conference, Bevan, by now shadow Foreign Secretary, stunned and dismayed his followers when he endorsed British nuclear forces and denounced unilateralism in a pungent speech. A furious quarrel followed with his most faithful lieutenant, Michael Foot and, with erstwhile Bevanites like Wilson and Crossman already having mended their fences with Gaitskell, a divided and demoralized left lost much of their influence. Labour entered its first electoral combat under its energetic new leader with high hopes. The Government's reputation (it was fondly assumed) had been battered by the Suez débâcle whilst Gaitskell fought what was seen as a skilful campaign. But hopes that a rejuvenated Labour Party would succeed at the polls were dashed. Its share of the poll fell from 46.4 per cent to 43.8 per cent, it lost another 200,000 votes and 19, seats whilst the Conservatives coasted back to power under the legend 'you've never had it so good' with a majority of 100.

In the immediate aftermath of the election defeat, Labour was torn apart by Gaitskell's bid to revise Clause IV of the constitution (the commitment to public ownership) The Leader reacted to Labour's third successive electoral defeat by calling for a widening of its appeal by discarding its commitment to common ownership. He claimed that Clause IV provoked needless fears of the Party's intentions, had been exploited by the Conservatives in the 1959 election who claimed that Labour had far-reaching plans to expand the public sector and was, anyway, a quite misleading statement of its ultimate purposes. Not unexpectedly, the initiative provoked passionate opposition from the left, and the Party probably was only spared a revival of hostilities between Gaitskell and an increasingly disenchanted Bevan by the latter's illness and death in 1960. More serious was the exasperation of several normal loyalist union leaders who felt that the Clause did little harm and regarded the whole episode as a needlessly provocative attack on tradition and the Party's sense of its own past. This view was (privately) shared by some of Gaitskell's own entourage (most notably Crosland) who regarded his move as tactically maladroit, chasing the shadow rather than the substance of power. It was also the view taken by 'reconcilers' such as Wilson and Crossman, who believed the Leader had failed to grasp the significance of symbols in cementing the party, was unnecessarily confrontational in his methods and was unduly rigid in rejecting the use of emollient and ambiguous compromises (Howell, 1980: 206). Reluctantly, he was forced to back down. Clause IV was retained, though, as a face-saver, supplemented by an additional, fuller (and rapidly forgotten) statement of principles. His prestige was damaged, the left and the unions were reassured, but in practical policy terms the retention of Clause IV had negligible effect

The episode distracted Gaitskell from the more explosive issue of unilateralism. A powerful and vocal movement, the Campaign for Nuclear Disarmament (CND), calling for the renunciation by Britain of all nuclear weapons had gained many adherents within Labour's ranks, mostly on the left. In 1956 the death of two right-wing leaders in quick succession gave a left-winger, Frank Cousins, the opportunity to win election as General Secretary of the TGWU. It took several years for the left to consolidate its position but the result was that by 1960 the votes of the largest union now attached itself to left-wing causes. Cousins was a unilateralist but the unexpected passing of a unilateralist resolution in that year was only possible because normally right-wing unions – for a variety of reasons – swelled the left-wing vote. It was the first real case of a power struggle between the Parliamentary leadership and Conference. Gaitskell's riposte to his defeat was uncompromising. Conference's decision was intolerable and must be overturned. In a celebrated speech he promised to 'fight and fight and fight again to save the Party we love'. He was as good as his word: the right mobilized effectively both in the constituencies and the unions and unilateralism was overturned by a large majority. His triumph the following year had profound effects for, as Minkin commented, 'Successful confrontation shattered the psychological bonds of the traditional view of Conference authority . . . The Party Leader, who had flatly refused to obey a Conference decision on the most contentious issue of the time, had survived with his prestige and power enhanced. The lessons of this were available to any future Party Leader' (Minkin, 1978: 287).

The Basis of Leadership Power

In the 1950s and early 1960s power in both the policy and managerial spheres was concentrated to an unusual degree in the hands of a ruling stratum dominated by the Parliamentary leadership. Upon what did this very substantial agglomeration of power at the centre rest? Not upon the hegemony of the Party machine. In fact Labour's organization, weak and poorly-staffed, bore few resemblances to a Weberian bureaucracy. Nor upon the lavishing of formal powers upon the parliamentary leadership. Constitutionally, as we have seen, it was the NEC and Conference which possessed the lion's share of power in both the policy and managerial spheres. Centralized control, in fact, rested on a range of contingent factors rather than upon any 'iron law' of oligarchy. The heart of the power system which prevailed for a generation after 1931 was elite consensus and the existence of a pattern of concurrent majorities: virtually all key institutions (the NEC, the Shadow Cabinet, the PLP, the major unions, Conference) were controlled by the right, knitted together by a shared ideology, a similarity of attitude on the main political issues and mutual enemies – the Communist and non-Communist left. This gave rise to a structure of integrated organizational control which enabled the parliamentary leadership to amass the powers that were constitutionally divided amongst a range of institutions. A decisive contribution to sustaining the structure was the staunch support afforded the parliamentary leadership by a solid block of right-wing unions, the so-called Praetorian Guard, against whose rock-like loyalty dissent would beat helplessly.

In voluntary organizations like political parties where the mass of members can neither be bribed, coerced nor suborned into conformity, systems of rule must ultimately rest on mass consent. The most effective by far is a sense of legitimacy, that is the belief that the existing pattern of authority is fairly and properly constituted and worthy of support. During this period Labour's authority structure enjoyed a broad degree of legitimacy, founded, firstly, upon agreement over the ground-rules and norms underpinning and validating the way in which power was distributed and decisions taken. It took the form of the doctrine of majoritarian democracy, in which although the Parliamentary leadership was afforded considerable leeway, Conference was regarded as the ultimate repository of authority and thereby responsible for setting the overall direction of the Party. It was reinforced, secondly, by a reasonable measure of substantive consensus: although there were sharp disagreements over important policy issues there was, nevertheless, a core of common purpose and ideals to which the great majority adhered: full employment, social justice and equality. Thirdly, the integrated system of control vested in the leadership a large measure of procedural power, that is the ability to affect decisions by influencing the way in which they were made. Thus the leadership was well placed in this period to stifle opposition by managing the Conference agenda: fixing its order of business, manipulating the rules governing the choice of resolutions to be debated such as compositing (the system by which the large volume of resolutions was reduced to a manageable number)[3] (Minkin, 1978: 320).[4] Yet impressive as it was, the power of Labour's Parliamentary elite was less securely rooted and more qualified in scope than it seemed to many observers at the time. It rested to a significant degree on contingent factors which might not always be present. When, in the course of the 1960s, the equilibrium within the unions and the Party shifted to the left, then fissures in the structure of leadership control soon began to show.

The Advent of Wilson

In 1962 Gaitskell was suddenly struck by a mysterious and fatal disease. A man who inspired intense personal loyalties, his followers – able young politicians like Roy Jenkins, Crosland and Hattersely amongst them – were dismayed, not only by his death but by the choice for the succession. Wilson - distrusted as much for his guile and ambition as he was admired for his mental agility and adroitness – emerged as the candidate of the left and centre. The major standard-bearer of the right was George Brown, a man of great talent and inexhaustible energy, marred by an unstable temperament and an ungovernable weakness for the bottle. As a result, a number of right-wingers persuaded another rising politician to enter the fray – James Callaghan. However, Wilson emerged as the victor and although Brown disappeared to sulk for a while it was these three men who formed an all-powerful trio in the early years of the next Labour Government.

Wilson was, both by background and experience, drawn to meritocratic themes. But he was also searching for policies which could heal the divisions which had troubled the Party for over a decade, reaching a crescendo in the battles over Clause IV and nuclear weapons policy at the start of the decade. At the same time, he wanted a message which could provide the Party with a sharp campaigning edge, impart to it a sense of mission and identity and, above all, galvanize the electorate.[5] The answer came in his much-acclaimed first speech to Conference as Leader in 1963 on 'Labour and the Scientific Revolution'. Far from being an outdated ideology, ran the argument, socialism ran with the grain of technological advance and scientific discovery. It was the application of purpose to politics, aiming to harness the scientific and technological resources of the country to modernizing society and the economy. The Tories were castigated as the party of amateurs and grouse-shooting aristocrats.[6] Labour, under the dynamic and youthful Wilson, would sweep aside the world of privilege and the 'who you know' society bringing in scientists and technicians fired by (in another Wilson phrase) 'the White Heat of Technology'. It was a virtuoso performance and Wilson was never quite able to repeat the excitement which he generated as Leader of the Opposition.

Notes

1   This section was excised from the published version, Newman suggests, because Strachey's friend Gaitskell objected on the grounds that it would lose votes (Newman, 1989: 150).

2   In 1956 Frank Cousins was elected to the leadership of the TGWU – traditionally a bastion of the right – after the sudden death of two of his predecessors. The popular myth – that overnight the union's block vote swung from right to left – has been proven to be without foundation by Minkin: it took several years before the union's vote moved firmly into the left's column (Minkin, 1978).

3   A favourite device was to ensure the defeat of critical resolutions by seeking to include in the final composited resolution extremely-worded sentiments unacceptable to the Conference majority. This could be achieved by astute management of the compositing process.

4   All this took a subtle and discreet form: it was 'an intricate process of "soundings" and cues' which rested upon 'assumptions about the management of a "good Conference" and involved shared perceptions and common purposes . . . ' (Minkin, 1978: 321).

5   Although (for quite different reasons) both former allies on the left and critics on the right were reluctant to admit it, Wilson's opinions on matters nationalization and economic policy were broadly similar to Gaitskell's (Pimlott, 1992: 254).

6   Sir Alec Douglas Home, formerly Lord Home, had just become Prime Minister and, in one unfortunate Party Political Broadcast sought to explain economic policy by using match sticks.

4 Keynesian Social Democracy in Power, 1964–1970

On his way out, [Maudling] put his head round the door carrying a pile of suits over his arm. His comment was typical: 'Sorry, old cock, to leave it in this shape.' ... And with that he ambled off down the garden path ...

(Callaghan, 1987: 162)

Strikes against the national interest are always to be condemned; strikes of capital are no less, and in certain circumstances infinitely more, damaging.

(Wilson, 1971: 32)

We are a world power and a world influence or we are nothing.

(Wilson in Whitehead, 1985: 3–4)

The New Age

The 1950s and 1960s are now commonly seen as 'the golden age of Keynesian social democracy'. Although, in this period, Labour only ruled from 1964 to 1970, it had – unlike most other social democratic parties – the great advantage of an absolute majority, thereby never being burdened with the wearisome task of compromising with coalition partners.[1] Furthermore, the achievements of the post-war Attlee Government represented a model for other social democratic parties and a firm foundation upon which a successor could build. But the performance of the 1964–70 Wilson administration was a disappointment, fulfilling few of the hopes it initially raised. Why this was so will be a major theme of this chapter.

After thirteen years in opposition, Labour had scraped back to office in October 1964 with a bare majority of four. This meant that a second election was likely in the near future, and electoral considerations inevitably coloured the thinking and actions of the new Cabinet. With George Brown as Secretary of State for Economic Affairs, James Callaghan as Chancellor of the Exchequer and like-minded politicians occupying most other influential posts, the Cabinet was predominantly right-wing. Although Wilson once compared himself to a Bolshevik revolutionary presiding over a Tsarist Cabinet, in reality there was little to divide him from the Cabinet majority.

Labour was elected in the crest of a reformist wave, upon which Wilson had skilfully capitalized. He argued that Britain suffered from a lower rate of growth than its main competitors because of the Conservatives' failure to tackle the underlying causes of a mediocre economic performance. Investment was too low, management often amateur and merit too frequently sacrificed to 'the old-school tie'. The Tory Government's 'stop–go' policies inflicted further damage. Orchestrated pre-election booms culminated in unsustainable balance of payments deficits as consumer demand sucked in imports and exports fell whilst the 'stop' stage designed to improve the external account through deflating the economy intensified the underlying problems by discouraging new investment and the introduction of new techniques (Woodward, 1993: 78). Wilson pledged that Labour would sweep away the musty networks of inherited privilege and obsolete attitudes (neatly symbolized by the grouse-shooting Tory leader, the former thirteenth Earl Home) modernize outdated institutions, instil a new professionalism and, through 'the white heat of technology', inject dynamism into a stagnant economy. The economy would be stimulated by a National Plan and the application of scientific and technological advances to industry would be furthered by a new Ministry of Technology. But the central components of Labour's programme were set by Keynesian social democracy: (1) the active management of the economy using the instruments of fiscal policy, indicative planning and prices and incomes policy to accelerate economic growth, foster the planned and equitable rise of incomes and maintain full employment; and (2) the enhancement of social justice and equality via a more progressive tax system and expanded public programmes on health, housing, personal social services and education to be financed mainly by the increments of faster economic growth.

The New Age Abandoned

Within hours of taking office, in October 1964, Wilson, Callaghan and Brown discovered that the economy was in even worst shape than they had imagined. They were informed by the Treasury that the pre-election boom, engineered by the Conservative Chancellor Reginald Maudling, had provoked a massive balance of payments deficit and firm measures were vital to avoid a financial crisis. They were presented with four options: devaluation of sterling, a stiff measure of deflation, import quotas and a temporary import surcharge. The majority of economic experts the new Government had brought in to advise it urged devaluation, as did Crosland, number two at Brown's Department of Economic Affairs and a professional economist. The Treasury and the Bank of England, however, pressed ministers to defend the value of the pound: 'for the officials, the defence of sterling had to be the test of Labour's self-discipline and economic maturity' (Middlemass, 1990: 114). The three senior politicians, without consulting the Cabinet, were all, for varying reasons, dubious about the value of devaluation and accepted the advice. As an emergency step, it was decided to impose an import surcharge – a controversial move since it was inconsistent with Britain's obligations to EFTA (the European Free Trade Association) and was much resented by its other members.

A budget was introduced shortly after in November which fulfilled several manifesto pledges, including the abolition of prescription charges and the raising of social security benefits and pensions. These were were balanced, in a fiscally neutral package, by increases in income and excise taxes (Ponting, 1989: 68). However, the budget was poorly received by the City and world financial opinion (Middlemass, 1990: 114). What then followed was a pattern that was to recur again and again throughout the life of the Government. The pound was engulfed by wave after wave of speculatory sales: in one day the Bank spent over 30 per cent of available currency reserves to staunch the flow out of sterling. The pressure was temporarily relieved by a combination of overseas borrowings from the main central banks, especially the US

Federal Reserve, standby credits from the IMF and higher interest rates (Ponting, 1989: 69–70).

This brought the new Government only a temporary respite. It was urged by the Treasury, the Bank, the US, the IMF and foreign central banks to take tough action to rein-in the domestic economy, but was loath to so quickly disenchant its supporters by slicing public expenditure programmes – which were mostly inherited from the Tories. Instead, it opted for a more gradual approach. The 1965 budget, which saw the introduction of the Capital Gains and Corporation Taxes, the raising of excise duties and steps to restrict overseas investment, was mildly deflationary (Ponting, 1989: 73). Despite additional borrowings, sterling was soon in the doldrums again following poor trade figures and wage settlements above the norm of 3–3½ per cent set by the Government's income policy. To stem outflows of sterling, the Government negotiated a further $1.4 billion from the IMF in return for a stronger squeeze on demand. The result was the July 1965 package of deflationary measures, including action to delay public sector investment projects and tighter higher purchase controls (Stewart, 1977: 53).

The 1964 manifesto had called for 'a planned growth of incomes broadly related to the annual growth of production'. This would apply to all incomes 'to profits, dividends and rents as well as wages and salaries'. In December 1964 the Government, the employers and the unions reached agreement over a *Joint Statement of Intent on Productivity, Prices and Incomes*. This declared that in order to rectify the balance of payments and increase competitiveness the growth of incomes had to be kept in line with the rise in output. Union wage moderation was intended to be part of a broader economic programme geared to higher growth, to be stimulated by the National Plan. Incomes policy on a voluntary basis was acceptable to the TUC but the policy had lasted no more than a few months before the Government – prodded by the Americans and a nervous foreign exchange market – decided that a purely voluntary system would not suffice.[2] Shortly after the deflationary measures of July 1965 the Government took powers to require early notice of wage claims, to refer them to the Prices and Incomes Board (set up to monitor pay and price trends) and to delay the implementation of wage agreements until the Board had reported. After tough talks, Brown obtained TUC approval for the proposed legislation in September 1965 and funds were duly forthcoming from the US and the main European countries to safeguard the pound (Stewart, 1977: 54). The TUC agreed to introduce its own wage-vetting system but the unions resented interference with collective bargaining and the substantial support that incomes policy initially attracted began to melt away. For the moment, loyalty to the Government, and a desire not to embarrass it in the face of a further electoral test, kept the unions in line.

By early 1966 Labour had built up a strong lead in the polls. An election was called in June 1966 and, after a quiet campaign, its support reached almost 48 per cent of the vote, it won an additional 46 seats and swept back to office with a majority of a hundred. It was only the second time in its history that the Party won a comfortable majority, a personal triumph for Wilson, whose reputation now stood at its peak. With the Government no longer having to scrape around for votes and manoeuvre for an imminent election, the aspirations of supporters were high that now many of Labour's promises would be fulfilled. But – despite the glowing picture painted during the election campaign – economic difficulties remained as intractable as ever. In July the industrial scene darkened with the outbreak of the seamen's strike. Like most major disputes, the strike was a complex one, the product of a long build-up of disaffection. As Wilson recorded in his memoirs, 'for years the National Union of Seamen had been little more than a companies' union, and ship owners and union officials had an equal responsibility for the utter frustration of union members, many of whom felt that that their interest had been entrusted to a union which was little more than a "stooge" of the employers' (Wilson, 1971: 227). An inquiry was set up which reported in favour of a compromise, but this was rejected by the union. Wilson, worried by the effect of the strike upon the country's fragile balance of payments, determined to fight the matter out.[3] On the basis of briefs from the security services alleging intense Communist activity in the union, he claimed that the inquiry's compromise was sabotaged by 'a tightly knit group of politically motivated men' set upon damaging the economic welfare of the nation (Pimlott, 1992: 407). Soon after, the strike ended but, notwithstanding, pressure on sterling continued to mount and the Government had a crisis on its hands.

For eighteen months devaluation had been firmly excluded from the Cabinet agenda. But with the prospect of yet another bout of deflation, the patience of a group of ministers from both right and left, including Brown, Crossman, Jenkins, Crosland and Castle was exhausted and they made a powerful call for devaluation. Wilson, backed by Callaghan and the Treasury, refused to budge. He had participated in the 1949 devaluation, believed that Cripps's reputation had been severely damaged by it and felt it was essential to prevent the Labour being dubbed the 'party of devaluation'. Both he and Callaghan feared that, in a fixed exchange-rate regime, devaluation of the world's second most important currency would have had a generally destabilizing effect, particularly on the dollar. Further, the future of sterling as an international currency and of the Sterling Area depended on the faith of overseas holders in the integrity of the pound. Above all, the strength of sterling was seen as a matter of prestige, a tangible embodiment of Britain's continued importance as a player on the world stage – 'almost' as Callaghan later acknowledged, 'a moral issue' (Callaghan, 1987: 159). Finally, behind the scenes, the Americans had made aid to prop up the pound conditional on the Government eschewing devaluation. Brown split the devaluers' camp by exploiting the dispute to make an intemperate bid for the premiership. The Prime Minister and the Chancellor manoeuvred successfully to surmount opposition and managed to obtain Cabinet approval for 'the biggest deflationary package ever' (Stewart, 1977: 73).

The £500 million worth of cuts included increases in indirect taxation, the tightening of hire purchase restrictions, and a £150 million reduction in public spending investment and overseas expenditure. This was coupled with a drastic six months' wages and prices freeze and a further six months of 'severe restraint'. Times come when awkward choices have to be made. July 1966 was such a moment as growth and the existing levels of employment were sacrificed in an effort to protect the pound. 'Faced with a range of options from import controls and defence cuts through devaluation to deflation, they chose to implement the standard Treasury deflationary package that had been used in every economic crisis for the previous ten years – except this time it was more drastic because the situation was worse' (Ponting, 1989: 200). It was a reversion to the Tory 'stop–go' policies so much deplored by Labour in opposition. The July measures had two major consequences: the additional resources which were supposed to accrue from higher growth to fund larger social outlays were now not going to materialize, meaning either heavier taxes, slimmed-down social aspirations or – as happened – both. Secondly, they

effectively pulled the rug from under the National Plan, upon which so
many hopes had been built.

Planning and Industrial Policy

The 1964 manifesto argued that the Conservative 'restoration of a "free"
market economy' was responsible for the laggardly rate of economic
expansion (Craig, 1975: 255). In its place, Labour promised to introduce
a National Plan to promote a more vibrant and efficient economy.
At the beginning of the 1960s there was a vogue for planning with
the success of the French economy attributed largely to its planning
system. Labour was running with the grain of mainstream thinking:
economic commentators in the quality press, and managerial and business circles were increasingly attracted towards a more pro-active role
for the government. The move towards planning had been begun
under the Conservatives: indeed, according to the economist Samuel
Brittan, 'much of the small print of the 1965 National Plan, and
Mr Wilson's own "purposive physical intervention" had already been
enacted before Labour came to office' (quoted in Hatfield, 1978: 28).[4]
'Only its evangelical language distinguished it from the Conservative
inheritance' (Middlemass, 1990: 123).

According to the Brookings Institution the National Plan was an
attempt 'to develop a co-ordinated, internally consistent set of projections of how the economy might develop to 1970 and thereby create
expectations that would induce private economic decisions to conform
to the projections' (quoted in Opie, 1972: 163). This mode of planning
did not involve any significant transgression of the market order or
business autonomy but sought to enhance the competitive position of
British industry in domestic and foreign markets by intensified and
institutionalized collaboration between government and industry. In the
eyes of George Brown, the man charged with the task of organizing
the plan, 'the whole point of the National Plan was to identify areas
where there were weaknesses in the existing situation and where we
should concentrate our resources. In that way individual industries and
sectors could see clearly what they had to do to enable this overall
national result to be achieved' (Opie, 1972: 162). The Plan aimed at
a 25 per cent increase in national output over the period 1964–70, an

annual rate of 3.8 per cent. The implications of the 25 per cent target were worked out for the various components of GDP such as private consumption and investment and 'a checklist was drawn up of the action required by management and unions if the overall and sectoral targets were to be attained' (Stewart, 1977: 50). The government would create the macro-economic conditions to facilitate growth by committing itself to a series of targets in terms of growth, fiscal policy, employment and the balance of payments.

To the proponents of planning, the Treasury's grip over economic policy formation was a major hindrance. Giving precedence to the control of public expenditure and protection of the exchange rate, it knew little about industry and was suspicious about expanding the state's role in the economy. In opposition Labour decided that a counterweight was required to act as a powerful and strategically-located force for modernization. Immediately on taking office a Department of Economic Affairs was established, headed by the number two in Labour's hierarchy, the unstable but dynamic George Brown. He rapidly emerged as a persuasive apostle for planning and the National Plan was unveiled to great fanfare. It was the means by which the sluggish British economy could be rejuvenated. 'If Wilson and his Government in the 1960s were remembered for something distinctive' Wilson's biographer wrote, 'it was for this' (Pimlott, 1992: 361). But its life-span was short and dismal. By the time it was published (in September 1965) it had ceased to be relevant and by the following year its emaciated remains were buried with discreet embarrassment.

Some doubt, in fact, must attach to whether the National Plan merited the appellation 'planning' at all. At a minimum, a plan requires clearly specified goals and mechanisms to induce relevant actors to conform to the behaviour expected of them, and an appropriate macro-economic policy. In each respect the National Plan suffered from major defects. There was a lack of precision in its thinking – words like 'target', 'forecast' and 'projection' were used indiscriminately (Leruez, 1975: 171–2). As the TUC commented in a paper to the NEDC in August 1965 'it is difficult to extract from [the Plan's] complexity a clear sense of the priorities underlying it' (Middlemass, 1990: 125). Furthermore, the Plan lacked any means of implementation, with neither the carrots nor sticks which planning authorities in France possessed. Investment incentives were non-selective and could not be used to promote the

Plan's sectoral priorities and the planners exercised no control over credit allocations, an essential condition of any workable interventionist strategy.

Finally, the DEA failed as a counter-weight to the Treasury. It was only with difficulty that Callaghan and Brown agreed a boundary between their two departments, based on the distinction between long-term planning and short-term policy. But the distinction was a false one: as Samuel Brittan predicted in 1964, if 'the Treasury remains responsible for the balance of payments, for taxation, for the Bank rate, and for the use of devices like the Regulator, it is likely to remain the effective economic ministry' (Walker, 1987: 204). All the means of implementation were left to the Treasury and 'the DEA had none of the powers of economic sanction or inducement over industry, trade, scientific policy or state infrastructure, let alone fiscal policy a full Ministry of the Plan required' (Middlemass, 1990: 122). Further, most key officials were recruited from the Treasury, injecting traditional Treasury thinking into a new department which was supposed to impart a fresh approach to economic management. Any lingering prospect of success disappeared with the decision to rule out devaluation. The deflationary bouts of July 1965 and July 1966 destroyed any possibility of reaching the targets set by the Plan, eliminated confidence in its projections and totally undermined its credibility. By selecting the defence of sterling as the chief object of policy, Labour constructed a macro-economic framework which forfeited any prospect of a faster expansion of the economy. 'The failure to accord growth priority over the preservation of the exchange rate doomed the Plan from the start' (Stewart, 1977: 51).

The 1964 Manifesto called for state-led modernization of the economy through government promotion of new technology and Research and Development and the creation of hi-tech public industries. One of the first acts of the new Government was the establishment of a Ministry of Technology, initially headed by the TGWU leader, Frank Cousins and then, after his resignation, by Anthony Wedgewood Benn, a vigorous young minister close to Wilson. However, Labour's approach to industry displayed little of the strategic thinking that appeared to inform Wilson's speeches in opposition. Industrial policy, after the demise of the National Plan, consisted of a collection of loosely-related policy instruments geared to incremental improvements in efficiency, investment and productivity.

Corporation tax was introduced in 1965 with the object of encouraging industry to plough back a larger proportion of profits into investment rather than into dividends. Selective Employment Tax, levied only on employment on the service sector, was designed to encourage the flow of manpower into manufacturing. Investment allowances replaced grants in the belief that they would be more effective in boosting new investment (Ponting, 1989: 279; Steward, 1977: 97). A new interventionist body, the Industrial Reorganisation Corporation (IRC), was established but in structure, scale and objectives bore little resemblance to Labour's thinking in opposition. With a board consisting almost entirely of industrialists, it was primarily a market-facilitating body, seeking to maximize industrial efficiency by creating large industrial units through encouraging mergers and takeovers. For instance, it provided funds to facilitate the amalgamation of two vehicle manufacturers to form British Leyland. It was expected to earn a commercial rate on its operations as a whole rather than taking account of activities from which broader economic or social benefits might accrue but that seemed unlikely to make a profit (Leruez, 1975: 215; Graham, 1972: 98–9). Industrial policy was also weak on implementation. The Government was unwilling, for instance, to make selective and discriminatory use of aid to alter corporate behaviour preferring to rely on co-operation between state agencies and the private sector. 'Such a consensual approach to industrial policy stands in striking contrast to the more *dirigiste* policies of Japan and France, where sectoral plans were drawn up by the state rather than industry, where individual firms were the direct objects of numerous programmes, and where a host of public sanctions were employed to enforce implementation' (Hall, 1986: 54). Indeed, the more the ambit of the state expanded, the more it became reliant on the goodwill of the corporate sector. The Industrial Expansion Act, 1968 empowered the Ministry of Technology to supply funds to firms that wanted to introduce new techniques that might not be immediately profitable or market new products for which there was no assured commercial future. It was a case of too little, too late, as time was now running out for the Government. Overall there was little evidence that any of the Government's initiatives in the areas achieved any very significant improvement in investment, innovation or productivity (Leruez, 1975: 215–16; Ponting, 1989: 273).

Little needs to be said about public ownership, since it hardly figured on the Government's agenda. The 1964 manifesto, *Let's Go with Labour*, contained a pledge to nationalize steel which was, by the 1960s, an ailing, inefficient industry succumbing to foreign competitors and this was eventually honoured, mainly for internal political reasons. Although the manifesto called for an expansion of the existing nationalized industries, this never materialized. In general, the Government displayed a distinct reluctance to extend public ownership, preferring to encourage private sector mergers and takeovers as a way of rationalizing the industrial structure in line with the ruling thinking that 'big was beautiful'. Furthermore, the performance of the nationalized industries and the yield obtained from them were impaired by a confusion of aims and policies. Effective corporate planning and modernization was constantly disrupted by delays and cut-backs in investment projects as the Government used the level of public sector investment as a mechanism of macro-economic management. It was not until 1969, when most of the nationalized sector came under the jurisdiction of the Ministry of Technology that a more consistent approach to investment and pricing policy evolved (Middlemass 1990: 173–4).

Devaluation

The external deficit shrank as a result of the July 1966 deflation but at the cost of stagnant output and rising unemployment. The six months' wages freeze followed by a period of 'severe restraint' was very reluctantly accepted and only by a wafer-thin majority at the 1966 TUC Congress (Stewart, 1977: 74). It was reasonably effective – in the year after July 1966 wages rose by only 2 per cent and prices by 4 per cent – but a complete freeze on wages and prices can only be short-term if the functioning of the labour market is not to be impaired. In the spring of 1967 a new Prices and Incomes Act adopted a zero norm, with wage increases only to be granted in 'worthy cases'. Rather than being part of a long-term policy to raise real incomes and narrow inequalities, it was now quite evident that incomes policy was simply a form of pay restraint. Restrictive economic policies seeking to uphold sterling at a rate that underlying economic realities did not justify stoked up opposition in the unions and also within the PLP were there were a number of backbench rebellions (Barnes and Reid, 1980: 87).

Nor did the improvement in the trade figures persist. In late spring 1967 a combination of the application for EC membership, poor trade figures and the Six Day War led to another massive run on the pound. The reserves and credit entitlements dwindled, trading performance remained mediocre and speculation against a fragile pound resumed. 'Despite all the loans and support operations, combined with a substantial deflation, the underlying position was as bad as it had been when Labour took office in October 1964' (Ponting, 1989: 289–90). The price of further loans would include statutory wage restraint, more deflation and strict IMF monitoring of the economy. After all the sacrifices made, many within the governing Party would not stomach yet another round of deflation and opinion both within the Cabinet and the Treasury now swung decisively in favour of devaluation.

But devaluation was a bitter pill. All the foreign borrowings, cutbacks in public spending, increases in taxation and restraints on wages now appeared to be wasted. Furthermore, Wilson had always regarded the sterling rate as a symbol of national standing and prestige. 'The Government had talked and acted for so long as if devaluation was a fate worse than death that it is hardly surprising that when it came people should have regarded it as a major national defeat and humiliation' (Stewart, 1977: 83). A crestfallen Callaghan immediately tended his resignation, but remained in the Cabinet as he swapped places with Roy Jenkins, the Home Secretary. Wilson's rather complacent assurance that the way was now cleared for economic recovery further damaged his credibility.

The City condemned the Government for its 'betrayal' of overseas sterling-holders; and salt was rubbed into the wound by the insistence of foreign creditors and the IMF on a further squeeze on the economy Financial markets felt that devaluation, having once been employed, might be repeated and doubted whether the new rate of $2.40 to the pound would stick (Stewart, 1977: 85). *Whatever* the Government did now appeared to foster speculative attacks on sterling. Furthermore, tremors in the foreign exchange markets were now becoming more frequent and more dangerous. During the next two years the franc, the Deutschmark and, finally, the mighty dollar were to come under intense pressure[5] – and, whatever the cause, the backwash was always the same: sudden and massive selling of sterling. Not only was the public left with the impression of continued mishandling of the economy, but the morale of ministers was battered as they tried desperately to avert the ultimate disaster of a second devaluation. Time and again the Cabinet was told by the new Chancellor, Roy Jenkins, that it had to endorse fresh packages of public spending cuts and tax rises – no less than five in the two years following devaluation. Wilson and Jenkins believed that a reduction in the level of domestic demand by means of a tight fiscal and monetary policy was essential to stabilize the pound and push resources into exports. The steps taken included stiffening hire purchase terms, increases in purchase tax, SET (Selective Employment Tax), corporation tax and excise duties; higher interest rates and limits on bank lending; and a steady reduction of public expenditure. Some measures were widely welcomed in the Party as long overdue, notably cuts in defence spending and withdrawal from East of Suez. Others were only agreed after prolonged struggle in the Cabinet – and to the dismay of many Party supporters outside – including the postponement of the planned raising of the school leaving age from fifteen to sixteen and the reimposition of prescription charges (Stewart, 1977: 87–9).

Eventually the tied turned. In 1970 there was a surplus on current account of £735 million, the largest in real terms since 1950; overseas lending was reduced by half and the reserves greatly replenished. The public sector borrowing requirement (PSBR) – which the Government pledged the IMF to reduce – fell heavily and in 1969–70, the last full year of Jenkins's chancellorship, the budget moved into surplus (Stewart, 1977: 87, 90). The effect of this 'marathon of taxing and squeezing' combined with the greater export competitiveness delivered by a lower pound was a considerable transfer of resources into the balance of payments at the expense of private consumption and public spending. Whilst export volumes grew by 27 per cent between 1967 and 1970, private consumption crept up only by 5.4 per cent and public consumption by less than 1 per cent (Stewart, 1977: 89). But the cost of this – as Castle and Crosland complained in Cabinet – was a growth rate low by both European and post-1945 standards and acquiescence in a level of unemployment higher than Labour had inherited (Castle, 1984: 562). Furthermore, the combination of a heftier tax burden and a laggardly growth in wages did much to undermine the respect in which Labour's economic capabilities were held by blue- and white-collar workers.

Post-devaluation, income restraint remained as important as ever. Depreciation of the currency inevitably imported inflationary pressures and higher taxes compressed take-home pay. From the Government's vantage point the build-up of wage pressure had to be resisted if the competitive advantage gained by a lower exchange rate was not to be lost and financial opinion overseas reassured. But, on the union side disenchantment was now rampant and at the 1967 TUC Congress a motion attacking statutory income restraint was carried by a sizeable majority (Taylor, 1993: 140–2). Jenkins riposted that, if incomes policy was scrapped, then there would be no alternative to even more austere polices. In early 1968 a further instalment of wage limitation was announced with a 3 ½ per cent limit on pay (and dividends) to be relaxed only on the grounds of 'genuine' productivity agreements. This was backed up by government powers to defer wage and price rises for twelve months. But the political credit that had bought union acquiescence in the past was now largely dissipated and a motion calling for repeal of pay policy was overwhelmingly passed at Congress. Between April 1968 and 1969 wage rates rose by 5 per cent and earnings by around 7 per cent. Barbara Castle, promoted in 1968 to the post of First Secretary and Secretary of State for Employment, tried to hold back wage advances well beyond the ceiling but by the end of 1968 the twin task of preserving the incomes policy without provoking serious strikes was testing the capacity of even so formidable a minister (Barnes and Reid, 1980: 104).

Wilson told the TUC Congress just before the 1964 election that a Labour Government would contribute 'three necessary conditions' to ensure the success of an incomes policy: 'an assurance of rising production and rising incomes ... equity and social justice' and the application of the policy to profits, dividends and rents (Taylor, 1993: 131). In practice, growth was very modest, progress towards more equity and social justice was seriously impeded by the scarcity of resources and no effective controls limited the growth of profits and dividends. With the Government's decision to give priority to the value of the pound, pay policy was disentangled from a general strategy for growth and welfare and became, instead, a part of a deflationary policy of curtailing demand and lowering wage costs. In these circumstances, the terms of co-operation were considerably less appealing to the unions. For other reasons, too, conditions were becoming increasingly less propitious for wages policy. Norms had been more rigorously applied in the public than the private sector where skill shortages were bidding up the price of labour, and wages drift enabled work groups with industrial leverage to maintain or increase their income whilst industrially weaker groups slipped down the pay table. All this provoked indignation and frustration (Coates, 1989: 51). Industrial radicals benefited from disaffection on the shop floor with figures such as Hugh Scanlon in the engineering union and Laurence Daly and Arthur Scargill in the NUM defeating right-wing candidates. Scanlon, Cousins and his successor, Jack Jones (elected in 1969) tenaciously upheld the right of unions to engage in free collective bargaining and were in no mood to acquiesce in policies which would reduce the living standards of their members.[6] In these circumstances, the ability of the Government to hold the line on pay visibly withered.

In Place of Strife

By the late 1960s the incidence of industrial disputes was growing rapidly. Between 1964 and 1967, the average number of days lost through strikes ranged from 2–3 million. The following year this doubled to 4.7 million and reached 6.8 million in 1969 (Whitehead, 1985: 19). Of these, a high proportion were unofficial (held without specific union authorization) and many were 'unconstitutional', that is in breach of agreed procedures. Orders were being forfeited through interrupted production, and the growth of plant-level bargaining was producing a rash of leapfrogging claims causing mounting levels of wage-inflation and undermining nationally-agreed pay policy. Further, there was growing anxiety in industry, the press and government about the damaging effect to industrial efficiency of overmanning, restrictive practices and resistance to new technology. The wave of strikes was extensively reported and as the unions incurred growing unpopularity, pressure built-up on the government to impose legal restraints.

At this point, the long-awaited report by the Donovan Committee into trade unions appeared. The Committee had been set-up in 1965 to investigate problems in the industrial relations system. Its report argued that the rising level of industrial conflict stemmed from the erosion of the established national structure of collective bargaining, increasingly displaced by a decentralized pattern of shop-floor bargaining. For Donovan, the essence of the problem was the widening gap between the informal and the formal systems of collective bargaining. The conflict between the two was the prime cause of 'the disorder in factory and workshop relations and pay structures' (Robinson, 1972: 319). The informal system was under-institutionalized and increasingly splintered. The breakdown of norms and procedures needed to sustain orderly labour relations – manifested in confusion over management rights, inadequate disciplinary and grievance procedures, chaotic pay structures and differentials – lay at the root of many of the unofficial strikes spreading across British industry. Further, the expansion of shop-floor bargaining had sapped the role and standing of full-time officials in collective bargaining as well as eroding managerial authority (Goldthorpe, 1977: 188). It followed that the remedy did not lie in imposing a legal framework but in encouraging employers and unions to undertake a programme of institutional reform designed to codify the informal shop-floor level of bargaining and re-establish a more harmonious, rule-governed framework (Goldthorpe, 1977: 189–90).

The Employment Secretary was sympathetic to the pluralist assumptions underpinning Donovan's analysis. She rejected calls from the Tories and business circles for the legal enforcement of collective agreements, the banning of sympathy action and the closed shop and favoured enacting recommendations from the report designed to strengthen collective bargaining. Thus the White Paper prepared in response to the report, *In Place of Strife*, included steps requiring employers to recognize and negotiate with unions, giving union representatives access to information for bargaining purposes and encouraging worker participation. It was hoped this would tempt the unions to accept the rest of the package. Here the White Paper departed from Donovan. The most contentious items were as follows: in cases of unofficial strikes, the government was empowered, if the effects of the strike appeared likely to be serious, to issue an Order requiring a return to work for 28 days, though on conditions existing prior to the dispute (to stop management from unilateral imposing changes). The pause was designed to enable the Department of Employment to secure a settlement but if it failed the parties to the dispute were free to act as they pleased. Further, the Secretary of State was empowered to require a union to hold a pre-strike ballot, 'where it was believed that the proposed strike would involve a serious threat to the economy or public interest, or there would be doubt as to whether it commanded the support of those concerned' (Robinson, 1972: 323). The Secretary of State would be responsible for the wording of the ballot. Finally, the Secretary of State would have the right to refer an inter-union dispute over recognition and bargaining rights first to the TUC and, if need be, to the new Commission on Industrial relations (CIR) and to require both unions and employers to accept the CIR's recommendation.

Why did Wilson, Castle and their supporters ignore Donovan and opt for legal regulation? Incomes policy was palpably faltering: in 1968 both the TUC and the Party Conference overwhelmingly rejected pay policy. The position of union leaders who had negotiated income regulation was being eroded from within as the rank and file turned increasingly to shop stewards, and local bargaining. Donovan appeared to offer no practical answer to high wage claims, strikes, restrictive practices, rigid job demarcations and over-manning, all issues which were increasingly disturbing ministers (Middlemass, 1990: 229). Further, the balance of payments had not yet responded to devaluation and foreign confidence, still very shaky, was bound to be further disturbed as the Government's retreat from pay policy became evident (Barnes and Reid, 1980: 105). Healey, then Defence Secretary, later recalled that Wilson 'came to the conclusion that his pay policy wasn't working, and didn't have public support, and therefore he'd go about it another way, and he made a cold-blooded calculation that he'd get more public support for a direct attack on union power . . . ' (Whitehead, 1985: 20–2). The Conservatives had recently published proposals for tough action against the unions and, given the swelling hostility to strikers and the unions, obviously intended to make political mileage. Ever the tactician, Wilson wanted to pre-empt the Tories: when he read *In Place of Strife*, according to Mrs Castle 'he was delighted. He thought it outmanoeuvred the Tories – he thought it first and foremost as a very skilful weapon for defeating Heath' (quoted in Pimlott, 1992: 528). As part of his attempt to transform Labour into 'the natural party of government' he saw an opportunity to demonstrate its 'national' credentials and distance it from the unions. Nor was he alone in his calculations. According to Sir Denis Barnes, then Permanent Secretary at the DEP, 'many Labour politicians considered the trade unions a liability rather than an asset' (Whitehead, 1985: 21).

Mrs. Castle, for her part, was much influenced by her involvement in industrial conflicts. Her diaries detail the immense amount of time and effort she expended in seeking to resolve industrial disputes and at the same time preserve the remnants of incomes policy. Whilst discussions over Donovan were taking place, a union demarcation row at Girling Brakes and a strike of ten men at Vauxhall led to thousands of layoffs in the car industry, there was unofficial action at Fords and in the steel industry there were inter-union disputes over negotiating rights (Barnes and Reid, 1980: 119). She saw the dispute at Girling (where a handful of machine setters, members of the engineering union, refused to accept the instructions of an ASTMS charge-hand) as 'typical of the industrial anarchy' pervading labour relations as a few workers strategically employed in a highly-integrated industry caused 'massive damage'. Unofficial strikes in the motor industry were spreading, she complained, and becoming more intractable 'and both the Government and the employers were in despair' (Castle, 1984: 508). In her diaries there is a subtle shift in the usage of the term 'industrial anarchy' from being a description to becoming an explanation of the problem. She became increasingly receptive to her officials' argument that the inflexibility of labour practices and the growth of shop floor power were major causes of economic weakness.

Government action which breached the much treasured trade union doctrine of voluntarism (that is, the absence of legal regulation in industrial relations) was bound to be contentious and, indeed, opposition from the unions to *In Place of Strife* was total and unrelenting. Singling out unofficial and 'unconstitutional' strikes did nothing to reassure them since, according to Department of Employment estimates, 95 per cent of recorded strikes were unofficial and an overwhelming majority were also 'unconstitutional'.[7] Union leaders also strongly objected to the principle of subjecting individual trade unionists to legal penalties, and to granting to the Secretary of State the right to frame the wording of a ballot and decide when a ballot was necessary because it would reduce the prospects of a successful strike call and sooner or later be used by a Tory minister (Robinson, 1972: 325). Though the conflict was presented by the media as a straight fight between the Government and the unions, opposition extended well beyond the industrial wing. The NEC – still with a right-wing majority – rejected the White Paper as did a growing number of MPs. This included not only left-wing MPs but also, more worryingly, many from the normally loyalist and right-wing members of the trade union group. Following the debate on the White Paper on 3 March 1969, fifty-five Labour MP's voted against and about forty abstained (Pimlott, 1992: 533). Many shared the unions' belief that *In Place of Strife* contained unwarranted threats to the right of working people to combine to defend their interests whilst others felt that any policy initiative that placed such tremendous strains on the loyalty of the unions to the Party was foolhardy. Principle, pragmatic judgement – and ambition – stirred dissent in the Cabinet too. The most dangerous opponent was the Home Secretary, Jim Callaghan. His reputation had been seriously tarnished by devaluation but in his next ministerial portfolio, at the Home Office, he adroitly retrieved much of it, in Crossman's words 'building up his position as a plain-style man of the people who will have no nonsense . . . easily the most accomplished politician in the Labour Party' (Howard, 1991: 590, 647). His additional post of Treasurer of the Party had given him the opportunity to establish friendly relations with many trade union leaders and he seized the opportunity to add another dimension to his political persona as the man who understood the unions: in Peter Jenkins's marvellous phrase, he became 'the Keeper of the Cloth Cap'. 'Behind the glad-hand charm, behind the beaming visage of Sunny Jim' was the politician with 'the cat-like speed of claw' (Jenkins, 1970: 82). With great shrewdness and dexterity, and not a little guile, he used the issue to bolster his personal position, presenting himself as the obvious successor if Wilson's obduracy precipitated his downfall.

Whatever had been the prospect of getting the legislation through the House more or less vanished after a speech from the respected and influential chairman of the PLP, Douglas Houghton, in which he warned that any benefits *In Place of Strife* might bring could not possibly outweigh 'the harm we can do to our Government by the disintegration or defeat of the Labour Party' (Ziegler, 1993: 307). When the Chief Whip, Bob Melish, was asked to report on the prospects of enacting legislation, he bleakly advised that a large percentage of the PLP would not vote for the bill (Pimlott, 1992: 540). By the summer of 1969, support within the Cabinet was cracking and Wilson and Castle became increasingly isolated. After one Cabinet meeting, the Prime Minister railed in a typical piece of bravado 'I don't mind running a green Cabinet but I'm buggered if I'm going to run a yellow one' (Ziegler, 1993: 309). His suspicions and accusations of disloyalty, one biographer wrote, 'were perfectly justified. His enemies were simply waiting for the right moment' (Pimlott, 1992: 535). With their hand so weakened, last minute attempts by Wilson and Castle to persuade the

TUC to alter its rules in ways that could meet some of the purposes of the White Paper failed and eventually they had to make do with 'solemn and binding' (soon dubbed 'Solomon Binding') pledges that the General Council would do its utmost to prevent or resolve inter-union disputes and unofficial disputes.

Barbara Castle continued to believe the package would have benefited the unions and her argument was in many ways persuasive: certainly in light of what was to happen after 1979, the unions would have done well to have been more amenable, especially over pre-strike ballots and inter-union disputes. Far from being too 'political', as often alleged, the problem was that the perspective of most union leaders rarely transcended the industrial relations field. Ironically, this was particularly so in the case of ostensibly left-wing leaders who, in practice, were content to reiterate the mantras of free collective bargaining whilst giving little thought to the impact of unfettered wage bargaining on employment, inflation and the pursuit of social justice. The characteristic attitudes and mentality of national officials and shop stewards were, in turn, strongly influenced by the unions' organizational structures and there was undoubtedly a strong case for their reform. But coupling organizational reform to an attempt to tilt the balance of industrial power from labour to capital had the predictable effect of rendering an arduous task more or less impossible. Seeking to restore industrial order by converting union officers into disciplinary agents of their own rank and file was equally misguided. As the Donovan Report had explained, trade union leaders 'cannot be industry's policemen. They are democratic leaders in organizations in which the seat of power has always been close to the members' (quoted in Hyman, 1989: 51). If union officials were seen to be co-operating with management to reassert control, then their *rapport* with their grass-roots would be put under even greater strain (Goldthorpe, 1977: 195). Finally, to conclude that the root cause of Labour's disappointing performance in office was union obstinacy and conservatism would be as unbalanced as ignoring it. Even if unions had been more accommodating over incomes policy, and less rigid over internal reform, there is little reason to believe, for reasons that will be developed later, that the basic thrust of Government policy would have altered much. The roots of Labour's problems ran deeper.

Wilson had described *In Place of Strife* as 'essential to our economic

recovery; essential to the balance of payments; essential to full employment' (quoted in Middlemass, 1990: 242). The issue inevitably was
portrayed by the media in terms of a contest between the Government
and union power and 'a test of [Wilson's] conception of Labour's capacity
to govern' (Walker, 1987: 199). Defeat meant that the Government
suffered public humiliation, Wilson's prestige plummeted further and
the political career of Labour's most dynamic minister, Barbara Castle,
never recovered. The legacy of *In Place of Strife* was not only badly
disrupted relations with the unions and disillusion throughout the Party
but a serious blow to the claim of Labour to be an effective party of
government.

Social Policy

The turmoil in Labour's ranks over industrial relations issues distracted
attention from its work in the social field, where its main accomplishments lay. A broad consensus existed within the Party that its primary
purpose in government was to create a more equal and socially just
society. This would be achieved by affording greater social protection for
the disadvantaged through the welfare system, enhancing and equalizing
educational opportunities, providing a decent standard of housing for all,
improving the National Health Service and promoting a more equitable
distribution of income and wealth.

Housing was a major issue in the 1964 election. Labour promised
to build half a million housing units a year, and the house-building
programme received a high priority in the allocation of public resources.
Though the target was never reached much building did occur, with
over two million dwellings completed between 1965 and 1970. The
problem lay in their quality: in the rush to build, and to overcome
shortages in funds, the Government succumbed to the fashion for
high-rise blocks of flats (Ponting, 1989: 122–4). The housing drive
pinpointed flaws in Labour's centralist brand of social democracy:
the assumption that the interests of ordinary members of the public
would be adequately safeguarded by public officials without the need
to consult them; a well-intentioned but short-sighted belief that pledges
could be honoured by spreading resources more thinly; and a 'social
engineering' approach to reform in which the calculation of the effects

of institutional reform neglected their impact upon the overall quality of people's lives. The consequence was that people were wrenched from their local communities and transferred to forbidding and isolating environments which often lacked basic social and commercial amenities and which hindered the revival of community networks. Far from being an instrument of social equalization, as Bevan the first of Labour's post-war housing ministers had dreamt, high-rise council flats intensified class inequalities by becoming a low-grade reserve for the poorer sections of the working class. High-rise flats reflected the extent to which Keynesian social democracy had departed from the traditions of ethical socialism, with its aspirations to construct institutions which would foster greater fellowship, a communal spirit and more altruistic forms of behaviour. This had been airily dismissed by Crosland and other practical reformers as backward-looking and utopian, but the new soulless working-class estates were soon to be the breeding grounds of a host of social ills, as socialists from an older generation like William Morris could have predicted.

By the 1960s education had come to be seen as a powerful lever for eroding class privileges. The eleven-plus and the split between grammar and secondary modern schools, introduced by the Butler Education Act, was widely regarded by Labour educationalists as an insuperable barrier to greater equality, with the bulk of working children being taught in lower quality, more poorly-funded schools in a setting which discouraged effort and dampened aspirations. Under successive Education Secretaries, especially Tony Crosland, local educational authorities were encouraged and cajoled into abolishing the eleven-plus and replacing grammar and secondary modern schools by comprehensives. However, the hopes of educational reformers suffered a setback when, in one of its periodic exercises in pruning public expenditure, the decision was taken to postpone the raising of the school leaving age from fifteen to sixteen.

However, the keystone of social inequality, a crucial conduit for the generational transmission of privilege, was the public school sector. Public schools, Crosland persuasively argued in *The Future of Socialism*, furnished not only a superior education but 'further crucial advantages of right accent, manners, and dependability of character'. These advantages were 'a major determinant of occupation, and hence of income, power and prestige' and their distribution was 'correlated almost exclusively with parents' wealth and class location . . . ' (Crosland, 1964: 140). Those with a public school education had a far better chance of securing places at Oxford and Cambridge, themselves part of the ladder to high-status, well-remunerated jobs; whilst the top echelons of finance, the professions and broadcasting contained a wholly disproportionate number of products from the elite public schools. Precisely for this reason, any measure to reduce the privileges of public schools was likely to be fiercely resisted and, for a cautious Government encumbered by many problems, an assault on the heart of privilege was not inviting. One or two reforms were considered but when their attention was drawn by their (largely public-school educated) officials to the very knotty 'practical difficulties' which would have to be surmounted, education ministers usually felt relieved of any obligation to proceed. Hence, no action was taken, even when Crosland served as Education Secretary.

More headway was, however, made in higher education. There was an unprecedented increase in the number of students in full-time higher education. 'A brief golden age for high-performing school-leavers' flourished with the universities (including the wave of new ones established in the 1960s) and the newly created Polytechnics 'funded with a generosity, and developed with an enthusiasm and degree of imagination, which British higher education would never see again'. The result was a major extension of educational opportunities (Pimlott, 1992: 513). One new departure, the creation of the Open University, bore Wilson's personal imprint, the measure, as he frequently professed, which gave him the greatest personal satisfaction. Making creative use of the broadcasting media, it was to afford a second chance for a university education to many thousands of adults.

One of the earliest pieces of legislation passed was also one of the most important. The Redundancy Payments Act obligated all employers to pay agreed amounts of redundancy pay, according to length of service and a range of other factors. It aimed to facilitate labour mobility, to reduce trade union opposition to job losses and to provide a cushion for workers by establishing the principle that workers have the right to be compensated for redundancy. The scale of compensation that a redundant employee stood to gain varied considerably, but at least all could be assured of receiving some offsetting payment for loss of income (Ponting, 1989: 134; Castle, 1993: 352).

In 1957, to considerable acclaim throughout the Party, Crossman had introduced a bold plan (drawn up by the three notable social policy experts, Richard Titmuss, Peter Townsend and Brain Abel-Smith) for National Superannuation. The 'pay-as-you-go' principle of the existing state pension system would be replaced by a fully funded scheme where all the benefits would be financed by earlier contributions. The levels of contributions and benefits would be linked to earnings though the payments would be progressive, as the lower paid would receive a higher proportion of their wages in benefits than those on higher incomes. Because of the restrictions placed on opting out and because of the high level of benefits provided, the scheme was designed to discourage the growth of private pensions. It would also make major inroads into wealth inequality and generate a valuable additional source of income for the state. Under the scheme 'the state pension fund would accumulate vast assets and be allowed to buy shares in the stock exchange, thus effectively increasing the level of state ownership'. This could have 'transformed society through its redistributive effects, the inevitable decline of private pensions and the use made of assets the state held' (Ponting, 1989: 138). A somewhat similar scheme had been successfully implemented by the Social Democrats in Sweden in the 1950s, substantially improving the quality of life of people of pensionable age, as well as significantly extending the electoral appeal of the Party (Esping-Andersen, 1984: 160–3). The resources that the Crossman plan would have diverted from the financial markets to the public exchequer would have contributed mightily to avoiding the later budgetary crises which so plagued the welfare state.

However, the measure developed by Crossman in office was a pallid version of the original scheme. The pay-as-you-go principle would be left intact; contracting-out into private pensions made easy, substantial funds would not be accumulated, and problems as to how the additional pensions would be financed in the future would inevitably arise. As Barbara Castle commented, the pass had been sold by the decision not to 'fund' the scheme as envisaged in the 1957 plan: 'we were once again proving that we had no policy for redistributing wealth. We couldn't even find a way of enabling ordinary people to share in the industrial increment. Everything had to be subordinated to the management of the economy and, in a capitalist one, that meant the continuation of inequality was essential . . . I am convinced that unless we get ourselves a policy for fairer shares we shall lose all momentum as a social democratic party' (Castle, 1984: 751, entry 19 January 1970). Progress with even this modest step was, furthermore, incredibly slow largely, according to Crossman, because of resistance within the department.[8] It took years before a White Paper was completed and a bill was only tabled in 1970. Not having reached the statute book by the time of the election, it was promptly dropped by the Conservatives (Ponting, 1989: 137–8).

The main additions to the infrastructure of the welfare state during these years took the form of improvements in the rate and scope of benefits. Family allowances were doubled and there were considerable increases in pensions and supplementary benefits. Furthermore, rates rebates were introduced benefiting about a million poorer households. Expenditure on social services rose from 16 per cent of national wealth in 1964 to 23 per cent in 1970, health from 3.9 per cent to 4.9 per cent and education from 4.8 per cent to 6.1 per cent (Ponting, 1989: 392). The growing proportion of GDP absorbed by public expenditure – and the charge that it was getting out of control – was shortly to become a controversial issue. However, the pace of expansion of publicly funded social programmes in Britain was not out of line with trends in the seven major OECD economies in the 1960s and early 1970s. 'In fact, of these seven countries the UK had both the lowest overall growth rate of social expenditure and the lowest rate of growth of real benefits' (Johnson, 1994: 294).

Another related objective of the Labour Government was a more even distribution of income and wealth. Disparities in the distribution of wealth (all types of assets) were substantially wider than in the distribution of income. However, the Government did little in this area. Though the Party was committed to the creation of a wealth tax, it was never seriously considered by either of the two Chancellors (Stewart, 1972: 84; Castle, 1984: 563). A Capital Gains Tax was introduced in 1965 but with so many exemptions that it merely retarded the rate at which wealth was accumulated (Ponting, 1989: 391). The distribution of net income was evened out a little due to a progressive tax structure, a shift from indirect to direct taxes, the expansion of public services and, in particular, increases in the value of cash benefits (Stewart, 1972: 88, 105). The Equal Pay Act, by establishing the principle of equal pay for equal work, was a first step towards more equal treatment of women (Ponting, 1989: 390). However, given the disappointing rate of economic growth, much of this additional spending was financed out of taxation with the share of national income collected in taxes growing from 32 per cent to 43 per cent during the period of the Government, a factor in the rising curve of wage claims in the late 1960s (Ponting, 1989: 392). Within the limits of the resources available, the social record of the Government was by no means as poor as depicted by its critics at the time. The real problem lay with an economic performance which failed to deliver additional resources.

Social Democracy, Constraints and Choices

The viability of Labour's project rested heavily on a faster rate of economic growth, for it was growth which set the pace at which it could 'build the fair and just society we want to see' (Labour Party *Economic Measures*, 1966, quoted in Beckerman, 1972: 44). But 'when it came to the ultimate choice, the Government preferred to sacrifice faster growth and full employment to the existing exchange rate' (Opie, 1972: 171). Nor did the Government change course after devaluation. Devaluation was not in itself a solution to the country's economic problems; nor would it, as many left-wing critics appeared to believe, have entirely dispensed with the need for some deflationary action to release resources for exports. But a more competitive pound was an essential condition for faster economic growth. In these circumstances, the failure to devalue, until forced in unfavourable circumstances to do so was, according to analysts of Labour's economic record, 'one of the major political puzzles of the 1960s' (Graham and Beckerman, 1972: 22).

How can the puzzle be unravelled? Why, in making strategic choices, did the Labour Government opt for policies that inhibited the pursuit of enhanced welfare and greater equality? The freedom of any state to pursue its chosen ends will be limited to some degree by its location in the global pattern of political and economic relations.[9] The viability of Keynesian demand management depended on the capacity of the state to control fiscal, monetary and exchange rate policy and a pattern of international financial and trading relations that did not expose national economic systems to uncontrolled capital movements. The Bretton Woods settlement reached at the end of the Second World War had established a regime of fixed, though alterable, exchange rates pivoted on the dollar standard, in which the movement of capital and currency was regulated by national systems of control. Because in the two decades or so after 1945 the amount of capital flows were relatively moderate and because of the existence of a battery of exchange controls supported by stand-by credits and lending facilities, fixed exchange rates could be upheld 'without seriously constraining national macroeconomic policymaking autonomy' (Webb, 1991: 311), enabling Keynesian social democracy to enjoy its 'golden age'.

Yet Britain was an exception. This was evident from the first months of the Labour Government. The increased social security benefits introduced in its first budget, Wilson wrote, 'provoked the first of a series of attacks on sterling, by speculators and others, which beset almost every action of the Government for the next five years' (Wilson, 1971: 31). As Callaghan recalled, 'In all the offices I have held I have never experienced anything more frustrating than sitting at the Chancellor's desk watching our currency reserves gurgling down the plug-hole day by day and knowing that the drain could not be stopped' (Callaghan, 1987: 167). Time and again cuts packages were justified – both before and after devaluation – by both Chancellors on the grounds that only by such means could the tottering pound be saved. The vulnerability of sterling was in part due to the size of the external deficit but it persisted even after the deficit narrowed. Thus by the middle of 1966 the imbalance on the current account balance was modest yet heavy selling of the pound resumed (Wilson, 1971: 250). Further currency crises were precipitated by virtually any untoward event, ranging from the seamen's strike in the summer of 1966, the dock strike in 1967, to the instability of other currencies, such as the dollar, the franc and the Deutschmark, and even unfounded rumours of ministerial resignations.

The Cabinet found itself under recurrent and intense pressure to modify policy and sacrifice cherished objectives in order to 'restore confidence'. Thus in a Cabinet meeting discussing a cuts package in January 1968, the Chancellor (Roy Jenkins) insisted on reimposing prescription charges (abolition of which was one of Labour's first measures in 1964) – brushing aside a compromise by which the cost of prescriptions would be met by tax rises – on the grounds that 'the issue had become a matter of confidence with the bankers' and 'a symbol, at home and abroad, of our determination to get the economy right' (Crossman, 1976: 637; Castle, 1984: 351). Losses to the reserves caused by speculative attacks meant that automatic credit rights were soon exhausted and the Government had to negotiate conditional loans from the IMF, the US Federal Reserve and other central banks, and the noose was further tightened.[10] As Wilson commented in his memoirs, for five years 'every action we took had to be considered against a background of the confidence factor, particularly against our assessment of what the speculators might do'. As a result – 'and this is not only inhibiting but humiliating for any government' – as late as 1969 when the external account was moving into surplus, steps such as increases in pensions, 'had to be timed in such a way as to minimise possible speculative consequences' (Wilson, 1971: 33).

Why was Britain so much more susceptible to pressures from the money market than other European countries? A key factor was sterling's role within the global monetary system. Whilst the dollar was the major reserve currency, the pound still retained its status as an international currency, held by other countries as part of their reserves and extensively employed for the settlement of international commercial and financial transactions (Strange, 1971: 202). Unlike the dollar – sustained by the resources of the world's strongest industrial economy – sterling rested on an exiguous economic base. Its status was mainly a residue of its historical role as the major medium of the international economy and financial system, which was given a new lease of life with the creation of the Sterling Area from the ruins of the world financial order in the 1930s. The end of the Gold Standard and the splintering of the global economy into rival blocks encouraged the formation of a separate area in which a number of countries (the UK, its colonies, the Dominions plus other countries with close trading ties with Britain) agreed to operate an enclosed multilateral credit and payments system. Members kept their foreign exchange reserves in London (the Sterling Balances) which they could withdraw at short notice, in return for which they received favourable treatment in terms of access to long-term capital. The international role of sterling greatly heightened the sensitivity of the national economy to international pressures. This was manifested in a variety of ways. Since Britain's reserves were inadequate to cover the Sterling Balances, finding means of dissuading sterling-holders from placing their capital elsewhere – and thereby causing a foreign exchange crisis – was vital. According to Keynes, 'the whole management of the domestic economy depends upon being free to have the appropriate interest rates without reference to the rates prevailing elsewhere in the world' (quoted in Helleiner, 1994: 164). But the main enticement for sterling-holders was above-average interest rates (Coakley and Harris, 1982: 33–5). In consequence, unlike other west European countries, interest rates were not used solely as an instrument to meet domestic policy needs. 'Balances that might have gone elsewhere for greater security were left in London because the yield was too attractive to give up. The resulting high interest rates in the UK inhibited investment and weakened the effects of tax incentives and subsidies to stimulate domestic investment' (Cooper, 1968: 187). Furthermore, the existence of the sterling balances meant that there were extensive sterling-holdings which could be – and almost invariably were – removed at the first rumour of a sterling crisis, which they thereby precipitated.

The role of sterling as a transaction currency worsened the problem since traders and dealers using the currency would also start selling if there appeared to be a possibility of a fall in the value of their holdings. This was compounded by the importance of multinational corporations (MNCs) in the UK economy. Since international trade in goods and services involved the buying and selling of foreign exchange, companies inevitably sought to protect themselves against losses and equally to exploit opportunities for gains as currency values fluctuated. MNCs could side-step controls on foreign exchange dealings by means of 'leads and lags', that is (supposing they anticipate a weakening of the pound) by advancing payments in foreign currencies and delaying payments in sterling.[11] The effect of 'leads and lags', moreover, could be self-fulfilling – as happened between 1964 and 1970 when sterling was periodically undermined as exporters' postponed payments due to them in foreign currencies whilst importers' advanced their payments (Wilson, 1971: 32). Multinationals also switched their working balances around to profit from the currency markets (Wilson, 1971: 440). However much they might rue the MNC's behaviour in the money markets, ministers felt they were hapless to prevent it. In June, 1968, during yet another speculative bout Peter Shore reported to a Cabinet sub-committee that Shell's capital outflow alone was £42 million and asked the Chancellor what criteria was adopted in authorizing it. He replied that 'capital restrictions would only have made Shell think this country was not a good base for an international oil company' (Castle, 1984: 461). As Callaghan commented in 1965 'The trouble was not, as we had always thought, with the bankers but with the big international companies who operated dispassionately in any country and had no national loyalties. It was almost impossible to curb their operations: if they were denied forward cover here, they merely instructed their agents in another country to get it for them' (Castle, 1984: 57). The net result was that large amounts of what was usually called 'speculative capital' were slopping around the international system though the 'professional speculators' whom Wilson excoriated for 'selling sterling short' were often holders of sterling balances and their advisors in the City (Wilson, 1971: 583, 448).

Finally, financial markets and foreign central banks regarded left of centre governments as innately too prone to worry about unemployment, too lax over inflation, too quick to levy taxation and too soft over spending. As a result, market behaviour tended to be more febrile and unsteady when Labour was in office. According to Wilson, the first major run on sterling in November 1964 originated in the belief of foreign owners of sterling that Britain now 'had a government of "softies"' They felt that, by helping pensioners and others in need, the Government was acting in ways Britain could not afford (Wilson, 1971: 33-4). Speculative attacks against sterling were often triggered off by rumours in the City, however ill-founded (Wilson, 1971: 586-7). 'Strikes against the national interest' Wilson observed in his memoirs, 'are always to be condemned; strikes of capital are no less, and in certain circumstances infinitely more, damaging' (Wilson, 1971: 32).[12]

Yet the Government's attitude to the City was ambiguous. On the one hand, it resented deeply-ingrained anti-Labour sentiment in the financial community and was unwilling to accede to all of its demands. But, on the other, it subscribed uncritically to the canons of financial orthodoxy and was wholly committed to the preservation of the City as an 'international financial centre of the first rank' (Cooper, 1968: 153). Thus anxiety that the reduction of the value of the sterling balances by devaluation would undermine the City's standing weighed strongly with the Prime Minister and the Chancellor. Although Wilson from time to time scolded 'international speculators' and the City's 'casino mentality', this was mostly rhetoric. One American authority concluded that 'London's role as a financial centre, with the resulting ease of undertaking large foreign exchange transactions, the ready flow of information (or misinformation) and the habit of acting quickly (or advising one's customers to act quickly) to take advantage of potentially profitable activities were prob-ably far more important than the existence of large sterling balances [in causing destabilizing speculative movements]' (Cooper, 1968: 186–7). Given the damaging effect this had on economic growth and social welfare, one might have anticipated efforts to reform the structure of the City, but these never materialized. The prime minister and his two chancellors largely endorsed the view of the Treasury/Bank of England complex that the interests of the City, in essentials, coincided with those of the nation. They never queried the desirability of a more free-flowing international financial order, though this trend amplified the ability of the financial markets to act 'as an arbiter of policy' (Gamble in Gamble and Walkland, 1984: 54). This is illustrated by a little noticed policy move which had profound consequences. The emergence of vast and highly mobile capital markets in the 1970s, as we shall see, contributed heavily to undermining Keynesian social democracy. A major cause was the creation of a huge Eurodollar market (that is, the market for dollars which are lodged outside the US) in London. 'This market provided an 'offshore', regulation-free environment in which to trade financial assets denominated in foreign currencies, predominantly dollars' (Helleiner, 1994: 168). The City quickly saw the potential of this new market. It grasped that its financial power could survive the post-devaluation decline of the pound's status as an internal currency if it succeeded in seizing the lion's share of the rapidly-growing Eurocurrency mar-kets.[13] The 1964–70 Labour Government greatly facilitated this crucial development by ensuring that the Eurodollar was given a physical base in the City and allowed to operate with minimal regulation. Indeed, Wilson commended the City's record in 'cornering a high proportion of the business in the rapidly expanding Eurodollar market' (Helleiner, 1994: 169; Wilson, 1971: 582).

Two of Labour's economic advisers noted 'the strange mixture of historical mystique and symbolism that equated the strength of sterling with the strength of the economy' concluding that 'the unwillingness of Labour to recognise that the exchange rate should be the means to other ends and not an end in itself was Labour's real mistake' (Graham and Beckerman, 1972: 25, 27). However, it *was* seen as a means, though to ends that sat uneasily was its social democratic creed. As Callaghan put it 'during the 1960s the pound sterling sign had been turned into a symbol of national pride' (Callaghan, 1987: 200) though without acknowledging that this was precisely how it was presented by the Wilson Government. In his Mansion House speech of November 1964, Wilson proclaimed 'our determination to keep sterling strong and to see it riding high. It is basic to all our plans for preserving values at home and for all we hope to do in world affairs . . . We are a world power and a world influence or we are nothing' (Whitehead, 1985: 3–4).

Governments in part construct their own environments and Labour Government *chose* to continue the pursuit of roles which intensified its vulnerability to external pressures. The belief that the UK's proper station in life was that of a global power was, for senior figures in the Labour Cabinet, as axiomatic as it was for their predecessors in the Attlee Administration[14] – testimony to the extent Labour's thinking was permeated by the established political culture. The pursuit of national grandeur helps explain the priority given – despite financial stringency and curbs on its social programmes – to military programmes. As Wilson explained to the Commons in December 1965, 'whatever we may do in the field of cost effectiveness we cannot afford to relinquish our world role . . . our "East of Suez" role' (quoted in Pimlott, 1992: 385).[15] But the cost was considerable. Military spending overseas incurred heavy foreign currency losses and therefore directly contributed to the fragility of the balance of payments. Throughout 1964–70 the private sector balance of payments was in overall balance. In contrast 'net spending abroad, almost entirely on military commitments, ran at well over £400 million a year: it was the major single cause of the balance of payments difficulties' (Ponting, 1989: 398; Strange, 1971: 184–5). The proportion of GNP devoted to military expenditure continued to be considerably greater than any of the UK's fellow NATO members in western Europe. Similarly, despite election pledges to shift the balance of R&D from military to civil purposes, the Government held military R&D at its existing levels (Crossman 3, 1977: 310). All these decisions were detrimental to Britain's economic health, aggravating the Government's difficulties in boosting growth and thereby generating the resources to fulfil its social objectives.

Although Wilson had, in opposition, attacked the 'so-called' independent deterrent, within days of arriving in office, after discussion only with the foreign and defence ministers, he decided to continue the Polaris programme. The reason given was that cancellation would incur 'inordinate cost' (Ponting, 1989: 88). In fact, the Prime Minister 'showed himself disconcertingly ready' to be convinced by 'mathematics [that] . . . were, to say the least, questionable' (Ziegler, 1993: 208). Taking Labour at its word, the Treasury had expected it to cancel Polaris and had 'deliberately refused to sanction major expenditure'. Whitehall estimated the costs of cancellation at about £40 million out of a projected budget of £300 million, so it would have brought major savings. The programme was only eighteen months old when Labour took office and was not due to become operational for another three years. The Admiralty, too, had anticipated cancellation and had prepared contingency plans to convert the submarines to conventional military use (Ponting, 1989: 88; Ziegler, 1993: 208).[16]

If cost was not the reason for carrying on with Polaris, what was? Was it an overriding matter of national security? It will be recalled that deterring the Soviet Union was not a factor in the original decision by the Attlee Government to build an Atom Bomb, and the notion that Britain would ever be in a position when it needed to rely on its 'own' nuclear arsenal (the missiles were of course bought from the Americans) to deter Moscow remained as far-fetched as ever; indeed, 'Wilson never deluded himself that it should be used by Britain in isolation against the Russians' (Ziegler, 1993: 208). In fact, the proposition that the USSR had any intention of invading western Europe was a highly dubious one, to which Healey, then Minister of Defence, for one gave little credence.[17] There was immense pressure from the Ministry of Defence, the Foreign Office and the military to stick with Polaris but the speed with which the decision was taken indicates that not much was needed to steer Wilson and other top ministers in the 'right' direction (Ponting, 1989: 88).

In a brief to President Johnson explaining the Labour Government's determination to hang on to its deterrent, US officials stated baldly that 'the reason is simple: the nuclear deterrent is the most important of the great power symbols still in British possession' (quoted in Ziegler, 1993: 210). To no one did this matter more than the Prime Minister: Wilson had 'an emotional attachment' to the UK's nuclear weapons as the 'ultimate virility symbol' (Ziegler, 1993: 208). The Johnson Administration in fact wanted Britain to integrate its nuclear weapons into a NATO system, but the Government refused. A small group of senior ministers actually took further steps in 1967 to guarantee the UK's continued nuclear capability by deciding, in absolute secrecy, to commission a new programme later known as Chevaline. It was designed to upgrade Polaris and was eventually to cost £1 billion. So, within three years of arriving in office, the Labour Government had not only reversed its apparent intention to cancel Polaris but 'embarked on a costly new modernisation programme to ensure its future until the 1990s' (Ponting, 1989: 94).[18]

The deterrent was intended to underpin Britain's status as a Great Power. Ironically, the Labour Government could only maintain the sterling parity and the UK's global commitments with American help (Ponting, 1989: 395). In September 1965 an informal bargain was struck between the British and American governments. Precisely what this entailed was never clarified but the basis of the agreement was that the US would do its best to support the pound on condition that the UK did not devalue, introduced firmer measures to control pay, maintained a tight fiscal stance, continued Britain's East of Suez role and supported American intervention in Vietnam (Ponting, 1989: 50–5). Over the next three years the Labour Party was under constant American pressure to impose stricter controls over wages, to cut public expenditure (except for defence programmes) further and – though on this point Wilson was obdurate – to dispatch British troops to Vietnam. During one Cabinet meeting, Douglas Jay, the President of the Board of Trade, blurted out that the Government could not 'reflate without breaking the pledges which James Callaghan made to Fowler [the American Treasury Secretary] in Washington'. Callaghan denied this but 'if ever a denial completely confirmed a statement it was Callaghan's on this occasion' (Crossman, 1975: 321, entry 1 September 1965). Wilson himself acknowledged that Fowler was 'apprehensive that if further central bank aid were required it would be difficult to mount' if we only operated a voluntary incomes policy. 'It was in these circumstances that we first began to think in terms of statutory powers' (Wilson, 1971: 131–2).[19] Washington's aid and the consequent need to accommodate its demands became permanent features of Labour's tenure in office. Thus, during the critical turning-point of the Government, the July 1966 crisis, the Administration indicated the terms on which it would receive much-needed US financial aid. According to the Treasury's representative in Washington, 'Johnson has made it clear that the pound was not to be devalued and no drastic action east of Suez was to be undertaken until after the American elections in November. In return, the pound would be supported to any extent necessary' (Ponting, 1989: 55). Of course, it does not follow that, but for American pressure, different decisions would have been taken. In reality, decisions are usually the outcome of a range of pressures and complex estimations of costs and benefits, risks and opportunities. However it is worth underlining the fateful consequences of the Wilson Government's reliance on the US, the corollary of its pursuit of national grandeur and its dedication to a strong pound. American pressure was always a factor when decisions were made to deflate and to introduce a statutory restraint of wages – decisions which extinguished its growth strategy, alienated the unions, led to public expenditure cuts, pushed up taxes to fund social programmes which, then, in a downward spiral intensified wage pressures.

After devaluation it became clear that the UK could no longer sustain its East of Suez role, though it was with great reluctance that is was finally abandoned (see record of Cabinet discussions in January 1968 in Crossman, 1976: 635, 646–50). At the same time, the political balance had changed. Jenkins, the new Chancellor, was a fervent advocate of EEC membership and (unlike Wilson and Callaghan) saw Britain's future as a European and not a world power. The Prime Minister, his political fortunes now inextricably tied to those of his Chancellor, threw his weight behind Jenkins's call for scaling down overseas commitments. The move towards a European vocation reflected a sea-change in thinking within the Treasury and the Foreign Office and, indeed, the establishment as a whole as faith in the country's capacity to sustain a global mission perceptibly ebbed.

The willingness to subordinate welfare goals to considerations of international status did not necessarily reflect majority opinion within the Cabinet. Critics included such ministerial heavyweights as Crosland, Crossman, Castle and Benn. However, none of these ministers exercised any significant influence over macro-economic policy, largely because its conduct was concentrated in the hands of the Prime Minister, the Chancellor and senior officials. The Cabinet (and its main sub-committees) acted less as a coherent policy-making body than a conclave of departmental ministers each primarily interested in their own concerns with little influence over crucial issues of macro-economic policy. In November 1968, contemplating one of the Cabinet's perennial cuts packages, Crossman noted: 'there has been no change from the original July 1965 meeting, the 1966 meeting or the 1967 devaluation meeting. All the way through we have had the same phenomenon of a small group saying to Cabinet, "This is it. Take it or leave it. It's too late to do anything else"' (Crossman, 1977: 270).[20] Crosland, like Crossman, a minister throughout this period, constantly complained about the failure to place economic decision-making in any strategic context. In a typical (and typically fruitless) intervention during yet another Cabinet session over cuts (in January 1968) he urged 'that at some stage we discuss the general strategy and rationale of the package: what total shift of resources was required; whether we had got the balance right between cuts and taxation, between defence and civil expenditure; and whether the balance was right between our civil priorities' (Castle, 1984: 353). The discussion never took place.

The minority of Cabinet members (like Crossman, Castle and Crosland) who took an interest in macro-economic policy found themselves continually frustrated. They lacked the time and expert assistance needed to grasp fully what was occurring outside their own briefs (Crossman, 1975: 280–1; Castle, 1984: 752). Their task was made more difficult by the ability of the Prime Minister and the top mandarins to manipulate policy-making procedures to maintain their control over strategic decision-making, for instance through their grip over the Cabinet agenda and the compilation of Cabinet minutes; by astute management of the structure, composition, and remits of the network of ministerial sub-committees; and by control over the supply and delivery of policy papers. In a comment that constantly recurs in the Castle and Crossman diaries, the former angrily reacted to the arrival of papers for the Steering Committee on Economic Policy the day before the meeting: 'Really, it is grotesque how one is expected to master massive wodges of economic and financial detail in one's odd moments and always at the last moment' (June 1968, Castle, 1984: 460). The effect was to entrench control over economic policy-making in the hands of the Prime Minister, the Chancellor and senior officials in the Treasury, the Bank of England and the Cabinet office. In March 1968 a disgruntled Crosland complained to his colleagues that during the three years he had been in the Cabinet devaluation had never appeared on the agenda, with all the real economic discussions taking place between the PM and the Chancellor. 'The rest of us were merely faced with the results when a crisis came and when the choice of action was inevitably limited' (Castle, 1984: 400).

Between 1966 and 1970 the Government was beset by evidence of its contracting electoral base. Even safe Labour seats were lost on massive swings, its urban strongholds collapsed as council seats fell in droves to the Conservatives and opinion polls registered the Party's massive slide in the public's affections. However, in the new decade, its fortunes appeared to revive and by the summer of 1970 it had collected a handsome lead in the polls. Wilson grasped the opportunity and called an election. But the recovery was brittle: for whatever reason – a freak set of trade figures, the quality of the Conservative campaign, even England's defeat in the world cup, large numbers of voters abandoned the Government at the last moment. Compared to the 1966 election, Labour was deserted by a million voters, its share of the poll shrank by 5 per cent and it lost 75 seats. The overall turnout fell heavily largely, it appeared, because of numerous Labour abstentions. Wilson could contemplate the failure of his ambition to transform Labour into 'the natural party of government' in the greater leisure of opposition.

With his 'science and socialism' speech delivered to an enthusiastic Conference in 1963 Wilson was acclaimed as a new visionary, infusing the Party with a new sense of purpose. But the besetting impression left of – to date (August 1995) – the last Labour Government to rule with a solid majority is of a rudderless ship. Wilson was a highly skilled political operator, a master tactician – but with no strategy. He was ' a tough politician who jumps from position to position, always brilliantly energetic and opportunist, always moving in zigzags, darting with no sense of direction but making the best of each position he adopts' (Crossman, 1976: 159). He was at his best in his first eighteen months, the deft and masterful trapeze artist, surviving crises, maintaining the morale of his troops and outwitting his opponents as he carefully prepared the ground for the 1966 election triumph. But once established in power with a handsome majority, his preference was for the role of the professional navigator content simply with keeping the ship of state afloat. To Healey – not, admittedly, one of his admirers – 'he had no sense of direction, and rarely looked more than a few months ahead.[21] His short-term opportunism, allied with a capacity for self-delusion which made Walter Mitty appear unimaginative, often plunged the government into chaos' (Healey, 1989: 331). A former Whitehall official himself, he admired the smoothness of the government machine and 'like the senior civil servants he too came to regard the efficient conduct of business within Whitehall as equivalent to success', and he increasingly relied for advice upon his officials, especially Burke Trend, the highly influential Cabinet Secretary (Ponting, 1989: 173, 174; Crossman, 1976: 296). 'I don't feel part of a Government pledged to fundamental change, with any idea of where it it's going' Crossman lamented in September 1966. 'Since 1964 nothing has really changed. We're still working from hand to mouth trying to overcome the immediate short-term problems' (Crossman, 1976: 51).

With the balance of payments in surplus, the Prime Minister and his Chancellor prided themselves in the healthy economy they left behind them. In reality, placed against the aims Labour had set itself – in terms of planning, industrial modernization and growth – the record was less comforting. One legacy was a significant expansion in social programmes, but even this fell short of what had been intended and, given the laggardly rate of economic growth, much of this was paid for in higher taxation with a large proportion of the working class drawn, for the first time, into the income tax net. The judgement by the leading theorist of Keynesian social democracy was a sombre one. Writing in 1972, Crosland stated flatly: 'nobody disputes the central failure of economic policy. In 1970, unemployment was higher, inflation more rapid and economic growth slower than when the Conservatives left office in 1964' (quoted in Hatfield, 1978: 30).

Notes

1   This was as much due to the electoral system – most west European countries used variants of Proportional Representation – as its own strength.

2   The US Treasury Secretary, Jo Fowler was, the Prime Minister recalled 'apprehensive that if further central bank aid were required it would be difficult to mount' if Britain relied solely on a voluntary incomes policy to resist inflationary pressures. 'It was in these circumstances' he added, 'that we first began to think in terms of statutory powers' (Wilson, 1972: 131–2).

3   Not all the Cabinet approved. Richard Crossman complained that the Prime Minister was resolved to defeat the union 'although we have just given huge concessions to the doctors, the judges and the higher civil servants.

It is an ironical interpretation of a socialist incomes policy' (Crossman, 1975: 538).

4   In fact, Labour's National Plan was prepared in very much the same way, and by broadly the same team of officials, as the Tories' 1962 planning proposal (Leruez, 1975: 171).

5   The Deutschmark for upward revision.

6   Thus at one meeting, Jack Jones denied that an incomes policy could ever redistribute wealth or help the lower paid. 'Nor could he accept that wages claims could ever be inflationary' (Castle, 1984: 735, entry 2 December 1969).

7   As Hyman has pointed out, the bulk of strikes originated in more or less spontaneous protest at the workplace with union authorization only following later, if at all. Indeed, since most strikes were of limited duration, they were usually resolved by direct negotiations between employers and workplace representatives (Hyman, 1989: 42).

8   Crossman's disaffection with the pace of progress is recorded in his diary. At one point, in exasperation, he complained to Wilson about 'the scandalous slowness of the Cabinet Pensions Committee . . . and how the official committee was deliberately making it grind to a halt'. He discovered that only four civil servants had been allotted to preparing 'the biggest piece of legislation' ever undertaken in the ministry (Crossman, 1976: 599).

9   'The political economies of modern western European states do not exist in isolation, but within a context established by the international system. In pursuing polices designed to facilitate economic growth and social cohesion, governments react not just to the interests and power of domestic groups, but to constraints and incentives provided by the world political economy' (Keohane, 1984: 15).

10 Thus a little later Jenkins, pressing his case for more spending reductions, 'described the terrible dangers we are now in and the pressure on the pound in the markets and also the pressure of the IMF . . . a second devaluation would occur within the next three months if the budget didn't restore confidence in sterling . . . ' (Crossman, 1976: 695, January 1968).

11 In his memoirs, Wilson cited the case of one company that purchased all its raw material requirements for twelve months ahead (Wilson, 1971: 440).

12 When asked on television in 1968 'to name some of the mistakes we had made as a Government, I said we had always underestimated the power of the speculators against a Government of whose politics, policies and even personalities they did not approve' (Wilson, 1971: 33).

13 The amount of dollar holdings in Europe swelled in this period because, as a consequence of the Vietnam war, the US was running a large balance of payments deficit. Once the world financial community recognized the

opportunities for speculative profit afforded by Eurodollars, other offshore currency markets sprang up.

14 Dismissing the charge that Wilson was simply an opportunist, his close associate Crossman argued that he had a number of 'long-term convictions' including keeping 'our military presence in the Far East, . . . our special relationship with the USA and to Britain remaining "great"' (Crossman, 1976: 159).

15 Attending a meeting in November 1967 with Wilson, Brown and Burke Trend, the Cabinet Secretary, discussing policy on Vietnam, Crossman recorded how 'I listened quietly and learnt a great deal about how the delusions of grandeur are the fatal defects of Harold and George and are constantly stimulated by Burke Trend. They believe that as acknowledged actors on the world political stage' they can influence President Johnson from a distance (Crossman, 1976: 564). Wilson, Brown, Callaghan and Stewart – the men in charge of Labour's foreign policy – he added a few months later, all believed it was their role to prove Labour could be relied upon to uphold Britain's mission as a great power as faithfully as the Conservatives (Crossman, 1976: 627).

16 Healey, the Minister of Defence, was informed that there was some disquiet within the Navy about cuts in their conventional budget if Polaris went ahead and that the submarines could easily and at no extra cost be converted into 'hunter-killers'. When he told Wilson he was asked not to let anyone else in the Cabinet know this, since he intended 'to justify continuing the Polaris programme on the grounds that it was "past the point of no return". I did not demur' (Healey, 1989: 302).

17 'I had never believed that the Soviet Union was bent on the military conquest of Western Europe since it had failed to challenge the Western airlift to West Berlin in 1948–9' (Healey, 1989: 309).

18 Ponting was a former senior official at the Defence Department.

19 Barbara Castle recorded a meeting with Wilson in November 1969, in which he stated 'that on the 2nd of September 1965 the Americans were insisting that we should introduce a statutory prices and incomes policy. Jim Callaghan . . . had caved in and sold out to the US Secretary of the Treasury, Fowler' (Castle, 1984: 724).

20 Similarly, in the discussion over the July 1966 deflationary measures, Crossman noted: 'Cabinet was a desultory affair. Nothing had been adequately prepared. Nothing had been thought out properly. We were fixing things once again, horribly inefficient, at the last moment' (Crossman, 1975: 578).

21 The quintessential Wilsonian phrase was 'a week is a long time in politics.'

5 Keynesian Social Democracy in Retreat, 1970–1974

During the Attlee Government, relations amongst the various components of the Party – the Cabinet, the NEC, Conference, the unions – were remarkable amicable but the pattern during the second majority Labour administration, particularly in its later phase, was strikingly different. Government policies were repudiated with increasing frequency by a restless Conference as the Government abandoned significant chunks of the Manifesto. Policy clashes soon began to express themselves in constitutional terms. The leadership's hold over Conference was seriously shaken by the rise of a powerful indigenous Labour Left within the unions.[1] Combined, the TGWU and the engineering union alone had about 30 per cent of the vote. There had always been disagreement over the precise circumstances in which Conference decisions were binding, but this was bounded, prior to 1964, by respect for its authority as 'the parliament of the movement'. Wilson, however, simply shrugged off adverse Conference resolutions. Conference had the right to express its views but, he insisted, 'the Government must govern'. Indeed, any attempt by an extra-parliamentary body to determine Government policy was, he maintained, incompatible with the principles of parliamentary sovereignty. To the mounting indignation of the rank and file, 'there was not the slightest verbal concession to the Authority of the Conference' (Minkin, 1978: 297).

This placed the Executive – in the past the reliable ally of the Parliamentary leadership but constitutionally accountable to Conference – in a difficult position. Its initial response was to seek to deflect and defuse criticism of the government as much as possible. However, slowly, in line with alterations in its composition – as ministerial representation shrank, and the number of left-wingers slowly grew[2] – it began to show greater responsiveness to grass-roots feeling (Minkin, 1978: 293, 297). But there were limits to how far the NEC (which retained its overall right-wing complexion) would exert pressure on Government and anyway there were no effective mechanisms by which a Labour Cabinet could be obliged to bring its policies more closely into line with those favoured by Conference or the NEC. By 1970 Conference appeared to have slipped into irreversible decline with its authority repudiated and with negligible impact on governmental policy (Minkin, 1978: 314).

However, forces were in motion that were dissolving the pattern of institutional integration and concurrent majorities upon which control of the Party by the Parliamentary elite rested. As a new breed of tough, left-wing leaders (most prominently Jack Jones of the Transport Workers and Hugh Scanlon of the Engineering Workers) came to the fore the bonds attaching the union movement to the Parliamentary leadership frayed. Pledged to free collective bargaining and to a left-wing stance on most political issues, they felt little of that instinctive sympathy with the predominantly right-wing Labour leadership that had characterized earlier generations of union leaders. Relations between the two wings of the movement were severely impaired by the several phases of statutory incomes policy and with *In Place of Strife*, virtually reached breaking point (Minkin, 1978: 297–8). Many right-wing union leaders were almost as indignant as their colleagues on the left and it was one of their number, Jo Gormley from the large and traditionally loyalist National Union of Miners, who moved the NEC motion rejecting Mrs Castle's White Paper.[3]

In June 1970, with Labour ahead in the polls, Wilson called an election and the procedure for producing a manifesto went into full gear. In theory, the NEC and the Cabinet shared responsibility for the task. During the Attlee administration, whilst day-to-day policy lay mostly within the province of the Government the responsibility for formulating future policy had devolved upon the NEC (on behalf of the wider Party). In the late 1960s, Richard Crossman sought to put a constitutional gloss on this division of tasks. With ministers immersed in the pressing contingencies of running the country, the Government was likely to run out of reforming steam. The NEC and Conference should accept that their role in shaping current policy was limited, concentrate on future policy and act as 'the battering ram of change' by injecting fresh ideas into the manifesto to prepare Labour for the next phase of governing. The spoke in the wheel was that Wilson was no keener to abandon control of future than day-to-day policy. Preparation of the manifesto was delayed until the eve of the campaign, when the NEC was under maximum pressure to show flexibility and there was little disposition to challenge a Government basking in the electorate's esteem. The net result was the type of bland and non-committal document the Prime Minister thought would help propel him back to power.

Whilst bearing the seals of office, the parliamentary leadership could afford to adopt a sanguine view of the shifting balance of forces in the NEC and Conference: it commanded the Government machine, was buttressed by the conventions of collective cabinet responsibility and enjoyed the status and prestige of public office. Wilson had treated Conference with disdain, had insisted on his right to place his own personal imprint on the 1970 manifesto and had regarded with indifference the withering of the grass-roots as Party membership plunged in the late 1960s. But Labour's unexpected defeat in 1970 stripped the parliamentary leadership of its protective shield and, for the first time since the war, it confronted an NEC and a Conference determined to reassert their prerogatives. The pain of Labour's departure from government in 1970 was not eased – as it had been two decades earlier – by pride in its accomplishments. Instead, the mood was one of disillusion, a sense of squandered hopes and lost opportunities. Wilson had asserted the superior wisdom of a Labour Prime Minister and Cabinet unfettered by Conference resolutions. The Government had failed – was not then the greater sagacity of the spurned and derided Conference vindicated? Was it not then time for the wider Party to lay claim to its rightful inheritance?

Circumstances were auspicious. Wilson's prestige had plummeted, many of his former cabinet colleagues were demoralized, the unions were less accommodating and the PLP leadership could no longer expect them to succour it in its hour of need. The constitutional prerogatives vested in the Shadow Cabinet were slight and the institutional conditions which had traditionally sustained the hegemony of the frontbench were no longer intact. In contrast, the NEC wielded a considerable range of powers. In the organizational sphere, subject to the final authority of Conference, it had overall responsibility for managing the internal affairs of the Party, including the interpretation and enforcement of the rules, oversight over candidate selection, election preparation and the maintenance of party organization. In the policy-making sphere, it was – again subject to the final authority of Conference – responsible for arranging the policy process and for policy formulation in its various stages, including the issuing of policy statements to Conference and (in conjunction with the Shadow Cabinet) the framing of the manifesto (Minkin, 1978: 320).

By the early 1970s, for the first time in Labour's history, there was on the Executive a rough parity in numbers between left and right. The left utilized their growing numbers to exercise to the full the NEC's prerogatives. Two key players were Ian Mikardo and Tony Benn. Tough, shrewd and sharp-witted, Mikardo had already served on the NEC (with a break of one year) for almost two decades, though previously as part of an impotent radical minority. His political skills and considerable intellectual prowess now began to make a mark on both policy and organizational matters. Benn had served on the NEC for a decade, although previously occupying a centre-left position. After 1970, he moved rapidly to the left and, a lucid and compelling speaker, he rapidly gained a large and enthusiastic following amongst the rank and file. A much higher priority was given to the detailed formulation of policy with the Executive drawing up for Conference a series of policy statements culminating in the comprehensive 'Labour's Programme 1973'. This effort was supported by a major expansion of the NEC's policy-making apparatus: an extensive network of sub-committees and study groups was assembled containing front and backbench MPs, trade unionists, pressure group representatives and academic experts. With the hold of the PLP leadership over the policy-making machinery undermined, the left-leaning Executive or, more accurately, its sub-committees and study groups, took the initiative in formulating policy. Traditionally those who performed the gate-keeping function – regulating the flow of inputs into the policy system – did so on behalf of the Parliamentary leadership. Now the system – for the first time ever – exhibited a greater receptivity to left-wing ideas and policy preferences. This was particularly the case in the field of industrial policy where left-wing specialists (such as Stuart Holland and Richard Pryke) and politicians, such as Mikardo, Benn and Judith Hart exerted considerable sway over the production of policy (Hatfield, 1978). Wilson who, according to his aide Joe Haines, had sunk into a 'apathetic and defeatist' mood after his unexpected defeat feeling became engrossed in compiling a memoir of his recently fallen Government (Ziegler, 1993: 372). No sooner had this been completed than he became increasingly preoccupied in trying to avert a disastrous split over the extremely divisive issue of EC membership. In consequence, until quite late in the day he figured only marginally in the NEC's deliberations (Hatfield, 1978: 24). Labour's most eminent intellectual luminary, Tony Crosland, forfeited influence by his irregular attendance of the Industrial Policy Committee, of which he was a co-opted member (Hatfield, 1978: 58). The potentially powerful Finance and Economic Sub-Committee inclined substantially more to the right but Roy Jenkins, Labour's Shadow Chancellor until his resignation in 1971, had so low a regard for the NEC that he largely ignored its proceedings. By dint of their own energy and the indifference and disdain of the right as much as by their growing numbers, the left gained a grip over policy formation greater than they had ever previously possessed.

Beyond Keynesian Social Democracy

The left was now in a position to challenge the intellectual and political ascendancy of Keynesian social democracy. Stuart Holland, an economist who had served as an adviser in Number 10 during the Wilson Government, wrote a series of papers for the Industrial Policy sub-committee arguing that Crosland's revisionism had been rendered obsolete by the rise of 'meso-economic' power, that is the dominance over the economy by giant multinational corporations. Keynesian efforts to manage the economy by fiscal and monetary policy were being systematically undermined by these corporate giants exploiting such techniques as transfer pricing, transfer payments and tax avoidance (Holland, 1975: 83–9). Holland's analysis exerted considerable influence. According to an NEC Green Paper the government's ability to achieve its objectives had been thwarted by corporate control over vital economic processes whilst the private sector had proved to be 'highly resistant to incentives, exhortations and the limited measures of control over private industry which are at the disposal of Governments' (Hatfield, 1978: 187–8).

The NEC contended that the interests of large corporations 'cannot be expected to coincide with the interests of the national economy' whilst 'social reform of itself cannot bring about effective progress towards equality' since the roots of inequality lay in the system of production. Since Keynesian methods alone were incapable of modifying the behaviour of these corporations, a future Labour government would have to 'act *directly* at the level of the giant firm itself' (Labour Party NEC *Labour's Programme 1973*: 13, emphasis in the original). The Party proposed two new instruments: a National Enterprise Board (NEB) and Planning Agreements. Planning Agreements – derived from continental experience – were designed to supply vital information on investment, prices, product development, exports and so forth to augment the Government's capacity to manage the economy (Hatfield, 1978: 184–5). The NEB would acquire substantial holdings in leading firms in the main industrial sectors in order to promote employment, investment, technological development and export growth (Hatfield, 1978: 188–9). Most radical of all, and in a dramatic break with Keynesian social democracy, the NEC called for the nationalization of a leading firm in each of the twenty-five or so industrial sectors on the grounds that only this would give government the ability – deemed vital for the attainment of Labour's economic goals – to influence corporate policies over pricing, investment, exports and location ('Labour's Programme 1973', 1973: 30).

Labour's Programme 1973 thoroughly alarmed the right. Crosland, belatedly entering the fray, dismissed 'the misleading assumption that a change of ownership of itself will produce miraculous results' emphasizing that 'there was no link between public ownership and equality, no link between powers and control' (Hatfield, 1978: 208; Benn, 1989: 38, entry 16 May 1973). But it was too late to wrest control of industrial policy-making from the left. Whilst on Wilson's insistence there was no mention of the 'twenty-five companies,' for the first time since 1945 an election manifesto contained a commitment to a significant extension of the public sector. *Let us Work Together – Labour's Way Out of the Crisis* called for public ownership of ship-building, the ports, aero-engines and development. It added: 'We shall also take over profitable sections or individual firms in those industries where a public holding is essential to enable the Government to control prices, stimulate investment, encourage exports, create employment, protect workers and consumers from the activities of irresponsible multi-national companies, and to plan the national economy in the national interest.' This would include pharmaceuticals, road haulage, construction, machine tools and North Sea oil. A 'powerful National Enterprise Board' would be set up and Planning Agreements signed 'to allow Government to plan with industry more effectively' (Craig, 1975: 191).

However, the left's ascendancy over policy did not extend to the crucial area of macro-economic strategy. Responsibility was placed with a new body, the TUC–Labour Party Liaison Committees, composed of representatives from the PLP, the NEC and the TUC (Minkin, 1978: 337–8). This was established (1) to co-ordinate the labour movement's response to the Heath Government's Industrial Relations Act of 1971, which was bitterly opposed by the unions, and (2) to prevent the recurrence of the Government-union fractures of the late 1960s by institutionalizing co-operation on major policy issues. The unions' priority was a pledge from Labour to repeal the Industrial Relations Act whilst the PLP leadership wanted to tie the unions to a commitment to wage moderation to lend credibility to its policy over the increasingly severe problem of inflation. Due to opposition from Jones, Scanlon and other industrial radicals this proved impossible to obtain. After protracted negotiations, the frontbench, the NEC and the unions reached an agreement which was labelled the 'Social Contract'. This recognized that incomes policy would only be acceptable to union members if it was part of a much broader bargain. Thus, if elected, the Party agreed to work towards 'a much fairer distribution of national wealth' and to curb 'high prices, rents and other impositions falling most heavily on the low paid and the pensioners' hence creating 'the right economic climate for money incomes to grow in line with production' (February 1974 manifesto; Craig, 1975: 1911). This fell considerably short of a clear promise to restrain wage demands, as the Party leadership wanted. Notwithstanding, the Social Contract contained pledges to repeal the Industrial Relations Act, to raise pensions, sickness, unemployment and other benefits within the first parliamentary session of Labour's return to power and henceforth to uprate all benefits annually in proportion to increases in average national earnings; to introduce a new system of child benefits, payable to the mother (instead of tax allowances paid usually to the father); to introduce strict price controls 'on key services and commodities'; to hold down the cost of living; to return to local authorities the right to fix council house rents, and to regulate rents in the private sector (Craig, 1975: 190).

The combination of the left's grip over the NEC's policy machinery and the strength of the left voice on both the Executive and the unions within the Liaison Committee produced the most radical platform on which Labour had contested an election since 1945. Yet a puzzle remains. In the years 1970–4 the left did not have a clear majority either on the NEC or at Conference yet the right, despite retaining their control over the PLP and the Shadow Cabinet as well as the backing of many unions, were unable to block the inclusion of key left-wing policies into the manifesto. The major reason for their weaknesses was a serious rift within the centre-right majority of the PLP over the issue of membership of what was then called the European Economic Community (EEC). In Government, Wilson had launched an application for membership which, however, was vetoed by President de Gaulle of France. De Gaulle resigned in 1969 and Wilson certainly intended another application: Labour's defeat meant that the initiative was taken by his successor, Edward Heath, an eager pro-marketeer. The issue aroused strong passions within the Party. A large minority of right-wingers, led by Roy Jenkins, were dedicated pro-marketeers. Regarding the matter as one of high principle they were prepared to do all in their power to ensure that the European Accession bill was safely navigated through the Commons. This meant helping to sustain the Heath Government because, faced with a minority of Tory anti-marketeers, it required Labour votes to enable it to survive vital divisions over the bill. There was an equally staunch minority of determined Labour anti-marketeers, mainly but not exclusively from the left. They were furious at the sight of pro-marketeers throwing a life raft to a Conservative Government enabling it not only to take Britain into the EEC but to push through legislation – for example over industrial relations and housing finance – which aroused fierce hostility in the Party. 'This treachery,' Barbara Castle, a resolute anti-marketeer recalled, 'caused immense bitterness' (Castle, 1993: 449).

Uneasily straddling the pro- and anti-market camps was a large group – including Callaghan, Healey and Crosland – composed of the undecided, the indifferent and the pragmatic, who agreed on taking a much more temperate view of the issue. Of these, Crosland had been most closely identified with the Gaitskellites and his (characteristically insouciant) refusal to regard EC membership as a matter of principle infuriated former close allies, such as Jenkins and Bill Rodgers. Neither the political nor the personal breach was ever wholly repaired (Crosland, 1981). Thus divided, the capacity of the right to resist the advance of the left – its ranks temporarily swelled by right-wing anti-marketeers – was enfeebled. The Jenkinsites were no less inflamed by Wilson's apparent *volte-face* (whose true purpose they could not or would not recognize). His priorities were, firstly, 'to keep the party united. All along I have believed that my duty was to be the custodian of party unity' (quoted in Castle, 1993: 448) and, secondly, to avoid at all costs an unequivocal commitment to withdrawal from the European Economic Community since his long-run objective was to win the Party's acquiescence to EEC membership whilst preventing an irreparable split. But for tactical reasons his speeches sounded a tone increasingly critical of the EEC, pouring scorn on the poor terms he claimed Heath had negotiated. But he knew the price he would pay for his tactics: 'the press will crucify me' (quoted in Castle, 1993: 448). So it transpired as he was denounced as unfit to be Prime Minister, derided even by the normally friendly (but pro-EC) *Daily Mirror* as a 'tethered sacrificial goat' to party unity. He was regarded with scorn and contempt by many Labour pro-marketeers and their numerous allies in the media. He was depicted as the man of no fixed principle, destitute of integrity and honour:

> A man so various, that he seem'd to be
> Not one, but all mankind's epitome
> > (Dryden, *Absalom and Achitophel*)

He was bitterly resentful. During one Shadow Cabinet, when Jenkins was rather pompously pronouncing how 'in all conscience' he could not support a particular issue, Wilson exploded: 'I've been wading in shit for three months to allow others to indulge their conscience' (Ziegler, 1993: 387).[4] Well aware that the Jenkinsites were conspiring to replace him with their champion, he was not prepared to alienate the left upon whose support he was reliant to repel a challenge from the pro-market right. Hence on domestic policy matters he strove to avoid hard and fast positions and (with the assistance of the erstwhile rebel Michael Foot) to conciliate rather than confront the left. His efforts to arrest the left-wing tide were concentrated on blocking those policies which he regarded as electorally most damaging whilst swallowing many others which he probably never intended to implement.

In January 1974, the Conservative Government was confronted, for the second time, by a miners' strike. A recent massive jump in the price of oil following the 1973 Arab–Israel war greatly bolstered the NUM's bargaining position. After raising the stakes by declaring a three-day week – ostensibly to conserve energy supplies – Heath sought to outmanoeuvre the miners by calling an election on the issue of 'who rules: the unions or the Government?' Most Labour leaders were deeply worried they would be soundly beaten if the election hung on this question, and Wilson tried assiduously to focus attention on prices, projecting himself as a Stanley Baldwin-type peace-maker in contrast to the abrasive Heath. But the outcome was much as feared: though turnout rose substantially, half a million voters deserted Labour, compounding its serious losses in 1970 when it was ejected from office. Its share of the poll fell by a hefty 6 per cent (down over 10 per cent on the 1966 figure) to 37.1 per cent, its worst score in thirty years. The myth that Labour 'won' the election, and that the combativeness of the miners catapulted it back to power, derived from an electoral system which produced a disparity between votes and seats greater than at any time since 1931. If elections were decided on basis of votes February 1974 would have appeared in the history books as almost as grim an election rout for Labour as for the Conservatives. The Tories, however, saw their electorate shrink even further; the only winners were the Liberals who, with 18 per cent of the poll and six million votes (up four million compared to 1970), secured their best result for half a century. With 301 seats (13 up from 1970) Labour had four more seats than the Tories[5] (though 200,000 or so less votes) hence, after Heath's efforts to reach an agreement with the Liberals had failed, Wilson was charged with forming a government. In short, Labour was back in power, despite the fact that it had been abandoned by many of its supporters, because of the distorting outcome of a highly unrepresentative electoral system. But from the outset, it lacked popular consent: Labour was in office by default.

Notes

1   Until the late 1960s (and with the exception of the TGWU) the left in the unions tended to be heavily influenced by Communists.

118 *Keynesian Social Democracy in Retreat, 1970–1974*

2 Union voting decisions for seats in the trade union and women's sections of the NEC are influenced by a range of factors, with bargaining over the disposition of seats on the TUC General Council, traditional arrangements, industrial alignments and rivalries all playing their part, so that shifts in the left–right balance take a little time to have an effect on its composition.

3 NEC minutes 26 March 1969. The motion was passed by the large margin of 16 votes to 5.

4 In fact, he demonstrated considerable tactical skill and managed to retrieve some of his reputation. Thus at the badly divided 1971 Party Conference, he concentrated his fire on the Tory party: 'I thought it was a cheap speech', a former supporter recorded, ' – most of Harold's speeches are – but he gets away with it and he is the old entertainer, the Archie Rice of the Labour Party. He knows how to press the right buttons and his position is strong' (Benn, 1988: 378).

5 If the Ulster Unionists had continued their previous practice of taking the Conservative whip, the Tories would have been the larger party and a Labour Government might never have materialized.

6 The Unravelling of Keynesian Social Democracy, 1974–1979

'The markets wanted blood . . . We didn't understand that at the time, we didn't know what they wanted was a humiliation . . . .trying to avoid humiliation was a waste of time.'
(Gavyn Davies, quoted in Whitehead, 1985: 187)

'We have to stop paying "danegeld"'.
(Crosland quoted in Benn, 1989: 668)

The Poisoned Chalice

Victory in February 1974 was a poisoned chalice. In 1972–3, in its 'dash for growth', the Heath Government had sent the economy racing ahead by boosting demand through highly expansionary fiscal and monetary policies. But this soon encountered capacity constraints, the boom sucked in masses of imports causing an alarming payments deficit, and inflation rose rapidly. Under the floating exchange rate regime, introduced in 1972, the pound sank steeply. The fourfold rise in oil prices in the wake of the 1973 Yom Kippur War, combined with rapid price rises in other commodities – part of the inflationary upsurge that predated the Middle East conflict – meant 'a drastic redistribution of real income from the consuming economies to the oil producers, a deficit in the collective balance of payments of the West *vis-à-vis* the oil producers, and a sharp twist in the inflation spiral' (Artis and Cobham, 1991: 4–5). To facilitate agreement with the unions over incomes policy,

Heath had introduced a system of threshold payments in 1973 in which pay increments were triggered off by each 1 per cent rise in the resale price index, further fuelling inflation (Artis and Cobham, 1991: 8). As a result, the outgoing Government bequeathed to Labour accelerating inflation, rising unemployment, a growing budget and a huge balance of payments deficit with the oil price hike yet to be fully absorbed.

Rather than pursuing restrictive policies that would exacerbate the deflationary effects of dearer oil, Healey, the new Chancellor, believed the major industrial countries should cover their deficits by borrowing whilst creating an international mechanism for recycling petrodollars. Hence in his first budget he increased pensions and other benefits, and raised food subsidies, funded by tax rises. However, virtually all other major economies deflated, with the result that the payments deficit grew even larger and pressure against the pound began to mount (Healey, 1989: 393; Coates, 1980: 20). Furthermore, though the Government moved quickly to repeal the Conservative Industrial Relations Act, the unions failed to deliver on their side of the Social Contract. In response to steps taken to regulate prices, price rises abated somewhat. But the new Government was greeted after the lifting of Conservative statutory incomes policy by an upsurge of wage militancy, especially in the public sector. Barbara Castle, the Secretary of State for the giant Department of Health and Social Security, was assailed on all sides by 'a clamour for higher pay' – from the consultants, nurses and ancillary workers, engineers and radiographers (Castle, 1980: 115, 147–8, 151, entries June and July 1974).

Projecting itself as a 'healing' administration for the election that could not for long be postponed, the new Government was anxious to avert further industrial strife. Its predicament was worsened by the swift implementation of manifesto pledges which pushed up public spending and by the decision to continue the inflation-boosting threshold payments: 'with hindsight . . . a disastrous mistake' (Wilson, 1979: 42). The election, called in October 1974, appeared to promise relief with the polls predicting a solid Labour majority. Not for the first time, nor for the last, they were wrong: Labour's vote crept up marginally by 2.1 per cent to a mere 39.2 per cent, it gained only 18 seats and found itself with a bare majority of four – which, within two years, had vanished. The point is worth underlining: from the first the Government was deprived of a bedrock of popular support, left to struggle on as the economic skies darkened further after an election in which three-fifths of all voters had disclaimed it.

By December the failure of the Social Contract was unmistakable. Earnings had risen by 29 per cent, prices by about 19 per cent. Inflation passed the 20 per cent mark, well above the OECD average and with British goods being priced out of markets, the trade deficit widened still further whilst unemployment continued to rise (Barnes and Reid, 1980: 201). Whatever the causes of inflation, it was clear that the inflationary spiral would persist unless union leaders could rein-in wage claims. The Treasury believed that a statutory incomes policy was essential, a view to which the Chancellor was soon converted, but, well aware of the strength of opposition within the Government, they stayed their hand until circumstances were propitious. In June 1975 a sterling crisis broke. Healey leapt in, insisting that only a statutory incomes policy could stop the pound crumbling. Wilson had condemned Heath's statutory policy but, desperately worried, now wobbled. At this point Donoughue and his Policy Unit – established for the purpose of providing an additional source of advice – interceded and, fully aware that union collaboration would not survive a statutory policy, challenged the Treasury arguments (Donoughue, 1987: 66–9). This afforded a breathing space for wiser counsels to prevail. With the survival of the Labour Government his priority, a seriously perturbed Jack Jones was now convinced that the surge of wage claims had to be restrained and, after discussions with the Policy Unit, he proposed a £6 flat rate pay policy. Shaken by the sterling crisis, the General Council agreed, though only by 19 votes to 13. The White Paper *The Attack on Inflation* announced a £6 a year increase from August for people earning below £8, 500; prices rises would be stayed by price controls and higher food and housing subsidies. Congress voted by 6.9 to 3.4 million to support the policy (Barnes and Reid, 1980: 206; Middlemass, 1991: 95). It was both the most equitable – with the low paid securing a significant enlargement in the earnings – and probably the most effective example of pay restraint with the Retail Price Index index falling from 24.2 per cent to 16.5 per cent between mid-1975 and mid-1976 (Middlemass, 1991: 97).

The Industrial Strategy and the Defeat of the Left

For the left, the radical industrial policy was the hub of Labour's economic strategy, the means by which output and productivity would be jacked up and the resources found to finance expanded social programmes. Though incorporated into the February 1974 manifesto it is doubtful whether Wilson or Healey ever seriously intended to implement it. However, in 1974 Wilson probably felt he had no option but to appoint as Industry Secretary the radical strategy's most powerful and persuasive champion, Tony Benn. Together with his junior minister, the doughty left-winger Eric Heffer and the industrial strategy's main author Stuart Holland, he worked on a draft White paper but the wary Prime Minister took the precaution of appointing a member of the Number 10 Policy Unit as a 'Benn-watcher' to keep a jaundiced eye on their progress. There was little sympathy for the radical industry strategy within the Industry Department. The Permanent Secretary, Sir Anthony Part regarded it as disastrous and, being left in no doubt that Wilson broadly shared his view, was given free rein to obstruct its progress. When the draft White Paper eventually emerged, the Prime Minister was dismissive. According to his Press Secretary, Joe Haines, 'Harold read it briefly, quite angry, said it was woolly rubbish and he would have to do it himself' (Whitehead, 1985: 129). 'As I had feared,' Wilson recorded in his memoirs, 'it proved to be a sloppy and half-baked document, polemical, indeed menacing, in tone . . . Under my chairmanship, a special committee of senior ministers rewrote the document' (Wilson, 1979: 33).

There followed lengthy and heated discussions in Cabinet as the Industry Secretary battled to stiffen up the White paper: 'two and a quarter hours of absolute agony and bloodshed' as Benn described one session (Benn, 1989: 210). At issue were two divergent views of the market economy. Reflecting the mainstream Keynesian social democratic tradition, the Cabinet majority supported industrial intervention in selected cases where the market could not be relied upon to achieve desired goals, such as improved export performance or regional balance, or where the social costs of market activity needed to be contained. But the co-operation of the private sector was, they insisted, vital. The left, in contrast, believed that the market suffered from endemic flaws and that both equity and industrial efficiency required a substantial enlargement of the public domain. Benn and his supporters had already retreated from their earlier policy of the outright nationalization of a leading company in all the main industrial sectors – an approach which had never even had the backing of the whole of the left. Their efforts were now concentrated on securing a well-funded NEB with the power to acquire a substantial stake in profitable manufacturing firms. Though opponents decried this as modelled on Soviet bloc economics, the proposal in fact drew heavily upon practice in the more *dirigiste* economies of western Europe.

The TUC rallied behind Benn's view. Len Murray, its General Secretary, told Wilson that 'the TUC attach great importance to the enterprise part of the NEB. We don't want the Government to be able to stop the NEB buying profitable companies' whilst David Basnett, centre-right head of the General and Municipal Workers Union urged that 'the NEB should be as free as private enterprise' (Benn, 1989: 336, 337, entries March 1975). But the unions did not regard the issue as a top priority. On the other hand, the Government was coming under relentless pressure from business. It denounced the package, objecting stridently to proposals for the disclosure of information, for selective and discriminatory industrial assistance and above all to the NEB's powers to secure control over a profitable firm by purchasing equities without the consent of the board of directors (Benn, 1989: 249, 315–6; Kramer, 1988: 7). The nationalization of the shipyards, British Leyland and British Aerospace were tolerated because these were ailing firms (or wholly dependent on government contracts) and generously compensated public ownership had in the past facilitated the movement of capital into more profitable areas. But business drew the line at profitable firms: the existence of a public agency with the right to use private sector techniques such as 'dawn raids' on the stock exchange was regarded as an inadmissible challenge to the prerogatives of capital. The Confederation of British Industry (CBI) contemplated tough action against the Government unless it backed down. Its chief, Campbell Adamson, later recalled that we 'certainly discussed an investment strike' as well as withdrawal from all government bodies and late payment of tax if Benn's views had prevailed (Whitehead, 1985: 131; Middlemass, 1991: 39–40).

To most of his Cabinet colleagues, Benn's behaviour was reckless and provocative. 'Tony has alarmed industrialists' Shirley Williams admonished. 'We must carry industrialists with us, they are on the edge of total non-cooperation' (Benn, 1989: 188, entry 28 June 1974). If business lacked the confidence to invest, output, productivity, the balance of payments and employment would all suffer and the Government would pay the electoral penalty. Healey warned of 'the collapse of business confidence' whilst Lever (a man with close contacts in the City) condemned 'a ruinous blow to industry' (Benn, 1989: 212). When Benn protested at the proposed emasculation of the NEB, complaining that even the IRC had been authorized to purchase shares without consent, Healey riposted:

> 'Well, we have to maintain the confidence of business.'
> 'Why just the confidence of business?' I [Benn] asked.
> 'Because the whole of our future depends on the confidence of business.'
>
> (Benn, 1989: 327)[1]

For the bulk of the cabinet, the logic of this was unassailable and Wilson acceded to the CBI's key demand, strict limitation of the NEB's powers to buy into private industry. The dilemma of the left was that 'politicians who sit at the organisational conjunction of a democratic electoral system and a capitalist mode of production face strong incentives to avoid policies that might discourage the owners of private capital from investing and expanding production' (Hall, 1986: 262). This bestowed upon business a systemic power which a government of the left could defy only at its own risk. Labour right-wingers understood this, but were not unduly discomposed since they had little sympathy for an interventionist industrial policy. Furthermore, Wilson was as eager as the CBI to see the removal of their *bête noire* from the Department of Industry. The outcome of the referendum on EEC membership, which Labour had promised to organize once the 'renegotiation' of the terms of entry to which it had been committed had been concluded, provided the opportunity for the Prime Minister to deliver the *coup de grâce*.

The decisive vote in favour of continued membership inflicted a major blow on the left from which it never really recovered. Brushing opposition from other left-wing ministers and Jack Jones aside, Benn was ousted from the Department of Industry exchanging places with Eric Varley, the Energy Secretary. Despite his one-time reputation as a left-winger, Varley, was far more pliable and the 1975 Industry Act which he oversaw accommodated many of the CBI's objections. The

Government reaffirmed its commitment to the mixed economy, declaring that 'we need both efficient publicly owned industries, and a vigorous, alert, responsible and profitable private sector, working together with the Government in a framework which brings together the interests of all concerned . . . ' (Wilson, 1979: 35). Wilson recorded with satisfaction: 'Contrary to the revolutionary hopes which surrounded the NEB when it was conceived in Opposition days, Eric Varley's department . . . ensured that it would not operate like an industrial rogue elephant . . . [but] within the existing rules governing the provision of industrial finance' (Wilson, 1979: 33, 141–2). Wilson chose Sir Donald Ryder, a well-known industrialist, as NEB chairman and then ensured that he personally appointed all Board members and approved all acquisitions whilst doing as much as possible to soothe the private sector (Middlemass, 1991: 83).

As had originally been envisaged, the NEB did operate as a public sector entrepreneur but only on modest scale through the fostering of small high-tech companies. Here it initiated some valuable new technological advances where the private sector had been slack, such as biotechnology and micro-electronics (e.g. INMOS) (Sawyer, 1991: 164; Hare, 1984: 54). But much of its limited resources were eaten up by the Government's insistence that it take responsibility for capsizing companies – above all British Leyland. The Government had decided to rescue the bankrupt firm since its collapse would have deprived at least 170,000 workers of their jobs and damaged the balance of payments (Sawyer, 1991: 162–4). But by placing the car manufacturer into the NEB's portfolio the Government not only drained the Board of much of its funding but ensured that it would act – in direct contrast to what had been intended in opposition – mainly as a casualty home for failed private sector companies. Not surprisingly, it was never able to do more than 'scratch the surface of Britain's deep-seated industrial problems'. Its funding was inadequate and too tightly controlled 'to transform the direction and structure of investment' (Hare, 1984: 53). Little needs to be added about the fate of Planning Agreements. The Government ensured that they were voluntary and not, as the left had wanted, compulsory. Only one such agreement was signed with a private sector company, the US motor manufacturer Chrysler and when it decided to sell-out its UK interests it took not the slightest note of its terms.[2]

In late 1975 the Government unveiled its own – though largely civil service-generated – industrial strategy designed (in the words of a senior official) to persuade 'industry to put its own house in order' (quoted in Grant, 1985: 63). Under the auspices of the National Economic Development Office (NEDO) Sector Working parties (SWPs) were formed with members from both sides of industry and were asked to identify bottlenecks and advise on how to improve productivity (Donoughue, 1987: 148). In Healey's words, it was less a strategy than a 'methodology, based on forty tripartite working parties' which sought to persuade industry to follow best practice of individual firms (Healey, 1987: 407). He had diagnosed the main faults of the economy as inadequate investment and low productivity, a reluctance to move out of declining industries or adopt new techniques and a financial system that discouraged long-term borrowing from banks and facilitated the export of capital (Healey, 1989: 405). But the Government possessed no effective means to act upon the Chancellor's diagnosis and relying solely on persuasion was a recipe for ineffectiveness. A workable industrial policy needed to be able to alter the behaviour of industry but the most effective lever – the selective manipulation of credit – was one over which the Labour Government lacked control (Zysman, 1983: 197–8). To acquire it meant challenging powerful vested interests in the City and there was little disposition amongst most senior ministers to do so. With the initiative left to the private sector, it was hardly surprising that the industrial strategy had negligible effects (Artis and Cobham, 1991: 274).

But the original interventionist strategy too was seriously flawed. There was a lack of clarity in setting objectives, and the concept of Planning Agreements was vague and ill-thought out. It was never explained how decisions arising from the planning process would improve the calibre of investment and the confidence it evinced in the superior wisdom of a central authority was never underpinned by empirical evidence. The case for a holding company operating as a powerful public sector entrepreneur was weakened by its connection with an ill-devised scheme for comprehensive economic planning. Furthermore, the problem of securing the co-operation of the private sector was never fully addressed. Reflecting upon the fate of the industrial strategy, Barbara Castle commented: 'Having had to face backwoodsmen like the consultants myself, I can just imagine what obstruction and downright sabotage we should face from industrialists if we tried to impose the party's polices on them' (Castle, 1980: 675, entry 8 March 1976). The argument between the left and the Government polarized over the issue of whether industrial strategy should be imperative – taking the form of compulsory Planning Agreements – or whether it should be voluntary. But it was a false polarity and, indeed, neither approach was likely to succeed. Seeking to compel industry to act in ways it regarded as incompatible with its vital interests would simply lead to a breakdown in co-operation and a curtailment of domestic investment, lower output and job losses whilst reliance simply on persuasion – the route taken by the Government – was a recipe for ineffectualness. However, even a more pragmatic interventionist strategy would provoke stubborn resistance from business which a Labour Government would have found it difficult to overcome. As Mrs Castle observed: 'The trouble is that we have just not got up a sufficient head of revolutionary steam in the country to win in a showdown. But,' she then pertinently added, 'the Varley's and the Healey's don't even try to win consent for more radical polices' (Castle, 1980: 675, entry 8 March 1976).

The Retreat from Keynesian Social Democracy

But events in the wider world soon consigned this dispute to the status of a sideshow. Throughout 1975 fears were being expressed with mounting urgency by the City, industry and (privately) the Treasury that public spending was spiralling out of control and that the ultimate disaster, financial bankruptcy, might be beckoning. During the Heath Government, public expenditure had risen rapidly, in real terms by 4.8 per cent compared to a GDP increase of 2.5 per cent per annum, and the incoming Labour Government inherited expenditure plans which maintained this rate of growth. Furthermore, the Conservatives had awarded substantial increases to nurses and teachers which were due for payment in the first year of their successors. Prior to the election, Joel Barnett the Chief Secretary of the Treasury[3] complained that spending commitments were made without any consideration by the Treasury team of how much money would be available and what the order of priorities should be (Barnett, 1982: 15). Notwithstanding, in March 1974, in fulfilment of election pledges, the Cabinet agreed to an extra £1,240 million for pensions and other benefits, £500 million for food subsidies and £350 million for housing (Barnett, 1982: 25). The problem of mounting public spending was then 'greatly aggravated' by the Treasury's £4 billion underestimate of PSBR, as a result of which a budget intended to be neutral was reflationary (Healey, 1989: 393). Different decisions would have been made, Barnett recalled, if the true figures had been known: 'indeed the whole course of the next five years might have been changed had we decided we could not plan for such a high PSBR and therefore not increased public expenditure to the extent we did' (Barnett, 1982: 24). Healey later described himself as 'too inexperienced . . . to appreciate the full horrors of the situation' (Whitehead, 1985: 127) whilst Sir Leo Pliatzky, a Treasury mandarin soon to be charged with control over public expenditure, pungently denounced the first year of the Labour Government, as 'a period of collective madness' (Pliatzky, 1982: 130–1).

From the spring of 1975, a key policy objective was to rein back expenditure as Healey insistently demanded 'real public spending cuts on a scale never before seen' (Jackson, 1991: 75–6). But initially he made slow progress. Ministers heading major spending departments, whose reputations were often measured in terms of the skill with which they protected and enlarged their budgets, were reluctant to put in jeopardy cherished programmes. Further, most ministers, immersed in their own portfolios, were slow to appreciate the gravity of the economic situation. But opposition to expenditure cuts ran even deeper. The left – including their representatives in Cabinet – regarded welfare programmes as the touchstone of socialism and their opposition was not as easily rebuffed as it had been in the previous Wilson administration. Their influence was rooted in three intersecting circles: the Cabinet, the NEC and the unions. The centre-left grouping within the Cabinet included a set of seasoned, determined and gifted ministers: Benn, the Industry Secretary, Barbara Castle head of the DHSS, Foot, the Employment Secretary and Shore, the Trade Secretary. Although the centre-left ministers as a whole met regularly (as the 'husbands and wives'), they were by no means a cohesive group, covering a wide spectrum of views, with uneasy personal relations which became increasingly soured over time. However, in Labour's first year of office differences were held very much in check by their common involvement in the campaign for withdrawal from the EEC, particularly as it became clear that the 'renegotiation of the terms of entry' promised by the Prime Minister was largely a stratagem to swing opinion behind continued membership. By acting in concert they were able to form an influential bloc opposed to cut-backs in public expenditure. Supporting the left were the Keynesian social democrats, headed by Crosland. Although they accepted the need for temporary restraint – indeed it was Crosland who, as Secretary of the Environment, announced to local authorities that 'the party's over' – on both economic and social grounds they rejected Healey's case for sweeping cuts. Time and again Crosland, who carried great weight in the Cabinet, contested the economic rationale behind the Chancellor's arguments. Benn, chairman of its Home Policy Committee, was the most influential figure on the left-led Executive. The powers the NEC possessed to influence the content and tone of Conference debates were used, not, as from 1945 to 1951, to mobilize support for the Government but to orchestrate criticism of it. This caused considerable embarrassment but what really buttressed Healey's critics was the firm support they enjoyed from powerful unions. Foot, the Cabinet minister most trusted by Jones and Scanlon, strenuously argued that putting the knife to social programmes would imperil the understanding with the unions, upon which the Government continued to vest its hopes for curbing inflation.

The Cabinet reached log-jam in the summer of 1975. In June Healey submitted to Cabinet a £3 billion package of cuts but was forced to compromise because of the strength of the resistance from the left and the Crosland group (Donoughue, 1987: 62–3). Yet if the Chancellor – and the Prime Minister – felt frustrated, their critics, whilst strong enough to block moves they disliked, were unable to push through an alternative; furthermore the failure of the unions to deliver on wages in the decisive first year of the Government's life was hastening the onset of a crisis which was very likely be tackled on the Treasury's terms. '"Politicians" a Treasury mandarin told Donoughue "never deal with serious issues until they become *the* crisis. So at the Treasury we're waiting till the crisis blows up"' (Whitehead, 1985: 128).[4] This point was reached at the end of June 1975 when a grave Governor of the Bank of England told alarmed Treasury ministers that sterling was about to slip into a headlong dive. Healey warned Cabinet that unless spending was sliced back, borrowing could stop overnight and a disastrous run on the pound could be triggered off (Castle,1980: 426). To restore the confidence of the markets, he insisted, a reduction in the PSBR was essential – which meant that the squeeze on public spending, first begun in the budget of April 1975, must be appreciably tightened. The political equilibrium by this time was becoming more favourable to the Chancellor. The turning-point was the EEC referendum.

The idea of a referendum had been aired during Labour's period in opposition by Benn – to be derided by virtually everyone else. Initially Wilson dismissed it as a 'nasty gimmick'[5] but then saw its value as a convenient device to patch up Party divisions for the next election (Ziegler, 1993: 38, 385). Although he had masqueraded as a critic of the EEC he had never much deviated from his desire for membership. His tactic was to commit Labour to a call for renegotiation of the terms of entry, a formulation which was sufficiently ambiguous to mollify the bulk of both pro- and anti-marketeers. Back in office, negotiations with Brussels were conducted by Callaghan, now Foreign Secretary, who reached agreement on 'new terms' which in practice only differed slightly from the original ones. Though the majority of the Party rejected the renegotiation package, the Prime Minister threw the Government's weight behind the powerful coalition (spanning Labour pro-marketeers, most Conservatives, the Liberals, business and virtually the whole press) urging a yes vote in the referendum. Though Wilson permitted the anti-market minority in the Cabinet to campaign for a 'no' vote, with the vastly greater resources at their command, there was never much doubt that the proponents of membership would triumph. The endorsement of the EEC by a two-thirds majority greatly sapped the influence of the left in the Cabinet. With the unifying bond of the referendum campaign removed, the many issues upon which the centre-left group was divided became more obtrusive, undermining its capacity for concerted action. Thus the majority of the left-centre ministers, like Foot, Castle and Shore strongly backed the £6 pay policy which left-wingers in the Tribune Group and on the NEC (and Benn privately) attacked. No real attempt was made to bring the left as a whole – in parliament, the NEC and the Cabinet – together to discuss an alternative economic strategy. Whilst Benn acted as an outspoken and fluent advocate, within Cabinet and outside, for a radical approach, his relations with other left-of-centre ministers steadily worsened.

Nor could left-wing ministers depend on left-wing union leaders as much as before. By 1975 the bulk of union leaders were doing their utmost, within the limits of their powers, to sustain the Government and rallied to defend ministers against the NEC, even when the latter was articulating Party policy in which they had had a hand in making. The growing acrimony between the Tribunite left and their former union allies was dramatically highlighted in October 1975 during the crowded Tribune rally, traditionally held during Conference. Speaking from the platform, Ian Mikardo was lambasting the Government, 'piling selective statistic on selective statistic to give a hostile distortion of the work of the Government. Suddenly out of the crowded aisle where he had been standing leapt Jack Jones, up onto the platform, jabbing an accusing figure at Mikardo like an Old Testament Prophet pronouncing his doom . . . he stood there for a full minute, jab following jab with inarticulate shout following inarticulate shout. It was electrifying . . . and there was pandemonium . . . ' (Castle, 1980: 512). By February 1976, Castle was confiding to her diary that 'we now have a situation in the party in which the Government has succeeded in detaching the trade union movement from the left-wing critics and Jack Jones is increasingly losing patience with them' (Castle, 1980: 662).

In July 1975 Healey received Cabinet backing for his proposal to introduce a cash limits system for controlling public expenditure. This replaced volume-based budgeting, in which departments were largely compensated for the effects of inflation, and had the effect of systematically encouraging underspending, intensifying the squeeze on public programmes (Ludlam, 1992: 720). In November Healey called for cuts of £3.75 billion – warning he would resign if he did not got most of what he wanted. This time Cabinet assented although only after much heated discussion (Ziegler, 1993: 448). By early 1976, as the £6 pay policy took hold, inflation was steadily falling, the balance of payments gap was narrowing and with the prospects of North Sea oil revenues providing a stream of foreign currency earnings within the next two years, the worst appeared to be over. Although the underlying problems of British competitiveness remained the current account deficit was down from £3.3 billion in 1974 to £1 billion in 1976 (Burk and Cairncross, 1992: 172–3; Healey, 1987: 427).

Wilson took advantage of this brief moment of calm in the spring of 1976 to announce his resignation. This took most people totally by surprise and far-fetched theories circulated to throw light on this apparently inexplicable decision. In fact Wilson had long intended to resign within a couple of years of returning to Number 10 and had told his closest aides. For much of his time as Party Leader he had lived in fear of a putsch by Callaghan but, such are the vagaries of politics, their mutual relationship had greatly improved since 1974 and of senior ministers he had been tipped off the earliest about the impending resignation. Five other candidates threw their hats in the ring: Foot, Jenkins, Healey, Benn and Crosland.[6] Foot emerged with the most votes on the first ballot, but well short of a majority. Three candidates withdrew or were eliminated leaving the second ballot to Foot, Callaghan and Healey which again failed to produce a winner. In the final run-off Callaghan scored 176 votes to Foot's 137 (Howell, 1980: 295). Two other figures who had played prominent roles over the last decade left Government along with Wilson. Jenkins, disappointed that his hopes for the leadership, which at one time he seemed destined to inherit, were finally dashed resigned to become an EEC commissioner; and Barbara Castle, one of Labour's ablest and most energetic ministers was effectively sacked for having crossed Callaghan once too often in the past.

The new Prime Minister enjoyed only a short respite. There was grave anxiety within the Treasury and the Bank of England over the effects of inflation in pricing British goods out of foreign markets, though there was disagreement over how best to respond. The majority view in the Treasury favoured a controlled fall in the pound. A stratagem was devised, in March 1976, to nudge the exchange rate down but, through a mixture of ill-luck and miscalculation, it totally backfired. The markets panicked and a precipitous fall in sterling occurred. 'It's a baptism of fire for Labour politicians when they first experience the power of the markets. It happened to Jim Callaghan in 1964 and now to Denis Healey in 1976' (an 'insider' quoted in Fay and Young, 1978). In June the Government hurriedly managed to arrange a $5.3 billion foreign loan with foreign central banks to buttress sterling. But the conditions were that the loan had to be repaid in six months and recourse would then have to be made to the IMF if further assistance was required (Allsopp, 1991: 32). The Americans helped arrange the loan but intended it as a bait. They calculated that market pressures would soon exhaust the loan and prevent it from being repayable by the due date, leaving Britain no option but to go to the IMF: 'what Healey presented to the House as a helping coil of rope for sterling half way down a precipice was to be a noose'. Top policy-makers in Washington regarded Labour as incorrigibly profligate, were convinced that the disease would only be

cured by 'a purgative dose of castor oil' – slashing public spending and
borrowing, and stiff controls on the money supply – but had no faith in
the willingness of the Government to swallow. The IMF would have to
spoon it (Fay and Young, 1978).

This was for the future. As part of the loan agreement, the Chancellor
presented the Cabinet with a fresh parcel of cuts totalling £2 billion.
Once again, he was opposed by the left-leaning ministers (Benn, Foot,
Shore, Stan Orme and John Silkin)[7] who called for import and exchange
controls to maintain the level of spending; and by the Keynesian social
democrats led by Crosland, and including Hattersely and Lever. Their
view was that there was no economic justification for a further clamp on
public spending, and that it would be counter-productive since slower
growth and higher unemployment would push up demand-led benefit
costs whilst reducing tax revenues. However, with Callaghan's support,
the Cabinet reluctantly agreed to prune £1 billion from public expenditure for 1977–8 and to raise a similar total from a National Insurance
surcharge on employers. It was anticipated that the PSBR would fall
to £10 billion though at the cost of an extra 200,000 unemployed
(Donoughue, 1987: 89–91). A meeting was held shortly after with
senior union leaders but, as Benn recorded in his diary, 'Not a peep
whatever from the TUC about the cuts, and that indicated the true
political position.' (Benn, 1989: 602, entry 26 July 1976).

The crisis, it seemed, was now over. But not for long. Senior officials
in Washington did not believed that the cuts went far enough, and
objected to tax increases as a means of lowering the PSBR (Burk and
Cairncross, 1992: 5). The money markets, too, were not placated and
after a Treasury leak claiming that official Government policy was
to allow sterling to drop to $1.50, the rush to sell resumed with a
vengeance. Further hikes in interest rates took them to 13 per cent
in October, imperilling investment, growth and job prospects. But
the flow would not be stanched, the pound sank to $1.60 with no
end to the selling in sight (Allsopp, 1991: 32–3). With the PSBR –
according to Treasury officials – well above forecast and money growth
substantially exceeding the Treasury's 12 per cent target, confidence
in the money markets slumped. 'The City would not buy gilts, the
foreign markets would not hold sterling, and the IMF refused to give
any more loans without a further dose of expenditure cuts as evidence
of self-discipline' (Donoughue, 1987: 93). A financial collapse seemed to

beckon. With sterling in a tail-spin, Healey – about to catch a flight to an international conference – suddenly turned round and hurried back to the Labour Party Conference and, in a fighting speech aimed more at the markets than at delegates, belligerently defended government policy. A further tightening of interest rates to 15 per cent restored gilts and stabilized the exchange rate but the Government had only bought time. With all prospect of repaying the six months' hard currency loan rapidly vanishing, and the pound still weak, the Government was under tremendous pressure 'to appease the markets and re-establish a claim to fiscal rectitude so as to improve the chances of desperately needed financial support' (Burk and Cairncross, 1992: 160). Callaghan grabbed the nettle, and in a seminal speech to Conference, drafted by his son-in-law and monetarist economist, Peter Jay, he declared:

> We used to think that you could spend your way out of recession and increase employment by cutting taxes and boosting Government spending. I will tell you in all candour that that option no longer exists, and that insofar as it ever did exist, it only worked on each occasion since the war by injecting a bigger dose of inflation into the economy, followed by a higher level of unemployment as the next step. (Callaghan, 1987: 426)

The Keynesian social democratic era was passing. Callaghan's stunned audience was not the real one – and the real one was impressed. 'Jim,' President Ford told him on the phone the next day, 'you made a helluva speech yesterday'. The speech 'demonstrated to us,' a senior US official commented, 'that the UK had changed course' (Burk and Cairncross, 1992: 56). At the same time Healey announced that he was applying to the IMF for assistance. Having already obtained two tranches of loans, Britain had reached 'third tranche conditionality' which required a full review of her policies and acceptance of IMF terms in exchange for a loan (Burk and Cairncross, 1992: 57).

The IMF's initial terms, backed by the US Treasury (and discreetly by elements within the Bank of England and the Treasury) were draconian, involving £5 billion of cuts spread over two years – an assault on spending of a scale that exceeded anything Mrs Thatcher was ever to mount. The price would have been a major economic recession and the ruin of the Labour Government. Callaghan responded by seeking to persuade the major western governments, especially the US and

Germany, to use their influence to moderate the IMF's stance. His 'great personal contribution', the head of his Policy Unit argued, was to resist these excessive demands and obtain agreement over a package which was sufficient to restore confidence in sterling without precipitating a serious recession (Donoughue, 1987: 95).[8] His efforts to ease the IMF's terms brought some relaxation, but they remained astringent. Although there were those in Washington who were sympathetic with his Government's plight, and rather more who feared pushing it so hard that the outcome might be (unrealistic as this scenario in fact was) the ultimate catastrophe of a left-wing government led by Benn, the majority view was that it was time for the medicine, however distasteful, to be administered. This left the Prime Minister with a complex juggling act as he sought to keep the Government intact by preventing ministerial resignations; to hold the Party together by making it clear that failure to support the Cabinet in its decisions would mean defeat in parliament and a general election, and to avoid a break with the TUC which would have destroyed the social contract (Callaghan, 1987: 433–4).

Callaghan discovered that two groups of critics were meeting – the left and the Keynesian social democrats. They were 'were playing a dangerous game which I was determined to circumvent' (Callaghan, 1987: 435). The tactic he adopted was to give all opponents full opportunity to express their views and thereby demonstrate that there was no viable alternative to his preferred course. No less than nine cabinet sessions were held over three weeks. The left group was by no means unanimous. Benn advocated a complete reversal of policy, including the imposition of import and exchange controls, control of bank borrowing and an interventionist industrial policy, but he was very much in a minority (Benn, 1989: 664). Shore concentrated on selective import controls whilst Foot pressed for another bid to tone down the IMF terms and risk rejecting them if the Fund was obdurate (Benn, 1989: 665–7, 673–4). Crosland argued that the IMF prescription would have a disastrous effect on investment and on wages policy: 'far from reducing the PSBR, the spending cuts would mean higher unemployment, which would in turn mean higher social security payments and lower tax revenue, thus actually increasing the PSBR'. They would also demolish the industrial strategy, alienate the public sector unions, and cause the collapse of the social contract. If the IMF refused to show more flexibility, the Government should install an import deposit scheme to reduce the payments deficit, and threaten to wind down defence commitments and introduce a siege economy. If they could keep their nerve they could limit cuts 'to window-dressing to appease the irritating and ignorant currency dealers'. He concluded: 'we have to stop paying "danegeld"' (Benn, 1989: 667–8).

The real danger for Callaghan and Healey was that all opponents would rally round Crosland. Tentative efforts were made for the two groupings of opponents to join forces but nothing came of this, though the reason why is not clear. By this time it was evident that Crosland occupied a pivotal position: if he could be induced to acquiesce, the opposition would be beleaguered and helpless. According to Barnett, his 'quality of objectivity, combined with his knowledge, experience and considerable ability, made him the Minister who had the greatest impact on Cabinet decisions on most issues' (Barnett, 1982: 47). He came under sustained pressure from the Prime Minister who lavished on him the full range of his considerable powers of persuasion, from flattery – 'I reminded him that he had great influence with a section of the Cabinet and must decide where to throw his weight' (Callaghan, 1987: 439) – via reasoned argument and appeals to Party loyalty to laying his authority on the line.[9] At the same time, the Crosland group began to dissolve – with, significantly, those later to form the SDP (Bill Rodgers and Shirley Williams) flaking away so that eventually Hattersley alone stood firm behind his intellectual mentor. A disconsolate Crosland eventually and reluctantly concluded that the price of defeating Callaghan and Healey would be too high: if the two most senior members of the Government were publicly rebuffed, a crisis of confidence would follow and the Cabinet would fall. In what seems a swan song for the Keynesian social democracy he had propounded for a generation (he was to die within a couple of months) he told Cabinet he thought the IMF package 'wrong economically and socially, destructive of what he had believed in all his life'. But he added 'the unity of the party depends upon sustaining the Prime Minister and the effect on sterling of rejecting the Prime Minister would be to destroy our capacity. Therefore I support the Prime Minister and the Chancellor' (Benn, 1989: 674, entry 2 December 1976). With the Foreign Secretary's capitulation, the effective resistance melted away. The package finally agreed included reductions in all items of spending – health, transport, housing, food subsidies, defence and so forth – except social security, totalling £2.5 billion from the period

1977–9 (Burk and Cairncross, 1992: 105). Despite the fact that taking the knife yet again to public expenditure undermined one of the major justifications for incomes policy, 'the working partnership [between the Government and unions] took the strain. Close contact between ministers and union leaders were maintained during the discussions with the IMF and the government measures, including cuts in public expenditure and higher indirect taxation, were accepted – though reluctantly – without any real possibility that the pay policy would be jettisoned' (Barnes and Reid, 1980: 211). As Callaghan commented, the Government obtained TUC backing with surprising ease (Callaghan, 1987: 443).

The Prime Minister emerged from the whole painful episode ironically with his prestige enhanced. He had fought tenaciously and skilfully – though with only modest success – to tone down the IMF terms. He then had managed the debate within the Cabinet with consummate ability, ensuring it was conducted with an unusual absence of acrimony and that it concluded without any resignations. His 'achievement in 1976 was quite remarkable' Donoughue later reflected. He had obtained both IMF and Cabinet approval of a cuts package smaller than IMF had initially wanted and kept the Cabinet together (Donoughue, 1987: 98). Benn, who clashed with him – as with Wilson – many times rather admired him, describing him as 'very charming . . . an agreeable and skilful politician, marvellous at getting his own way . . . a shrewd political figure' (Benn, 1989: 62). But the future was not to be gentle to Callaghan, for a high price was eventually to be exacted.

The Crisis of the Keynesian Welfare State

As now enshrined in popular folklore, the crisis was about how a bankrupt Labour Government was forced to go, 'cap in hand' to the IMF to be 'bailed out' by international bankers. This was the translation into a popular idiom of an influential body of academic thought which contended that the crisis in public spending was the predictable outcome of the contradictions of Keynesian social democracy. It had given the state responsibility for full employment, economic growth and constructed an elaborate system of social protection. But the more the government sought to regulate the more it became dependent on the consent of powerful organized interests: 'the enormous new powers that government exercises over producer and consumer groups at the same time puts these groups in a position to frustrate these powers by refusing their co-operation and consent' (Beer, 1981: 14). Thus strengthened, these groups – notably trade unions and social spending lobbies – gained more leverage to extract resources from the Government. The civil service also possessed a bureaucratic self-interest in adding to their responsibilities since this way more staff, better promotion prospects and more power could be amassed. More staff, in turn, facilitated the growth of public sector trade unionism. Unlike unions representing employees in the private manufacturing sector, the pay of public sector employees was funded directly from the public purse. This gave them a vested interest in higher spending since it paid their salaries, boosted their numbers and enhanced their bargaining power. Because the effectiveness of departmental spending ministers was judged by their ability to enlarge their budgets, this gave another twist to the upward spending spiral (Beer, 1981: 27–8). Finally, reducing public spending was far more difficult than increasing it since both bureaucratic providers and recipients would fiercely resist attempts to withdraw new entitlements (Rose, 1979: 357). The billowing cost of public programmes drove up taxation and government borrowing which undermined incentives, pushed up high interest rates, crowded out private sector investment and fuelled inflation.

To many commentators the excessive power of the unions, their capacity to bid up the price of labour and extract costly policy concessions from the Government, was the major cause of government 'overload' of the state and 'exorbitant' public spending. 'The overwhelming power of the trade unions in the Party,' wrote a former head of the Department of Employment, 'the almost total dependence of the Party on trade union money, the reliance of trade union organization in elections, the block vote at the Labour Party Conference, the substantial number of parliamentary seats within union gift' meant that the relationship between the unions and the Government was inevitably at times 'that of patron and defendant' (Barnes and Reid, 1980: 222). The Social Concept as a strategy for containing inflation – the concept of exchanging wage restraint for a higher social wage and an institutionalized union presence in the policy process[10] – aggravated the problem as the government sought to assuage powerful trade unions with new spending commitments (Lehner, 1987: 64). Jack Jones was widely seen as 'arguably the most powerful politician within the Labour Party' (Barnes and Reid, 1980: 192) and several cabinet ministers complained of the Government's supine attitude (Barnett, 1982: 94). 'The climate of the time,' according to Jenkins, 'was that of ministers finding out what the TUC wanted and giving it to them' (Jenkins, 1991: 392).[11] This interpretation has imprinted itself on the modern Labour Party where claims are regularly made that 'New Labour' will never again be 'in thrall' to the unions, never again over-tax, over-spend and over-borrow.

Ultimately, the argument ran, the burden of the Keynesian welfare state would become non-sustainable – and the chickens came home to roost in Labour Britain in 1976 as an uncontrollable escalation in public spending consumed a frighteningly high proportion of GDP. By 1975, according to the 1976 Public Expenditure White Paper, spending had risen to 60 per cent of GDP (Pliatzky, 1982: 161), a much higher proportion than virtually any other western country. The weight of public spending, Roy Jenkins pronounced, was endangering 'plural society' (Barnett, 1982: 80).[12] One senior (unnamed) economic policy-maker concluded: 'the public sector's demand's on the GNP had to be contained, the public sector borrowing requirement had to be reduced in order to lower interest rates, business profits had to be raised, and the influence of the unions on government policy had to be lessened in order to revitalise the British economy' (Scharpf, 1987: 82).

The account this argument offered of the IMF crisis, plausible on the surface was, in fact, rooted in unproven assertions, highly questionable causal connections and a one-dimensional grasp of the realities of power. The thesis expounded here is quite different. The IMF crisis was not, in essence, an ideological or even primarily an economic crisis: thus it was *not* the consequence of a public spending running out of control, *nor* of an unbridgeable payments deficit, *nor* of excessive borrowing. The IMF crisis was *not*, in short, caused by a seizing-up of the economy. The key indicators – the inflation rate, the money supply, the external account – were all moving in the right direction whilst revenue from North Sea oil would soon be providing funds for the exchequer and large amounts of foreign currency earnings (Artis and Cobham, 1991: 271). Even on narrow monetary criteria, the Government's record was better than any major western government other than West Germany (Burk and Cairncross, 1992: 93). Kalecki had pointed out, in 1943, that full employment would never be to the taste of business. 'The workers would "get out of hand" and "the captains of industry" would be anxious "to teach them a lesson."' He predicted that, at some point in the future, 'a powerful block is likely to be formed between big business and the rentier interest ... [which] would most probably induce the Government to return to the orthodox policy of cutting down the budget deficit' (Robinson, 1962: 89). The rapidly expanding power of the financial markets, the globalization of production and the ideological advance of the new right provided propitious conditions for a conservative counter-offensive to reoccupy the lost ground conceded in the post-war decades. The crisis, then, was essentially a political one, the root cause a new *constellation of power*, in which capital and the political right could commence the dismantling of the Keynesian welfare state.

In Thrall to the Unions

To the extent that the unions failed to deliver on wage restraint, the initial Social Contract of 1974–5 was, as often alleged, a one-sided exchange. Indeed, it is arguable that many of the spending commitments which the Government respected deepened the crisis – although it should be added that Healey himself initially favoured maintaining demand in the (forlorn) hope that other industrial powers would do so too. Undeniably in the first year of the Government the unions exerted considerable power. But – notwithstanding received wisdom – this soon waned and the unions had little influence over crucial economic policy decisions after the summer of 1975. In general, on issues which they regarded as priorities the Government took great care to consult with them and offer concessions involving some increases in spending (e.g. training and job creation measures to hold down unemployment). But on all-important economic matters it rarely acted on their advice and union leaders became increasingly disheartened (Keegan and Pennant-Rea, 1979: 123; Taylor, 1993: 243). They could not prevent substantial cuts in public spending, nor were they able to induce the Government to boost the economy in order to cut jobless totals (Keegan and Pennant-Rea, 1979: 123).

There was a wide gap between the economic policies espoused by the TUC and actual Government policy, but in fact little pressure was exerted by union leaders on ministers. The TUC Congress resolutions urging an alternative economic strategy did not express the real views of Jones and Scanlon, who regarded them 'as at best a bargaining pressure in relations with the Government and, at worst, sloganising impracticalities'. In private, TUC officials articulated scepticism about the alternative strategy whilst Jones disliked what he saw as the 'posturing' of left-wing middle class 'theorists' who ducked practical problems (Minkin, 1991: 170). They were largely reliant for advice from the TUC Economic Department, which was heavily influenced by Treasury thinking. In contrast, contact with the Cabinet left was sporadic. 'Indeed, at this time on key issues of macro-economic policy, an avalanche of advice was showered on the union leaders, all pointing to the common sense of the Government's general approach' (Minkin, 1991: 170). Whilst Jones did have some qualms about the Cabinet's increasingly Treasury-driven economic strategy he could see no real alternative. In contrast, Scanlon – previously the more radical of the duo – underwent a profound change in his outlook. He 'accepted the Bacon–Eltis thesis – heavily pushed by economic journalists and by the Treasury at this time – that high levels of public sector expenditure were starving the market sector of resources, causing deindustrialisation and weakening the economy' (Minkin, 1991: 170).[13] The real significance of the institutionalization of the union role in government lay in the opportunity it afforded to ministers and civil servants to socialize union leaders and TUC officials into *their* way of thinking, to the extent that many came to accept *their* definition of the problem and to believe there was, in practice, no alternative to the Treasury view.

The Treasury

The Treasury had for long been the most prestigious and powerful department in Whitehall and constituted the central nervous system of the economic policy machine. Its institutional power derived from the vital importance of the functions it performed – ranging from control of public expenditure, to fiscal and (together with the Bank of England) monetary and exchange rate policy. In an uncertain and unpredictable world the greatest opportunity for the exercise of Treasury influence was in providing the Chancellor with forecasts – above all projections for public spending and the PSBR – and in briefing him on the options implied by them (Keegan and Pennant-Rea, 1979: 80, 86). Forecasting, however, was a very inexact science, rooted – as Healey trenchantly put it – 'in the extrapolation from a partially known past, through an unknown present, to an unknowable future according to theories about the causal relationships between certain economic variables which are hotly disputed by academic economists, and may in fact change from country to country or from decade to decade (Healey, 1989: 38). This gave plenty of room for the exercise of presentational and arithmetical skills in which the Treasury demonstrated an impressive mastery. 'I though I had done a fair amount of juggling with figures as an accountant,' the then Chief Secretary wrote in his memoir, 'but when it came to the sort of sophisticated "massaging" and "fudging" I learned as Chief Secretary, I realised I had been a babe in arms by comparison' (Barnett, 1982: 22). 'The prevailing belief among [Treasury officials],' he added, 'was that our poor industrial and economic performance meant that we must restrain the growth of public expenditure. Consequently, all their considerable efforts in presenting the figures would be geared to than end' (Barnett, 1982: 21).

Intriguingly, after the July 1976 cuts, which elements in the Treasury regarded as insufficient, the estimate of the PSBR was actually revised upwards (in discussions with IMF) to £11.2 billion (Burk and Cairncross, 1992: 183). This apparently put Britain way out on a limb amongst western countries. Donoughue, as head of the Number 10 Policy Unit, noticed that the PSBR for 1977–8 was higher than any other current forecast 'creating suspicion in our minds that the amount had been inflated to create an atmosphere of crisis enabling the Treasury to "bounce" large cuts through Ministers' (Donoughue, 1987: 94). In fact, public expenditure absorbed a much higher proportion of GNP in the UK compared to other OECD not because more was spent but because *the figures were compiled in a different way*. Sir Leo Pliatzky, who was promoted second Permanent Secretary with specific responsibility 'to impose a Draconian change in public-sector practices' (Fay and Young, 1978) later recalled: 'in the same way that the theory of gravity came into Isaac Newton's head when the legendary apple dropped on it' so with a sudden flash of insight he realized 'we were double counting on a large scale' (Pliatzky, 1982: 164).[14] Not only this: the inclusion in the public expenditure figures of capital spending by nationalized industries was 'peculiar to the UK and inflated both public expenditure

and the borrowing requirement' (Burk and Cairncross, 1992: 137).
And further: even that portion of public sector companies' investment
programme financed from internal resources – making no claims on
the public purse – was incorporated in the overall spending total
(Pliatzky, 1982: 162). When account was taken of the proportion of
the gross debt interest in the public sector as a whole financed by
interest receipts and other offsets – once, that is, the Treasury dropped
double counting – then the debt interest figure for 1975–6 calculated at
£5.5 billion shrank rather dramatically to £1.1 billion (Pliatzky, 1982:
164).[15]

The outcome was that the 'alarming' figure of 60 per cent of GNP
absorbed by public spending contracted to just under 46 per cent
(Pliatzky, 1982: 166). As Barnett commented, 'it rather made a mess
of Roy Jenkins's endangered "plural society" argument'. The following year (1977/78), as – *pre-IMF* – cuts took hold, the figure fell
to around 40 per cent (Barnett, 1982: 81). An OECD study published in 1978 indicated that the percentage of public expenditure in
the UK was not out of line with OECD countries as a whole. It
was a little higher than the average (brought down by low social
spending in Japan and the US) but on a par with Germany and well
below the Scandinavian countries and the Netherlands (Pliatzky, 1982:
166–7).

The claim by many commentators that the rapid rise in the relative
size of the public sector between 1974 and 1976 meant that public
expenditure was out of control was also inaccurate. Two factors unrelated
to the volume growth of public spending – that is, the actual output
of goods and services – accounted for much of the increase. Firstly,
in these years, real GDP fell by 2.6 per cent so the public spending
proportion automatically grew. Secondly, the prices at which public
expenditures were valued tended to rise faster than the prices at which
the GDP was valued – the so-called relative price effect. In particular,
the public sector was very labour intensive, hence it was affected
disproportionately by wage increases (Jackson, 1991: 76). In addition,
the form anti-inflationary policy took – subsidies on food, housing, fuel
and rates designed to hold down prices – contributed to the spending
totals (Jackson, 1991: 77). Nor did the growth of public spending differ
much from other countries. Both in the proportion of GDP accounted
for by public spending and the rate of increase in spending between

1972 and 1976, the main distinction was between the USA and Japan on the one hand, and the west European countries on the other. In the latter year, using OECD figures, the percentage for the UK was 46.3 per cent (including, of course, an above-average defence budget), 43.9 per cent for France, 47.9 per cent for Germany, 52.9 per cent for the Netherlands and 51.7 per cent for Sweden (Burk and Cairncross, 1992: 223).[16]

The Cabinet and Spending

Healey declared in his autobiography that 'I can't forgive' the Treasury 'for misleading the Government, the country and the world for so many years about the true state of public spending in Britain. Indeed I suspect that Treasury officials were content to overstate public spending in order to put pressure on governments which were reluctant to cut it' (Healey, 1989: 402). Ministers more strongly committed to publicly-funded welfare were a little more sceptical – at the time – about the Treasury's statistics than Healey professed to be. 'I remain firmly convinced,' Barbara Castle wrote in July 1975, 'that half the elaborately detailed public expenditure calculations are phony in economic terms' (Castle, 1980: 462).[17] It is a matter of conjecture whether or not the street-wise Healey was quite so misled. He was, however, sympathetic to some Treasury attitudes about 'the soft underbelly' of social spending. At the Labour Clubs, the Chancellor at one point confided to his Cabinet colleagues, there was a lot of support for cutting public expenditure. 'They will all tell you about Paddy Murphy up the street who's got eighteen children, has not worked for years, lives on unemployment benefit, has a colour television and goes to Majorca for his holidays' (Benn, 1989: 461).[18] He warned his critics that people would 'be shocked, not pleased, when they saw how much we were spending on social services. "Which ones?" I [Barbara Castle] demanded. "Name them." "Schools for one, and other forms of education." Suddenly as I listened to him I lost heart totally . . . I felt a sense of hopelessness engulf me. The only strategy that will be before us . . . will be one which commits us to unemployment levels continuing at 3 per cent right up to 1978–9 . . . this is a scenario,' she added presciently, 'for another Tory victory just in time for them to reap the harvest of our bitter self-sacrifice. And the price will be the destruction of all our social polices, so that a Labour Government will preside over the biggest cuts in public services since 1931' (Castle, 1980: 457–8, 462, 463).

The Government's assault on public expenditure had 'no parallel in any other period in the post-war years' (Burk and Cairncross, 1992: 190). However, some programmes escaped the knife. *Britain Will Win with Labour*, the Party's October 1974 manifesto, had stated that the Government would reduce the proportion of the nation's resources spent on defence to bring it more closely in line with that of 'our main European allies' (Craig, 1990: 254–5). The Heath administration had authorized further development of the Chevaline project – first mooted by the previous Labour Government. Wilson secured the Cabinet's approval for its continuation (it could have been cancelled quite cheaply) though its real cost was estimated in 1975 at £595 million, more than twice the figure given to ministers (Ziegler, 1993: 460). By 1977 the real cost had reached £800 million and Joel Barnett, who as Chief Secretary of the Treasury was supposed to authorize all spending, only got to know of the project after Labour had lost office, by which time the cost had almost doubled again to over £1,000 million, 'the largest matter in recent years not to have gained a passing mention in the annual defence estimates' (Freedman, 1980: 55). Healey later described his failure not to have insisted on the cancellation of Chevaline, whose costs soon 'escalated beyond control', 'as one of my major mistakes' particularly since he could detect no military justification for it (Healey, 1989: 455, 313). This was part of a general pattern for, despite the endless sequence of public expenditure cuts, the Cabinet felt that the defence budget must be held firm at a percentage of the GDP well above that of its main European allies: in 1977 Germany was spending 3.1 per cent of its GDP on defence and 11.5 per cent on social security whilst Britain was spending 4.9 per cent on defence and only 8.9 per cent on social security. This 'exceptionally high' expenditure, Healey recalled, 'imposed a heavy strain on [Britain's] resources of skilled manpower and of foreign exchange' (Healey, 1989: 412, 411). Indeed, in 1977 the Government went one step further. Contrary to its manifesto pledge it accepted NATO decision to *increase* defence expenditure as from 1979 (Keohane, 1993: 29).

The Financial Markets

'The single most important structural change in the world economy in the second half of the twentieth century', Sir Douglas Wass, then Permanent Secretary at the Treasury observed, was that 'the ability of national governments to pursue a policy of their own choosing was being steadily narrowed by the increased integration of the world economy' (quoted in Burk and Cairncross, 1992: 165). During the 1970s there was a 'quantum jump' in the power of the money markets (Keegan and Pennant-Rea, 1979: 131). This was due to a range of factors, most notably the rapid expansion of the unregulated London-based Eurodollar market, the removal of quantitative controls over interest rates by the Heath Government's Competition and Credit Control Act, and the replacement of fixed by floating exchange rates. In consequence the markets were rapidly emerging 'as the most important influence on policy' (Keegan and Pennant-Rea, 1979: 131).

The growth in the magnitude and velocity of currency markets undermined the economic autonomy of national governments. 'Once monetary flows came to dominate exchange rates it was less the state of the current account that provided a test of equilibrium than the view taken by financial markets of a country's economic prospects.' Thus a trade deficit might be ignored or an exchange rate crisis might develop even when trade was in surplus 'depending on the fears and expectations of market operators' (Burk and Cairncross, 1992: 165). To the money markets the only figures that really mattered were those for the PSBR and money supply and these they watched 'like hawks. They have become the symbols and accepted measures of fiscal and counter-inflationary rectitude' (Keegan and Pennant-Rea, 1979: 134). Furthermore, expectations derived from monetarist theorems were often self-fulfilling, since if enough market players were persuaded that the money supply was growing too quickly and/or that the PSBR had now reached such a size that it could only be financed at a higher rate of interest, then sales of government securities would dry up – the so-called 'gilt strike' – placing heavy pressure on the Government (which in the absence of sufficient sales of public debt has to issue Treasury bills which automatically increases the money supply) to raise interest rates to restore market confidence (Keegan and Pennant-Rea, 1979: 133).

Healey recalled in his autobiography that Crosland had argued in Cabinet that the situation was already under control. 'So in fact it was,' he now conceded, 'but the markets would not believe it' (Healey, 1987: 431). Strachey, we may recall, had warned of 'a social ejection mechanism' which would, in a free flowing international financial order, destabilize governments of the left. Since he wrote, the power of the financial markets had swollen beyond anything he could have imagined. The roots of the crisis the Labour Government confronted in 1976, and the key to the unravelling of Keynesian social democracy, lay (as Strachey had foreseen) in the crumpled confidence of the financial markets. In the July 1976 measures the Government had agreed £1 billion of cuts plus a 2 per cent surcharge on employers' National Insurance Contributions to reassure the markets. These measures, according to Healey, 'were sufficient to get our economy into balance . . . I thought enough had been done, but that didn't mean that it was enough to satisfy the markets' (quoted in Whitehead, 1985: 187). Gavyn Davies, a prominent City economist and at the time a member of Number 10's Policy Unit recalled: 'the markets wanted blood, and that didn't look like blood. We didn't understand that at the time, we didn't know what they wanted was a humiliation . . . trying to avoid humiliation was a waste of time' (quoted in Whitehead, 1985: 187). Over a twelve-month period public spending had been repeatedly cut, unemployment had reached a level not known since the 1930s and the Treasury was already using monetary targets to manage the economy. Notwithstanding, it was increasingly evident that 'no matter what the Government did, short of repudiating both its history and its supporters, the market would continue to demonstrate its total lack of confidence, unless and until an approach was made to the IMF' which, as all the players well understood, meant in the circumstances submitting to the Fund's supervision of the economy (Burk and Cairncross, 1992: 54). 'An agreement with the IMF is like the Seal of Good Housekeeping: it is regarded by the markets as a guarantee of responsible economic management . . . ' (Healey, 1987: 435). Without the IMF seal of approval the Government 'was almost certainly sunk', Donoughue reflected. 'The markets would have panicked, sterling collapsed and even bigger cuts would have been needed, or Government would have had to adopt protection (Donoughue, 1987: 96, 97).

The IMF and the USA

The IMF was, however, not as formidable a force as many assumed – it was more a conduit than an actor in its own right. Since the 1950s Washington had 'consciously used the IMF to try to impose its will in the international monetary area' as it was generally easier for a country to take unpleasant medication if prescribed by an international organization like the Fund (Burk and Cairncross, 1992: 8, 6). The Ford Administration also had a clear idea of what needed to be done. The three most influential figures in the shaping of US monetary policy were, at the time, all very right-wing. Arthur Burns, the Governor of the Federal Reserve System described himself as a 'Neanderthal conservative and naturally suspicious of a Labour Government' which he saw as 'profligate'. William Simon, Secretary of the Treasury, was a bond dealer with 'an absolute faith in the market'. Edwin Yeo, Under-Secretary for Monetary affairs, was resolutely anti-Keynesian: national economies were no different from households so income must balance expenditure. 'Our role,' he announced, 'was to persuade the British the game was over. They had run out of string.' All three men 'trusted that the IMF could enforce the financial and political discipline which they believed the British so sorely needed' (Burk and Cairncross, 1992: 37, 42; Fay and Young, 1978). This meant taking the knife to public spending and borrowing, and a squeeze on the money supply.

The State Department was more sympathetic to Britain,[19] but Simon managed to convince President Ford that 'a fundamental shift in British economic policy' must be achieved. Whilst groups within the Administration disagreed over how harsh a line the IMF should take, these were tactical conflicts: 'all those surrounding Ford believed Britain could not go on as she had been: they only differed over the extent of the pain required' (Burk and Cairncross, 1992: 45, 64). That the Labour Government be impelled to take action was seen as a vital American interest. To William Rodgers, the Secretary of State, 'it was a choice between Britain remaining in the liberal financial system of the West' or, under the prodding of Benn, turning its back on the IMF. Then 'the whole system might fall apart . . . So we tended to see it in cosmic terms' (Fay and Young, 1978).

Domestic pressure reinforced external ones. Much of the detailed negotiations with the IMF were conducted by Treasury officials: all ministerial participants attested to their skill and high calibre – and all were left with a lingering mistrust of the part that, at least, some played. Barnett, a right-wing Labour Minister and firm proponent of expenditure reductions, had 'no doubt in my own mind that there were some senior Treasury officials who felt more strongly than others that the IMF was needed to keep a check on this profligate Labour Government. I have no doubt about that. There are some who suspect sabotage by at least one official, senior official. I have no evidence to support that view, although I think it's fair to say that I would share the suspicion' (quoted in Whitehead, 1985: 193). Callaghan himself became increasingly convinced that 'the British and US Treasuries were in league to force still more deflation on Britain' (Fay and Young, 1978; see also Healey, 1987: 50). Donoughue has described how, during the crisis, he went to the US Embassy for a secret meeting with a top official who said, 'you should be aware of something, which is that parts of the Treasury are in very deep cahoots with parts of the US Treasury and with certain others in Germany who are of a very right wing inclination and they are absolutely committed to getting the IMF here and if it brings about the break-up of this government, they will be very, very happy' (Burk and Cairncross, 1992: 244).[20]

Though there were significant divisions within the Treasury (whilst one strand of opinion was worried about unemployment another was determined on a sweeping cuts package) (Healey, 1987: 430) there was a general belief that public expenditure was excessive and that a very substantial reduction was essential to economic recovery. Keynesianism was out of fashion and with the City and the Bank of England already eager proselytizers, many within the Treasury too were rediscovering the virtues of monetarism and laissez faire. To the markets, the IMF, the US Administration and key Treasury officials a commitment to social welfare and full employment through publicly-funded programmes – the core of Keynesian social democracy – constituted loose and wanton management of the public finances. In theory, borrowing could have been narrowed by tax rises but, as Whittome, a senior IMF official, commented, 'psychologically a cut in public expenditure is worth a great deal more than an increase in taxation' (Burk, 1989: 44). According to Harold Lever, a right-wing Labour Minister and financier, 'my judgment after innumerable discussions with contacts I had at various

levels in the Treasury and so on, was that the position at the top of
the Treasury and the Bank . . . [was] that the Government was wildly
extravagant and that the only way of curbing it was to get them into the
IMF . . . the idea was that the IMF would bring the Cabinet to order'.
Lever contended that he could have arranged a stand-by loan from other
sources without IMF-type conditions attached but that opposition from
within the Treasury, the Bank of England and the US Administration
scuppered his efforts, convinced as they were that the discipline of the
IMF was needed to make an irredeemably lax Labour Government
'behave' (Burk, 1989: 45).[21] The economic case for another stiff dose
of deflation might have been shaky but what counted was the bleak
reality of power: with such forces as the financial markets, the US and
the Treasury all mounted against it, the costs of resistance would have
been high.

Pay Policy, 1976–1978

Reducing inflation to single figures was now the Government's pre-
eminent goal, and in addition to tight fiscal and monetary stances
it continued to lean very heavily on incomes policy. In response to
complaints over the compression of differentials during the flat rate first
phase of incomes restraint, the second phase was percentage based. The
General Council agreed to a new norm of 5 per cent with a £4 ceiling
and a £2.50 lower limit, with tax concessions attached. Stage Two was
'remarkably effective . . . It produced the most severe cut in real wages
in twenty years' (Barnes and Reid, 1980: 208, 210). By 1977 after two
years of declining real wages the purchasing power of the average worker
with two children had fallen 7 per cent (Whitehead, 1987: 257–8). With
their rank and file becoming restive, union leaders felt unable to commit
themselves to a third formal agreement, hence the TUC could only
promise that no union would seek more than one increase per year.
Healey pledged that, if the growth of earnings were held to a 10 per cent
increase, taxes would be cut. Though the tax concessions were granted,
by July 1978 wages had increased by about 16 per cent compared to
about 8 per cent for prices. Nevertheless, the annual rate of inflation
had fallen to about 8 per cent (Barnes and Reid, 1980: 211–12; Healey,
1989: 398).

Whether restraint could survive a further year was a question anxiously debated in Government. The signs were not encouraging. At the 1977 TGWU conference, Jones's support for an incomes policy was resoundingly rejected by delegates who passed a resolution favouring the immediate resumption of free collective bargaining. Both Jones and Scanlon – the 'terrible twins' of earlier years who had since 1975 thrown all their energies behind keeping Labour in power – were due to retire shortly. A number of disputes in 1977 and early 1978 (such as the fire-fighters strike) were only settled with great difficulty. But Callaghan and Healey were determined to embark on a fourth phase of restraint to bring inflation down to the level of the UK's main competitors. A 5 per cent limit on basic pay was considered to be the highest figure compatible with keeping inflation within single figures (Donoughue, 1987: 154–5). The fact that the third phase had survived without formal TUC approval 'blinded us to the growing anomalies which it had created, and to the groundswell of opposition from the shop-floor' (Healey, 1989: 398) although there was no shortage of advice from within the unions warning that a further stage was tempting fate. A limit of 5 per cent after a period of three years of stagnant (or falling) living standards was beyond the capacity of even the most sympathetic union leaders to deliver. The Cabinet was by no means united: some ministers wanted a higher figure whilst the more left-leaning ones opposed setting any figure (Callaghan, 1987: 522). According to Healey the Prime Minister had become 'obsessed by inflation' and indeed, he would have preferred a zero norm (Healey, 1989: 398).

Yet initially criticism from the unions was very muted. The Government had been in office for four years and, although the Conservatives remained ahead in the polls, their lead was narrowing. Election fever began to spread and union leaders were convinced that the 5 per cent policy was only a campaign ploy and that the Prime Minister intended to go to the country in the autumn of 1978. Then – to their astonishment, and then indignation – Callaghan announced that the Government would carry on into 1979. It was a supreme tactical misjudgement. Even if Labour had lost in the autumn of 1978, it would have been by a narrower majority, the Winter of Discontent would not have occurred and the civil war into which the party was soon to be plunged might have been averted. As it was, union leaders felt 'snubbed' and 'badly let down' by the decision not to call an election and extremely disturbed by a 5 per cent limit to which they did not feel committed and knew they could not uphold (Donoughue, 1987: 166).

Arduous negotiations followed with the 'Neddy six' group of senior trade unionists to try and reach some kind of arrangement. One which met some of the Government's objectives was eventually patched up but, to its dismay, it was rejected by the General Council of the TUC.[22] This was a major blow: the unions were now under no obligation to restrain wage claims. 'The Government's moral authority,' Callaghan brooded, 'was undermined' (Callaghan, 1987: 533). The first challenge to the 5 per cent policy was, as anticipated, the Ford pay negotiations. The company had made handsome profits in the preceding year and the unions called for pay rises well above the limit. After a protracted nine week strike, the company conceded a 17 per cent pay increase: a serious breach of the norm as the firm was a traditional pace-setter in the pay year. Other disputes soon flared up. Oil tanker and road haulage drivers demanding a 25–30 per cent pay increase went on strike which the new leader of the TGWU, Moss Evans – despite assurances that he would help the Government – soon made official. This raised the serious threat of oil, food and other shortages which could have a crippling effect on the economy. Eventually the lorry drivers were induced to accept 15 per cent.

Then followed a massed wave of industrial action from low paid public sector workers. 'A million and a half public service workers went on strike, closing hospitals, schools and local authority services across the country. The railways came to a halt' (Donoughue, 1987: 176). Hospitals were picketed, the rubbish accumulated in the streets and – in one incident in Liverpool – the grave diggers went on strike.[23] 'There was a curious, feverish madness infecting industrial relations and in some cases unions actually went on strike before their pay claims had been submitted' (Donoughue, 1987: 171). To compound everything, the country then fell into the grip of a harsh winter, with fierce blizzards grinding traffic to a halt. The Government appeared overwhelmed. 'There was a deadly calm in No. 10, a sort of quiet despair . . . Ministers were clearly demoralised. Moving among them as they gathered for Cabinet in the hallway outside the Cabinet room, their sense of collective and individual depression was overwhelming' (Donoughue, 1987: 176). Although pressed by some of his Cabinet colleagues and advisers to take tough action and lash out at the unions,

Callaghan was reluctant to do so, because – the head of his Policy Unit suggested – he found it difficult to break a lifetime's habit of working alongside them (Donoughue, 1987: 177). Other ministers, such as Bill Rodgers, later to be a member of the SDP's 'Gang of Four' were privately highly critical of the Government's failure to come out against the unions, guns blazing. Eventually the strikes petered out, as the Government reached a 'concordat' with the unions, but the Winter of Discontent was to inflict devastating political damage on Labour and the unions for years ahead. There were a number of reasons for this. The disputes were highly visible and those who suffered most were not the employers but the public. Further, the picketing of hospitals, the heaps of garbage, 'bearded men in duffel coats huddled around braziers' (Healey, 1989: 463) all presented dramatic TV images. To the tabloids, uninterested in the poor pay and conditions that lay behind them, the public sector strikes were a gift: '"Has everyone gone mad?", "No Mercy", "Pickets Rule", "Target for Today – Sick Children" – headlines like these poured out of Fleet Street' (Whitehead, 1987: 282–3). The Government appeared listless and indifferent – 'crisis, what crisis?' queried Jim Callaghan (it was alleged) as he stepped off the plane, suntanned after a conference in Guadalupe.[24] The effect upon the Government was debilitating. Its fortunes went 'cascading downhill', Callaghan gloomily recalled, 'our loss of authority in one field leading to misfortunes in others just as an avalanche, gathering speed, sweeps all before it' (Callaghan, 1987: 540).

Why had it all gone so sour? Why did the Social Contract self-destruct in so catastrophic a manner? The experience of social democratic governments in countries like Sweden, Norway and Austria suggested that the optimal conditions for corporatist arrangements were the existence of a powerful peak association able to formulate policies and negotiate on behalf of labour as a whole, centralized and cohesive unions and nation-wide bargaining with employer associations. Under such conditions sectional definitions of employee interests – in terms of protecting differentials, leap-frogging pay claims and demarcation disputes – were discouraged; conversely more weight was given to interests that workers held in common, such as full employment and social advances. The task of ensuring the membership abided by an agreement was eased which in turn gave added union leverage in securing policy gains. In Britain in the 1970s few, if any, of these conditions obtained. Since the early

1960s collective bargaining systems had become progressively more diffused and decentralized. With the growth of workplace bargaining workers' allegiance was increasingly confined to the immediate work group, sectionalism spread and class solidarity was eroded. One study of a car plant found that 'a sense of solidarity amongst workers in the factory was of a tenuous, limited, or even grudging kind. There were attitudes and feelings not merely of apathy but of antipathy towards other groups of workers' (quoted in Lane, 1974: 174; see also Turner et al., 1967: 291). There was little sense of an overriding class interest. In Hyman's words, many workers were 'ready to accept the virtually universal condemnation by press and politicians of *other* workers' disputes' (Hyman, 1973: 126).[25] Corporate bargaining entailed shifting distributional struggles from the industrial to the political plane, but the legitimacy of union involvement in politics was widely queried (Butler and Stokes, 1974: 198; Nichols and Armstrong, 1976, 194; Bain et al., 1973: 141). Mackenzie and Silver found that 'for all but a few working people unions appear to be valued only for their specific bargaining functions'; they were seen as 'useful instruments rather than cherished objects of loyalty' and attracted considerable criticism for their wider political and economic interests (McKenzie and Silver, 1968: 130). In reaction to the autocratic methods of right-wing union leaders, some of their left-wing successors, most prominently Jack Jones, encouraged organizational decentralization but the effect was to reinforce the parochialism of shopfloor bargainers. It was commonly believed on the left that the expanding role of shop stewards and greater shopfloor militancy indicated a more radical and combative class outlook. In fact 'far from being concerned with the liberation of a thwarted and frustrated idealism and the emergence of a sense of purpose on the shop floor, decentralisation tended to inflame the underlying fragmented tendencies of what were often diverse and competing work groups' and failed to generate any sense of class solidarity or political consciousness that could stimulate a socialist perspective (Taylor, 1993: 150).

To Healey the Winter of Discontent stemmed not from the frustration of ordinary workers after a long period of wage restraint but from 'institutional pressure from local trade union activists who had found their roles severely limited by three years of incomes policy agreed by their national leaders' (Healey, 1989: 467). This view overlooked the way in which incomes policy *extended* the role of shop stewards. Since wage norms made it difficult to take account of such factors as variations in profitability and productivity, and skill shortages, workplace bargaining with shop stewards compensated for the absence of national or industrial agreements. Indeed, a Warwick University study calculated that in the 1970s the number of full-time shop stewards quadrupled, outnumbering union officials for the first time.[26] Finally, with its limited authority over affiliated unions the TUC was unable to act as an effective co-ordinating body, 'The intractable nature of the so-called trade union "problem" stemmed not from the supposed overweening strength and pretensions of organised labour at the national level, whether inside or outside the TUC, but from the TUC's fundamental weaknesses . . . ' (Taylor, 1993: 261). The departure of Jones and Scanlon worsened the problem by depriving the unions of leaders who had a broader understanding of the issues at stake and the authority which may have restrained the outburst of militancy.

On the other hand, Healey overlooked the fact that the unions were receiving diminishing returns for wage restraint. To balance the sacrifices union members made the Social Contract imposed dividend restrictions and price controls, and provided a range of subsidies. Dividend restrictions were not very effective since they simply pushed up share prices and income in the form of capital gains, which were, furthermore, taxed at a lower rate than dividends (Hare, 1984: 58). Price controls were awkward to administer and, as a result of pressure from liquidity-strapped firms, the Government progressively relaxed them. 'Thus, increasingly, both price and dividend control took on a cosmetic appearance with very limited real effect' (Hare, 1984: 58). Pay policy was also designed to reduce the share of wages in favour of profits in order to boost competitiveness through lower labour costs and increased investment. But there was no way of guaranteeing that higher profits would bring workers any compensating benefits since they often flowed into overseas investment or property acquisitions, or were distributed in higher dividends.

The heart of the Social Contract was a trade-off between wage limitation and improvements in the 'social wage'. The problem was that this was incompatible with the Government's squeeze on spending. The knot was further tightened by pressure to keep within PSBR targets based on inaccurate forecasts and calculations which, as we have seen, substantially exaggerated real spending patterns. The outcome was considerable shortfalls in actual expenditure, and cuts that bit even deeper than planned. Thus although the expenditure White Paper of February 1976 forecast that public expenditure would rise by two and a half per cent in real terms in 1976/7, it actually declined by 2 per cent (Jackson, 1991: 84). In other words, unions were obtaining few tangible gains for their members. 'It was these stringent measures on public sector pay, in order to deliver the IMF cuts, coupled with the existing incomes policy, that so aggravated public sector unions' (Jackson, 1991: 85).

Notwithstanding, it could be argued that the lower inflation produced by wage restraint was in the interests of all, including trade unionists. However, particularly for lower paid workers whose living standards had been stagnant or had fallen, this point would not have seemed so persuasive, whilst the victories of Ford and road haulage workers appeared to prove the effectiveness of industrial action in boosting wages. The sectionalism of better paid workers with more industrial muscle rather than the frustration of the more poorly paid was the real problem.[27] Union leaders were more painfully aware than many Cabinet ministers that they lacked the power to impose a 5 per cent limit on their members. Callaghan and Healey failed to appreciate that, as elected heads of pluralist organizations, with their freedom circumscribed by executives and conferences and by shop floor power, union leaders were not in a position to shepherd their members in whatever direction they chose to go. As Healey later reflected, the insistence on the 5 per cent policy exhibited a 'hubris' to which all governments could too easily succumb.[28]

As in Greek tragedy, in May 1979 the Government suffered its inexorable fate. Although, on a higher poll, the total number of Labour voters remained static at eleven and a half million, its percentage of the poll fell by 2.2 per cent whilst the Tory score leapt by over 8 per cent. Compared to the last election the Party lost fifty seats and the Thatcher Government emerged with an overall majority over forty.

Conclusion

Overall, the record of the 1974–9 was by no means as poor as has been commonly portrayed. In 1979 inflation was lower (though rising) than in

1974, growth had been resumed, the balance of payments was far stronger and the exchange rate stabilized (Artis and Cobham, 1991: 276). Whilst it was dogged by very high inflation, a severe recession, recurrent sterling crises, and whilst there was little growth in productivity and personal disposable income, notwithstanding 'the Labour Government left the economy . . . in better condition in 1979 that they had found [it] in 1974' (Artis and Cobham, 1991: 277).[29] Further, measures taken by the Government, particularly in its first year and mostly enacted by that most determined of social reformers, Barbara Castle, protected some of the poorest and most vulnerable groups from the effects of economic austerity. Thus not only did the elderly benefit from the largest ever increase in pensions but legislation (subsequently repealed by the Conservatives) guaranteed annual uprating in line with the increase in average earnings or prices, whichever was the higher. Families gained by the replacement of child tax allowances, paid usually to the father, by child benefits which were paid directly to the mother, ensuring for the first time that mothers received a regular income. For the first time, too, attention was paid to the plight of the growing numbers of the disabled and infirm, and those who struggled to care for them, with the introduction of new benefits. Mrs Castle also fought valiantly to remove inequities from the health service, for instance the phasing out of private treatment in NHS hospitals (pay beds) but the obduracy of the consultants and her own dismissal from office in March 1976 meant that progress was painfully slow. The much-reviled employment legislation also provided valuable new rights for traditionally neglected sections of the community. These included maternity leave and job security for pregnant women, guaranteed payments for workers on short-time and temporarily laid-off, and a strengthening of equal pay provisions. The many victims of accidents or ill-health caused by poor working conditions, whose plight had always been routinely ignored by the media, gained a protector in the Health and Safety Executive coupled with a more effective system of workplace inspection. Industrial tribunals also provided protection through compensation for unfair dismissal, though here, as elsewhere, there were problems of weak implementation. The Advisory, Conciliation and Arbitration Service performed so obviously a useful function in the management of industrial disputes that it even survived a decade and a half of Conservative rule, unlike so much else of the constructive work of the 1974–9 Government.

But these gains were extracted in the teeth of circumstances. From 1975 onwards, social spending came under relentless pressure. The Government 'presided over the largest cuts in real public expenditure that have occurred in the last fifty years' (Jackson, 1991: 73–4). The proportion of GNP spent on education, health and the social services actually fell between the financial years 1974/5 and 1978/9 (Bosanquet, 1980: 36). Unemployment rose steadily and never fell below a million – which, for those accustomed to the full employment of the post-war decades, was an intolerable level.[30] One is left with the impression of a Government struggling to do its best in extremely bleak conditions, where the familiar landmarks were vanishing, and where few of the levers used in the past to control events any longer worked.

Notes

1 At one Cabinet meeting an exasperated Crosland declared 'I must say I am very cross that Tony Benn should criticise businessmen. You can't expect them to invest now' (Benn, 1989: 329).

2 'The British Government was taken to the cleaners by the American business. Chrysler ran through £150 million of [a government] subsidy, and sold out to Peugeot Citroen, without waiting for British approval' (Whitehead, 1985: 145).

3 A post which carries responsibility for control of public spending.

4 The technique was known as the 'bounce', a traditional Treasury practice in which the Cabinet would be presented with a package of cuts and advised that a rapid response was vital, to restore confidence, or avert yet another speculative attack. Ministers who might be skeptical of the Treasury line would have little time to critically analyse the proposals and to present properly researched alternative ways of handling the problem.

5 With greater acumen, Callaghan commented: 'Tony has launched a rubber dinghy into which we may all one day have to climb' (Ziegler, 1993: 382).

6 In this period the right to participate in leadership elections was confined to Labour MPs.

7 By this time the redoubtable Mrs Castle was out of the Cabinet, whilst Orme and Silkin were new members.

8   Given that a year later the IMF was prepared to destroy the social demo-
    cratic Soares government in Portugal in pursuit of its polices, Donoughue
    wrote, the Crosland strategy of out-bluffing the IMF would have failed
    'and we were right' since the Fund showed itself fully 'capable of launching
    economic "remedies" which could destroy governments (especially govern-
    ments of the left)' (Donoughue, 1987: 95). But would Britain have been
    treated the same way as Portugal?

9   According to Donoughue, though previously he had been tolerant, Callaghan
    then called Crosland (and Lever) bluntly 'more or less ordering them' to
    support the package (Donoughue, 1987: 97).

10 'The entry of union leaders into Whitehall was a disgrace' one former
    top Treasury official later recalled, 'a complete disgrace'. (Institute for
    Contemporary British History seminar, July 1995).

11 As early as 1974 Callaghan (regarded as the senior figure on the right
    most sympathetic to the unions) stated that the unions 'have got too much
    influence on all governments and we must rectify and remedy the situation'
    (Benn, 1989: 239; Crosland shared a similar view, ibid., 240).

12 At one Cabinet session he launched a 'great diatribe against public
    expenditure . . . It was "absurd that public expenditure should have risen
    to 58% of GNP"' (Castle, 1980: 427).

13 Castle records how, at a meeting of the TUC–Labour Party Liaison
    Committee in February 1976, Scanlon, once the arch-opponent of incomes
    policy, now was 'almost abject in his support of the Government'. 'The
    level of wages has fallen well below purchasing power' he noted, whilst
    prices were not being effectively controlled. But he added that he felt
    no need 'to apologise for accepting that, because [he] was convinced that
    the [Government's] overall economic strategy was correct' (Castle, 1980:
    659, 660).

14 This was because 'both the debt interest on loans raised to build council
    houses and the housing subsidies which went towards paying this interest'
    went into the total. But if the object was to calculate the 'net amount of debt
    interest which had to be met out of taxation, the interest costs of public
    housing had to be excluded altogether, since either they had already been
    charged up to the taxpayer once in the subsidy figure or else they were a
    charge on the tenant and not on the taxpayer at all'. This also applied to
    debt interest in the nationalized industries (Pliatzky, 1982: 164).

15 After lunch with the then Deputy-Secretary at Treasury in charge of public
    expenditure, Benn recounted that Pliatzky 'sees himself as one of the really
    tough officials who keep Ministers on the straight and narrow'. He adduced
    two factors which motivated the Treasury to seek deep expenditure cuts:
    pressure from the Bank of England and the fact that the Department had

been 'deeply wounded by the general charge that public expenditure was out of control' (Benn, 1989: 593. Entry 9 July 1976).

16   The figure for the US was 33.4 per cent (Burk and Cairncross, 1992: 223). From the US perspective, it is easy to see why the public take in Britain was seen as lax, though this was even truer of Sweden and the Netherlands. The *significance* of these figures is a different issue: the question of their economic effects is a matter of contention amongst economists; on the social front, the variation in spending patterns reflects, broadly-speaking, the difference between the advanced welfare states of Northern Europe and the 'private affluence, public squalor' more characteristic of the US.

17   At a Cabinet meeting in March 1976, at the onset of the IMF crisis, Barbara Castle asked Think Tank members present to provide international comparisons for public expenditure as a whole. She added (as a dig at Jenkins): 'There have been some sweeping statements recently to the effect that the level of public expenditure is so high that democracy is threatened and it would be interesting to know if democracy is collapsing all over Europe.' 'Roy smiled rather sourly, while Michael and Joel chuckled openly. "That was very funny," said Tony Crosland afterwards. "Of course, the figures will show that other people's public expenditure is as high as ours."' However, the figures were never provided (Castle, 1980: 670, entry 4 March 1976).

18   He also argued that unemployment benefits may have created a disincentive because the gap between the level of the benefit and low wages was insignificant (Foreign Relations Committee, 1977: 7).

19   The State Department feared that, if the Labour Government was driven too far, the Benn line might prevail. According to Brent Scowcroft, the US National Security Adviser who shared these fears: 'I spent more time on this matter during those weeks than anything else. It was considered by us the greatest single threat to the Western world' (quoted in Burk and Cairncross, 1992: 77).

20   Donoughue recalled that 'Some American sources would come through to us at No. 10 and report to us what some people in the UK Treasury were allegedly saying to the IMF in terms of "keep firm and really make sure that you impose big expenditure cuts"' (quoted in Whitehead, 1985: 193). According to Simon, the US Treasury Secretary, 'the people in the Bank of England and the people in the UK Treasury knew what had to be done. While they would never say it, because they were fiercely loyal, I think they were secretly rooting for us, that we hold fast our ground' (quoted in Whitehead, 1985: 193).

21   As Gordon Pepper, a leading City commentator observed, Treasury officials, 'desperately anxious about the UK', had no 'political' preference

over which party composed the government as long as the government produced 'responsible' fiscal and monetary policies (Contemporary Record, 1989: 44).

22   Because of the absence on holiday of two supporters of the agreement who felt their votes would not be needed.

23   In Donoughue's account, this became 'in many places' and the heaps of the unburied dead piling up around the country has become part of the folklore of the Winter of Discontent.

24   As reported by the *Sun*. The report was false, but nevertheless it struck a chord.

25   There was no link between the growth of industrial militancy and 'heightened class consciousness'. See, for example, Timperely and Woodcock, 1971: 27–9; Cousins and Brown, 1975: 75; Nichols and Armstrong, 1976.

26   Furthermore, research indicated that management played a crucial role in the expansion in the number and role of shop stewards, just as they often favoured closed shops and check-off forms of payment (Taylor, 1993: 246).

27   In contrast, wage solidarity, in which wage gains were more evenly spread, was a central aspect of the Swedish corporatist system.

28   He added that if ministers like himself had been more flexible and opted for a formula like single figures, settlements would have been lower and the Winter of Discontent avoided (Healey, 1989: 462–3).

29   Ironically, for the first eight years of the Thatcher Government, the ratio of government spending to GDP exceeded that which they had inherited from Labour, largely because of the much heavier cost of the dramatically-increased level of unemployment (Jackson, 1991: 85).

30   Not all ministers were as bothered in private as they appeared to be in public. 'We have taken the heartache out of unemployment,' Roy Mason, the Northern Ireland Secretary announced. 'Male unemployment in Northern Ireland is almost 30%, and there is no trouble there' (Benn, 1990: 321).

7 Time of Troubles, 1979–1987

A Fractured Party: 1979–1983

Between 1979 and 1983, Labour was wrenched apart by ruptures of an unprecedented ferocity which inflicted enduring harm on its public image and contributed directly to the electoral disaster of 1983. Disagreements within political parties are usually depicted by the media as unpleasant and pathological: the bickering and petty squabbles of self-interested politicians. In fact, they are normal and, indeed, a sign of a healthy and pluralistic organization. But within the Labour Party from the years 1979 to 1983 they acquired an intemperate quality as an unrestrained struggle for power between left and right and a massed insurgency by grass-roots activists against the parliamentary establishment broke out. The Party was split into two hostile camps which were locked in combat over an extensive range of issues and the fault lines were deep and mutually reinforcing. The crisis was both political and institutional, an ideological clash and a power struggle as the institutions of the parliamentary and extra-parliamentary parties contended for supremacy. Left and right subscribed to radically different conceptions of the Party's role and purposes, viewing each other as antagonists not as competitors striving after the common good. As a result attachment to the rival camps often overshadowed that to the Party and the capacity of the leadership to maintain unity by appeals to loyalty and solidarity disintegrated.

The turmoil with the Party after 1979 had its roots in the Government's failure to reduce unemployment, the cutbacks in social spending and the shift to monetarism (for a more detailed account, see Shaw, 1994a). It was accused of abandoning the 1974 manifesto, flouting Conference and treated the wider Party with contempt. The NEC protested over these departures from the manifesto but its influence over the Government had been negligible and it was never consulted before ministers embarked on major policy innovations. The status of the NEC *vis-à-vis* the Labour Government, the Party's Research Secretary, Geoff Bish complained, had been no more than that of 'a mere pressure group, just one amongst many (NEC paper 'Drafting the Manifesto' reprinted in Coates, 1979: 164). The battle over the 1979 manifesto had further worsened relations between the Cabinet and the NEC. The National Executive had sought to assert its constitutional prerogative to decide (along with the Cabinet) the contents of the manifesto and a number of NEC–Cabinet Working Groups had been established to iron out differences. But at the crucial Clause V meeting called to decide the manifesto an entirely new 'Number 10' draft was produced which formed the basis of the final, and rather anodyne, document.[1] This experience 'laid the basis for much of the bitterness and recrimination which was to follow' ('Drafting the Manifesto', Coates, 1979: 164).

The lesson appeared to be, once more, that whatever the formal rules, in practice it was the parliamentary elite which, in the final analysis, determined policy. Yet, if the extra-parliamentary Party lacked the means to enforce its policy preferences, it did have one undeniable power – to alter its own rules. And rules, in turn, had an effect on the internal balance of power. A campaign for constitutional reform masterminded by the Campaign for Labour Party Democracy (CLPD), an organization of grass-roots activists set up in 1973, was already being pursued before Labour's loss of office. It sought three main reforms: mandatory reselection of Labour MPs so that they would have no automatic right to remain as Labour representatives beyond the life of one parliament; the placing of the right to frame the manifesto solely in the hands of the NEC; and extending the franchise for selecting the Leader beyond the PLP to the Party at large. The aim was to weaken the hold of right-wing Parliamentary leadership on the Party and to redistribute power to the rank and file. The central reform, mandatory reselection, was designed to enforce MPs' accountability to their individual parties – in the knowledge that constituency General Committees were predominantly left-wing; a wider franchise aimed to render the leader more sensitive to Party and union opinion, and NEC control of the manifesto to remove the leader's power of veto.

The Parliamentary leadership and the right in general stridently opposed these reforms but were were unable to deflect Conference from approving two of them (NEC control over the manifesto was narrowly rejected) or from adopting left-wing positions on major policy matters (unilateralism, withdrawal from the EEC, public ownership, economic strategy), reversing many of the policies pursued by the 1974–9 Government. The parliamentary leadership, deprived of its key resource, control of the government machine, and discredited both by Labour's drubbing at the polls and by the low esteem in which its performance in office was held, was in no position to resist. Callaghan resigned the leadership before a new leadership election procedure was implemented in the hope that, with the franchise still precariously in the PLP's hands, Healey would enter into the inheritance for which, by experience and talent, he seemed eminently well-qualified. But he was narrowly defeated by Foot, by 129 votes to 139, largely because sufficient numbers of right and centre MPs feared that the abrasive Healey would so infuriate the left as to finally rupture the Party. In addition, a number of MPs intending to quit Labour's ranks and form a breakaway voted for Foot on the grounds that he would be less formidable as a leader than Healey.

Once an unrepentant rebel, Foot had for a decade performed the role of conciliator. But even his emollient gifts proved inadequate to the task. He could neither end the civil strife that still raged within the Party nor prevent a large segment of the right seceding. In February 1981 a special conference was held at Wembley because the annual Conference the previous October had accepted the principle of a wider franchise for electing the leader but failed to agree on a method. After some deft manoeuvring by CLPD activists, a majority was garnered for an electoral college divided 30 per cent for the PLP, 30 per cent for the CLPs and 40 per cent for the unions. For four former Labour ministers (David Owen, Shirley Williams, Bill Rodgers and Roy Jenkins lately returned from a stint as a member of the EEC Commission) unwilling to acquiesce in the adoption of a raft of left-wing policies, this was the final straw. To a blaze of enthusiastic publicity, the so-called 'gang of four' announced the formation of the Social Democratic Party; eventually two dozen other Labour MPs and one Conservative signed up. It was the worst split in the Party for half a century and the electoral consequences were to be devastating.

Scarcely had this grim news slipped from the headlines than Benn decided to challenge the incumbent Healey for the deputy leadership in 1981, hence activating the electoral college for the first time. He had played an increasingly prominent role in mobilizing the left. He carried immense prestige as a highly experienced and capable former Cabinet minister who (it was widely believed) had battled almost single-handedly for Party policies in the last Labour Government. And he was one of those rare politicians upon whom the label charismatic could accurately be pinned, with his exceptional ability to communicate his views in a vivid and compelling fashion and to inspire great loyalty and enthusiasm. However, equally he aroused extreme enmity amongst his opponents and from the press, where he was frequently (and absurdly) portrayed as wildly ambitious, mad and a fanatic. A man of courage and determination, unutterably convinced of the rightness of his cause, he could be stubborn and wilful and he ignored the appeals of those – including the Party Leader and some within his own camp – who pleaded with him to desist from a course bound to deepen divisions.

> Pleas'd with the danger, when the waves went high
> He sought the storms; but for a calm unfit,
> Would steer too nigh the sands to boast his wit.
>
> (Dryden, *Absalom and Achitophel*)

There followed months of blood-letting, in which partisans of the two candidates lashed out at each other in the most uninhibited fashion: Healey and his supporters were charged with blind opportunism and treachery in betraying the Party's ideals in the recent government; Bennites were depicted as dangerous zealots, totalitarians bent on erecting a Stalinist state. In the end, Healey very narrowly prevailed – by less than 1 per cent – largely because a number of left-wing MPs, including Neil Kinnock, decided to abstain The battle, fought under the spotlight of intense media interest, offered to the public a spectacle of a party tearing itself apart and Labour's poll ratings tumbled as millions of its supporters flocked to the SDP.

The 1983 Manifesto and the Election

The tumult in the Party did not entirely distract the NEC from an ambitious programme of policy development (though to a greater extent than usual the process was driven by Head Office officials and advisers) which culminated in *Labour's Programme 1982*. In the aftermath of the election in 1979, a Policy Co-ordinating Committee bringing together representatives of the NEC and the Shadow Cabinet was set up. But only very late in the day was it presented with lengthy drafts for Labour's Programme 1982 and an aggrieved Shadow Cabinet felt that it had been effectively by-passed. In spring 1983, with her party way ahead in the polls, Mrs Thatcher called an election. The Clause V meeting to frame the manifesto was the shortest ever: it agreed (with only Peter Shore dissenting) to reprint as the manifesto (entitled *New Hope for Britain*) Labour's recently published Campaign Document, itself largely a distilled version of *Labour's Programme 1982*.

The 1983 manifesto promised a massive programme of public sector-led reflation to regain full employment and refurbish the public services. To cope with the problems of currency and capital flight and to stabilize the balance of payments, Labour called for the reinstatement of exchange controls and the introduction of selective controls on imports. Since this was clearly in breach of the Treaty of Rome it also proposed withdrawal from the Community. All privatized industries were to be restored to the public sector 'with compensation of no more than that received when the assets were denationalized'. Furthermore it contemplated 'a significant public stake in electronics, pharmaceuticals, health equipment and building materials; and also in other important sectors, as required in the national interest' (New Hope for Britain, 1983: 12). The manifesto also outlined schemes for a new partnership with the unions under the so-called National Economic Assessment, the installation of a complex system of economic planning and a series of proposals to promote industrial democracy. It sought not only the traditional social democratic objectives of full employment, greater equality and social justice but also to transcend them through the pursuit of 'a fundamental and irreversible shift in the balance of power and wealth in favour of working people and their families' (New Hope for Britain, 1983: 9). This was to be achieved not only through the established methods of fiscal policy but also through its proposals for planning, industrial democracy and the involvement of the unions in public policy-making.

It was a highly ambitious programme which would have encountered the most determined opposition if attempts had ever been made to implement it. But the prospects for this, with Labour badly trailing in the polls, were slight. This helps to resolve a puzzling feature of the Clause V meeting: the remarkable ease with which the manifesto had been agreed despite the fact that the left lacked a majority. At elections in 1981 and 1982 seven left-wingers – a quarter of the total membership of the NEC – had been replaced by right-wingers whilst the Shadow Cabinet had never lost its right-wing majority. Furthermore Benn had been deposed as chairman of the key Home Policy committee and succeeded by the tough and shrewd right-wing trade union MP, John Golding. It seems highly probable that the right's willingness to virtually nod through a manifesto stuffed with left-wing ideas was a calculated move: if the Party was going to capsize, it might as well sink to the ocean bed with a red flag tide to its mast. The calculation was correct, for the fact that Labour was trounced on a left-wing manifesto did much to engrave upon its mind the view that it could never win on a left-wing platform.

The untenability of engaging in electoral battle under a manifesto of which the bulk of the Shadow Cabinet disapproved anyway rapidly became evident. Given the nature of Britain's parliamentary system, it was Labour's parliamentary spokesmen who were regarded by the media as the authoritative exponents of Labour's policies and were the Party's major channel for relaying its messages to the voting public. As Geoff Bish, the Party's Research Secretary, bluntly pointed out after the election: 'The Shadow Cabinet clearly felt that they had been bounced into accepting a document they did not want. They did not like the policies and it showed' (Paper to Home Policy Committee quoted in *Guardian*, 25 July 1983). Furthermore, the immersion of the Party in internal matters had led to a serious neglect of electoral preparations and the 1983 campaign was so disorganized and incoherent that it managed to transform defeat into disaster – Labour's worst electoral performance since it had emerged as a serious contender for power. Though 209 MPs were elected, its vote was a mere 28 per cent. Labour had been driven back to its heartland in Scotland and the North and the council estates. What was especially disturbing was that the party tended to perform least well amongst the expanding social groups, employment sectors and geographical areas. It escaped from the catastrophe of being relegated, in terms of votes, to third party status by only 2 per cent as the Liberal–SDP Alliance won no less than 26 per cent of the poll though the electoral system awarded it no more than a paltry 23 seats. The Conservatives, in contrast, despite a loss of 1.5 per cent, emerged triumphantly with a huge majority of 144.

The Coming of Kinnock

Foot resigned soon after the election. Of the two main contenders for the succession, Neil Kinnock and Roy Hattersley, the latter would probably have won if the election had been confined to the PLP. However, under the new system, Kinnock was elected leader by a handsome majority in all three sections of the electoral college. The new leader had first arrived in Parliament in 1970 at the youthful age of 28. Claiming the mantle of Bevan, he rapidly made an impression as a fluent and witty speaker espousing the standard left-wing causes. In 1977 he was elected to the NEC and voted on most issues with the left majority. His rhetorical skills and congenial manner soon brought him promotion and he was appointed chief education spokesman by Foot, whose protégé he had become, in 1981. At this point he openly broke ranks with the Bennite left by publicly attacking Benn's candidature for the deputy leadership. By abstaining he, along with a number of other left-wing MPs, ensured Healey his knife-edged victory earning himself vitriolic abuse from some but the gratitude of many others. With Benn a casualty of the recent election and hence out of the running[2] Kinnock was well-positioned to capture votes on both the left and the centre.

Essentially a pragmatist, the new Leader soon concluded that the Party had to be steered to the middle ground if it were to extend its appeal and regain the many voters who had abandoned it in the last two elections. This, he believed, entailed taking much more heed of the opinion polls and stripping Labour's platform of the left-wing policies which, the polls instructed, estranged voters. This appeared more essential than ever as the external environment had become much more threatening: social and economic changes appeared to be wearing away the basis of the Party's support; competitive pressures had intensified as it found itself squeezed by a resurgent Conservative party and a potent new centre-left formation, and all the while it was under the the relentless spotlight of a largely hostile media.

Kinnock's predicament was that his command over the Party was insufficient to accomplish his goals. In opposition, the power of the parliamentary leadership had traditionally rested on a structure of integrated organizational control, underpinned by a pattern of concurrent right-wing majorities in all major institutions, in which it was able to concentrate in its hands the powers that were constitutionally more broadly dispersed. Membership compliance, in turn, was rooted in a considerable degree of procedural and substantive consensus, that is broad agreement over the ground-rules, principles and objectives of the Party. In the Party that Kinnock had inherited these conditions no longer obtained, for a range of reasons. It is vital to recall that the formal powers of the PLP leadership, whilst in opposition, have always been limited. As we have seen, the major responsibility for both formulating policy and managing the Party lay with Labour's extra-Parliamentary institutions. Thus whilst on most issues Kinnock received the backing of the Shadow Cabinet, the agency equipped with the capability to engineer change was the NEC (Kinnock, 1993: 17) where, despite its recent setbacks, the left still maintained a substantial presence. In the first two years of his leadership no major initiatives could be planned or launched without an extensive process of consultation, patient efforts to mobilize support and assiduity in steering them through myriad committees as well as the annual Conference. It was not until 1985 that he felt sufficiently confident that he could get his way on the Executive, though even then 'a certain amount of pressurising' was required (Kinnock, 1993: 16).

In 1984 a reform was passed that was, in due course, to have a profound effect upon the decision-making system. With the rise to ascendancy of the left in the early 1970s the prime function of NEC altered from being a mobilizing agent on behalf of the frontbench to being an institutionalized critic. With the creation of an extensive network of sub-committees and study groups, the left for the first time in the Party's history controlled a policy machine that enabled them to challenge the right's historic rule. The sharpening conflict between left and right gradually transformed a pluralistic system into an adversarial one with the frontbench and the Executive operating as rival command posts of Labour's two bitterly antagonistic wings. In the wake of the

1983 disaster, it was widely agreed that the existing system exacerbated tensions and a new tier consisting of joint NEC–Shadow Cabinet policy committees was created in order to institutionalize co-operation between the two bodies. Kinnock's ultimate objective was not, however, joint policy determination but the full restoration of the power of the leadership and to accomplish this he pursued a double course: to deprive the NEC of its autonomous policy-making capability – hence its ability to act as an effective voice of Conference – and to gain personal political mastery over it. Thus at the same time as the policy process was reformed a complacent NEC acquiesced in the scrapping of its elaborate network of study groups and working parties with their large number of co-opted advisers. Initially the system did operate on the basis of reciprocity but as far as Kinnock was concerned this was a transient phase until he had reduced the NEC to an instrument of his will. But this was to take a number of years.

In his early years Kinnock faced a restive membership which was quick to denounce any sign of backsliding by the leadership. The new cohort of activists which had entered the Party in the 1970s and early 1980s were predominantly young, educated and employed in public sector white-collar occupations. They were not exposed to the types of socializing experiences that had inculcated the traditional labourist norms of loyalty and solidarity. They were far more assertive and more rebellious than earlier cohorts, much more impatient of the rules and those who sought to enforce them. Imbued with a participatory ethos far from being deferential, they were extremely mistrustful of any form of authority: 'To lead was to betray. Leadership itself was an anti-social act, an indictable offence. Leaders would sell out – unless they were stopped' (Mitchell, 1983: 35). Members are more likely to feel bound by leadership decisions to the extent that they believe that it is has the right to make them, that is that power was legitimately exercised. To most constituency activists the source of authority was Conference, representing the will of the Party, but it was evident to them that most senior frontbenchers regarded it with little short of scorn. MPs, they claimed, who were elected to exercise their judgement and discretion, should not be trammelled by Party mandates and were only to be accountable to the voters. MPs, constituency activists countered, were in practice accountable to no one but the leadership, bound to it by ties of ambition, patronage and discipline. Since the parliamentary leadership was arrogating to itself powers that properly belonged to Conference, activists felt under no obligation to accept its authority.

Within the unions, too, they were numerous elements who viewed the parliamentary leadership with wariness and suspicion. Although the engineering union had moved sharply to the right its place had been taken by the National Union of Public Employees (NUPE) which had expanded rapidly in the 1970s, the size of its Conference vote quadrupling from 150,000 to 600,000 between 1974 and 1980. The NUM and then the NUR also moved to the left whilst the merger of ASTMS and TASS created MSF (the Manufacturing, Science and Finance union), another sizable left-wing union. With the TGWU still solidly aligned to the left, this formed a powerful grouping: any attempt by Kinnock to wrench the Party too openly or too far to the right would encounter stiff resistance from Conference.

Any doubts Kinnock might have felt on this score were dispelled by his first, ill-fated moved to alter the system of parliamentary reselection. For parties operating in a liberal democracy, the ability to influence the recruitment of parliamentary representatives is bound to be a major source of power. In mandatory reselection constituency activists possessed a powerful mechanism to influence the conduct of the Labour MPs and early in 1984 Kinnock came under strong pressure from the Shadow Cabinet and right-wing members of the PLP to alter the rules (*The Times*, 1 March 1984). Kinnock recognized that scrapping the mandatory element was not a viable option so he advocated what came to be called 'OMOV' (One Member, One Vote) which involved transferring the right to select Parliamentary candidates and deselecting MPs from constituency General Committees (composed of delegates from branches, affiliated trade unions and other organizations) to the more 'moderate' passive members. Under pressure of time – delay would mean that the next round of selections would be well under way before the rules could be modified – Kinnock cobbled together a compromise system of 'voluntary OMOV' in which General Committees could, if they so choose, delegate the right to determine the fate of a sitting MP to Party members as a whole. He calculated that his personal prestige would swing enough trade union votes behind the proposal but it provoked almost universal hostility from the left in both the Party and the unions. He secured a majority on the NEC only with difficulty and although the two most senior figures in the TGWU, Moss Evans and Alex Kitson, were sympathetic they were outvoted by the union's Conference delegation. As a result, the proposal was rejected at the 1984 Conference by 3,992,000 votes to 3,041,000 (LPCR, 1984: 66). Kinnock had staked his personal prestige on the issue: his defeat was an unwelcome reminder of the limits of his power.

But during the following year he faced even tougher tests as his gradual efforts to wean the Party from the radicalism of the early 1980s and project a more moderate image were derailed by two serious conflicts, both springing from Government initiatives. As part of its drive to cut public expenditure, the Tory Government in 1984 assumed the power to 'rate-cap', or set legally-binding limits to the amount that rates could be raised, as a result of which 'overspending' councils would have to cut services or manpower. A group of prominent left-wing local government leaders including Ken Livingstone of the GLC (Greater London Council), Ted Knight of Lambeth and David Blunkett of Sheffield jointly agreed to defy the Government by refusing to set a rate (the so-called tactic of 'non-compliance'): a course which entailed defying the law and could lead to fines and disqualification from office. Dwarfing in importance even the squeeze on public spending was the Thatcher Government's determination to break the industrial power of the unions. The prime target for a collision was the NUM, the union which had allegedly destroyed the Heath Government. Although no longer one of the largest unions, with its esprit de corps and its traditions of solidarity and self-discipline it remained one of the most powerful and combat with it would amount to a trial of strength – by proxy – with organized labour as a whole. Hence the most thorough and meticulous preparations were made to use all available means to win, whatever the cost. In the early summer of 1984 the inevitable battle commenced as the union struck in protest against a closure programme.

On issues as controversial as these, whatever the Party did would inevitably affect its national standing, but the frustrated national leadership was pushed to one side and the initiative was taken by extra-parliamentary forces, the left-wing Labour local authorities and the NUM led by its militant President, Arthur Scargill, a man of impressive fluency, total dedication and unblinking dogmatism. The radical left had little time for Kinnock's middle of the road strategy and these two disputes offered an opportunity to rally support for and test their own strategic conceptions. The key to Labour's defeat, they believed, had been the desertion of working-class voters disaffected by the record of the 1974–9 Government and the subsequent equivocations of the leadership, and they would only return if they were convinced of the Party's determination to stoutly defend their interests. Both the rate-capping struggle and the miners' strike offered an opportunity to mobilize the working class by energetically campaigning on behalf of the local authorities and the miners. If both triumphed, the Government would be demoralized and Labour would be swept back to power.

This strategy cut right across the efforts Kinnock had been making since his election but he was helpless to prevent Conference's enthusiastic endorsement in 1984 of radical left positions. Rodney Bickerstaffe, NUPE's new General Secretary, moving one motion carried against the leadership proclaimed: 'The question is not should we break the law, but which law shall we obey?' (LPCR, 1984: 129). Conference also adopted a series of resolutions, to which Kinnock was personally opposed, condemning the behaviour of the police during the miners strike (LPCR, 1984: 55) Despite the leadership's serious reservations about Scargill's refusal to hold a national strike ballot such was the emotional temper that it hardly risked raising them. With his unstinting commitment to the principle of legality, all this was thoroughly unpalatable to Kinnock but he lacked the means to assert his will. He regarded both disputes as immense distractions, a squandering of the energies of the Party. But left-wing influence was strong in all sections of the wider Party and he found himself ground between opposing pressures: from the media to disassociate himself from the 'illegality' of non-compliance and the violence for which (almost universally) they held the miners responsible, and from the left to provide unequivocal support for the miners and local authorities. Despite his total opposition to extra-parliamentary methods he felt he had to modulate his response. He feared that any too overt criticism, in particular of the NUM, would later be exploited by the hard left to blame him if the strike failed (as he believed it would). As he later recalled, during this period 'I had to bite my lips a lot' (interview with David Dimbleby, BBC 2, 5 December 1992), though by then he regretted his 'gross mistake' in not calling, publicly and unambiguously, for a miners' ballot (interview with Roy Hattersley, Channel 4, 22 May 1993).

Eventually both the non-compliance protest and the much more formidable miners' strike disintegrated leaving a triumphant Government in command of the field. The crushing of the NUM in particular had a profound impact, demoralizing the trade union movement and greatly enhancing Mrs Thatcher's prestige. The effects on Kinnock were more mixed. Personally, the Leader paid a high political price for what was perceived as his evasiveness, his lack of temerity and his subservience to 'militants' and 'trade union barons', precisely the reputation he was seeking to escape. But the rout of both extra-parliamentary struggles discredited the left's radical strategy and – together with the fate of the radical 1983 manifesto – was seized upon by those who argued that the only feasible strategy was a return to moderate, mainstream politics. Further, it also soon became apparent that the miners' strike had but temporarily retarded a growing fissure in the ranks of the left over a wide range of policy, organization and strategy matters. The process dubbed 'the realignment of the left' witnessed the emergence in 1985 of two separate currents, the 'soft' and the 'hard' left. Amongst activists, it was represented by the LCC, in Parliament by the Tribune Group, within the NEC by a group around David Blunkett, Tom Sawyer and Michael Meacher and it had the support of the Tribune weekly. Ranged against it were the hard left, organized in CLPD, the Campaign Group of Labour MPs with the backing of about a quarter of the NEC and with various Trotskyist bodies as outriders.

The friction between the two currents first really flared into the open over how to handle the Trotskyist Militant Tendency (for a detailed account see Shaw, 1988: 259–90). The influence of this organization was much exaggerated in the media, which indeed rarely bothered to distinguish between Militant, a tightly disciplined body with its separate leadership and objectives which owed no loyalty to Labour, and left-wingers as a whole. Initially the left were united in rejecting tough action against the Trotskyist group and Foot's drive against it in 1982 came to little, but its ruthless and intimidatory tactics, and its abusive and sectarian style increasingly alienated opinion. By 1985 a growing number of soft leftists came to share the right's conviction that debate with such an organization was fruitless and that disciplinary measures were necessary to arrest its advance. For Kinnock destroying the influence of the Trotskyist far left was essential if Labour was to regain political respectability and the likely backing of the soft left now rendered feasible the major assault he had long been contemplating. A golden opportunity then appeared when, in the autumn of that year, in a major tactical blunder, the Militant leaders of Liverpool city council issued redundancy notices to all its employees. This was designed as a ploy to intensify pressure on the Government but instead angered the unions and its own workforce. Wasting no time, Kinnock launched an impassioned attack on Militant at the 1985 Conference:

> I'll tell what happens with impossible promises. You start with far-retched resolutions. They are then pickled into a rigid dogma, a code, and you go through the years sticking to that, outdated, misplaced, irrelevant to the real needs, and you end in the grotesque chaos of a Labour council hiring taxis to scuttle round a city handing out redundancy notices to its own workers. *(Applause)* . . . You can't play politics with people's jobs . . . *(Applause and some boos)* (LPCR, 1985: 128)

It was, according to *The Guardian* 'The bravest and most important speech by a Labour Leader in over a generation' (*The Guardian*, 12 October 1985). As one frontbencher gleefully commented, 'with one speech [Kinnock] lanced a boil' (*Observer*, 6 October 1985). What was perhaps less expected was the speech's reception from predominantly left-wing constituency delegates: according to one observer, most eagerly applauded and 'drowned the scattered boos almost completely' (I. Aitken *The Guardian* 2 October 1985). Whilst Kinnock was furiously denounced by the hard left, the soft left soon swung behind his determination to clamp down on the entryist group. Though the disciplinary drive against Militant was only completed after a long, protracted process it eventually culminated in Militant's decision to abandon entryism and quit Labour. The electoral benefits were probably ephemeral, since few voters distinguished between the Militant Tendency and the left and 'militants' in general, but the eventual end to entryist burrowing and the rancour and divisiveness it had caused made a significant contribution to reviving a spirit of harmony within the Party.

Co-operation over Militant solidified the alliance between Kinnock, the right and the soft left. As long as the right lacked the strength to reassert its traditional control over the Party, and as long as the hard left still posed a threat to the leadership, he needed the soft left and they played an influential role in the internal politics of the Party. The soft left–right axis afforded him for the first time a solid and reliable majority in all key institutions but, at the same time, further intensified the limits on his freedom of action on the more sensitive policy issues set by the need to negotiate the approval of the centre and left-wing unions. The problem, as Kinnock defined it, was that he had inherited a series of radical policy commitments which had to be shed if he was to pilot Labour back to the middle ground. From late 1985, with the appointment of the astute and wily Peter Mandelson as Communications Director, Labour's approach to campaigning and communication underwent a transformation (for a detailed account, see Shaw, 1994). Policy was increasingly subordinated to strategic considerations, as the leadership sought to winnow out those commitments – most notably the Party's stances on the sale of council houses, membership of the European Community, repeal of Tory industrial relations legislation, the reversal of privatization and unilateralism – which opinion polls indicated lacked public support. Policy over council house sales and the EC was swiftly abandoned with negligible opposition, but on other matters Kinnock had to move with greater circumspection. As he later recalled, 'to have changed all policies simultaneously would have fractured the Party' (interview, *Kinnock-The Inside Story*, ITV, 25 July 1993). This was illustrated by the Leader's haltering progress over what came to be known as the 'modernization' of Party policy.

The privatization of publicly-owned industries, a direct attack on collectivist ideology, was one of the most far-reaching of Conservative policy departures. Labour's policy, reaffirmed in 1984, was that all privatized industries would be returned to the public sector with compensation paid on the principle of 'no speculative gain' – that is, not at market price (*A Future that Works*, 1984: 15). Since then British Telecom had been privatized and British Gas was next on the cards. Though the bulk of shares were acquired by the financial institutions the Government had succeeded in attracting millions of new shareholders eager for the easy pickings shares sold at discounted prices guaranteed. Established policy seemed certain to alienate many voters but with feelings running high in public sector unions like NUPE and the GMB and with the leadership unwilling to jeopardize its alliance with the soft left, it did not feel sufficiently self-confident to meet the issue head on. Eventually a compromise was negotiated: the 1987 manifesto proposed that shares in BT and (the by now privatized) British Gas would be converted into special new securities which would be tradable on the market and 'carry either a guaranteed return, or dividends linked to the company's growth' (*Britain Will Win*, 1987: 6). Whilst this meant that Labour was now pledged to pay full compensation the policy of returning the utilities to the public sector still held. This still left the leadership worried since it feared that the policy could easily be portrayed by Conservative propagandists as threatening the millions of privatized shareholders but the compromise represented the limits of what was attainable in the circumstances.

Labour's established policy on industrial relations was the repeal of all the laws, which were designed to weaken the unions, enacted by the Thatcher Government. However, the consistent message of opinion research was that the new framework was applauded by the bulk of the electorate – and, indeed, by a majority of trade union members (Minkin, 1991: 319). Repeal, an anxious leadership felt, would be pounced upon by the press and the Conservatives to intensify fears that under a Labour Government the union 'barons' would once more stalk the land, afflicting more 'winter's of discontent' on a hapless country. If Kinnock had possessed full freedom of action he almost certainly would have dropped the policy but labour law was a matter of immense concern to the unions and whilst they were prepared to give considerable leeway to the frontbench on most issues, on this they inspected its actions with an eagle eye. An open rebuff, Kinnock believed, would not only be exploited by the Conservatives as proof that Labour was in the pocket of the unions but would boost the standing of his union and left-wing critics (Kinnock, 1993: 7). Hence he proceeded gingerly. After protracted discussions, the eventual compromise was that much of the existing framework would be repealed, but the obligation upon unions to hold ballots over strikes and for union executive elections would be reaffirmed. (*The Guardian*, 14 August 1986; TUC–Labour Party Liaison Committee *People at Work: New Rights, New Responsibilities*, 1986). However, aside from falling short of what Kinnock wanted, these policy changes were too narrow and too nuanced to have any impact on public opinion, which continued to see Labour as too attached to union interests.

Labour's commitment to unilateralism was the trickiest issue of all because though it was regarded by many on the right as unsellable to the electorate Kinnock had not only personally championed it for years but was convinced that any attempt to abandon it would tear open Labour's wounds (Leapman, 1987: 149). A NEC–Shadow Cabinet Joint Policy Committee produced a report in 1984 (*Defence and Security for Britain*) which in essentials reaffirmed the policy and was overwhelmingly endorsed by the radical Conference of 1984. For many on the left, both in the unions and the constituencies, allegiance to unilateralism had become a litmus test of socialism and while prepared to compromise on most other issues on this they were adamant. Kinnock concluded that his 'commitment on this issue has to be beyond question if he is to have the room for manoeuvre that he needs on other policy issues' (*The Guardian*, 14 October 1985). However in late 1986 qualitative research conducted as part of a campaign to promote the non-nuclear policy produced the disturbing finding that a large majority of the electorate was vehemently and emotionally opposed to it. Kinnock's own faith began to wilt. Yet a reversal of policy was politically not feasible, given the existing balance of forces within the Party. Powerful unions, including the TGWU, remained firmly committed to unilateralism, and such was the feeling that the issue aroused amongst many activists that an attempt to discard it would probably have incited a mass rebellion. Furthermore, any last-minute alteration of policy would lack credibility. Instead, the leadership sought to present the non-nuclear policy as a step towards a more effective NATO strategy (*The Guardian*, 3 December 1986) and savings from the cancellation of Trident, which it had been originally intended would be used to fund social programmes, were now committed to expanding conventional military spending. But none of this swayed public opinion which seemed utterly persuaded that Labour could not be trusted to protect the nation. Defence policy remained an exposed flank which was mercilessly harried during the 1987 election campaign and, it was widely felt, was a key factor inhibiting those who otherwise felt some affinity towards the Party from actually voting for it.

The 'Loony Left' and the 1987 Election

Notwithstanding, throughout much of 1986 Labour led in the polls. With its new pastel shades, red rose, slick commercials and neat media management hopes were raised that it could stage a major political recovery. But then the following year all seemed to go to pieces.

The radical left had expanded rapidly in London since the late 1970s. Libertarian in outlook, they actively pursued equal rights policies to improve the status of ethnic minorities, gays, lesbians and women. But at times the councils they controlled behaved in an obtuse and insensitive manner which grated on the sensibilities of the general public. In the autumn of 1986, the Conservatives mounted virulent attacks against these councils, loudly, repeatedly and often adroitly echoed by the Tory tabloids. Countless examples were offered to demonstrate their intolerance and capriciousness, most of which were distortions or fabrications though the accurate ones lent credibility to the campaign (Media Research Group, 1987). The attacks reached a crescendo during the Greenwich by-election for which, to Kinnock's anger, a hard left candidate had been selected and which was disastrously lost to the SDP. The leadership had few doubts about what had gone wrong. In a leaked letter Patricia Hewitt, Kinnock's influential press secretary, declared: 'It's obvious from our own polling, as well as from the doorstep that . . . the 'loony Labour left' is taking its toll; the gays and lesbians issue is costing us dear amongst the pensioners; and fear of extremism and higher taxes/rates is particularly prominent in the GLC area' (*The Guardian*, 6 March 1987). Kinnock had been dismayed and embarrassed for some time by the actions of radical left councils and would have preferred to have brandished the stick but, although the NEC was equipped with powers to suspend or reorganize constituency parties, political realities at the time rendered their use hazardous. The hard left were solidly entrenched in London, in the mid-1980s, and such action would have precipitated an outbreak of internecine strife which the leadership was desperately seeking to avoid.

The 'loony left' offensive – much of it geared to exploiting racist and homophobic sentiments – was strikingly successful and afflicted cruel damage on Labour's image. Its standing in the polls slumped and when Mrs Thatcher called an election there were real fears that Labour would slide into third place. This fate was avoided by a highly professional and skilfully executed campaign which, with its mastery of modern communication techniques and the cohesion and discipline it displayed, impressed media commentators and did much to restore the Party's battered morale. However, the campaign was derailed over two crucial issues, defence and tax. On defence Labour's policy was wildly misrepresented as pacifist and defeatist. In a highly effective advert a full-page picture appeared in the press of a soldier with his hands in the air and the simple caption 'Labour's policy on arms'. A post-election poll revealed that defence was the second most important issue after unemployment (cited by 35 per cent) and twice as many

Labour defectors mentioned the issue as Labour loyalists (Crewe, 1987b). On tax, Treasury ministers claimed that Labour's pledges would cost a crushing £35 billion (the same figure, having proved itself, was wheeled out for the next election) whilst Labour's response was hesitant and ill co-ordinated.

Even with these stumbles, the result came as a shock. The Party's gains were disappointingly small, its share of the vote rose a mere 3.2 per cent to 30.8 per cent, though it gained a million and a half votes on a higher turnout. It only added 20 seats to reach a total of 229 – its second worst result since 1945. The one objective that was fully achieved was the winning of the battle of the opposition, as the gap between Labour and the Alliance widened from 2 points to 8. Labour's share of the working-class vote remained discouragingly low in the south and amongst home-owners (both growing groups) and highest in those sections (like council house-owners, union members, public sector workers and workers in manufacturing industry) which were shrinking. Crewe concluded that it now represented a declining segment of the working class. Its pulling power was much weaker amongst the more affluent workers living in owner-occupied estates and employed in the new service economy of the South. 'It was party neither of one class nor one nation; it was a regional class party' (Crewe, 1987a; Crewe, 1987b). The Conservatives, whose share of the vote was static, romped home again with a majority of just over a hundred.

Notes

1   G. Bish, RD 2902, NEC minutes 1983.
2   Fortuitously, Benn's constituency had, by boundary changes, become a marginal and he lost his seat in 1983, preventing him from standing as a candidate for the leadership. If he had stood, Kinnock might have been squeezed out on the first ballot and thereby improved Hattersely's chance of winning. Benn returned to the Commons as MP for Chesterfield in 1984.

8 The Abandonment of Keynesian Social Democracy, 1987–1995

Unless Labour addresses the issue of taxes 'it can say little that is positive and even less that is radical . . . Radical decisions will certainly disadvantage some members of the higher-income groups.

(Roy Hattersley, *Observer* 15 January 1995)

New Labour will no longer tax for taxation's sake.

(Gordon Brown)

The Policy Review

The driving force behind programmatic renewal in the Labour Party since 1987 has been the search for votes. In 1983 a strife-torn party ineptly led had run a ramshackle campaign. Four years later the smooth professionalism of Labour's campaign had won acclaim – but the Party was not spared another crushing defeat at the polls. Not only were there several points at which it was still at odds with popular feeling, but the pervasive lack of trust in the Party, the lack of confidence in its ability to govern and manage the economy competently all convinced the leadership that a major overhaul of policy was essential. It was fully aware that it faced a daunting task. Labour's score of 31 per cent was one of its worst ever. With social trends mostly adverse it was vital for it to 'widen our appeal to embrace new occupational groups' (Labour Party NEC 'Moving Ahead', 1987: 4). An elaborate exercise entitled the Policy Review was launched in 1988 with seven Policy Review

Groups, composed mainly of representatives from the Shadow Cabinet and the NEC, charged with examining the whole gamut of issues. Unlike continental parties like the Swedish and German Social Democrats Labour's policy-makers did not embark upon a systematic reappraisal of values and objectives. The Party did publish at an early stage of the exercise a statement entitled *Democratic Socialist Aims and Values* to furnish some ideological moorings, but it was almost immediately forgotten. Policy innovations occurred in an incremental way, registering the shifting balance of views and interests within the Party and reflecting a step-by-step attempt to grapple with altered economic, political and social circumstances.

Four Policy Review reports were published between 1988 and 1991. The object of the first, *Social Justice and Economic Efficiency*, was to produce a statement of values, goals and major policy themes. It was the least influential and had no impact. The detailed elaboration of policy was left to the second phase; its report, by far the bulkiest, was entitled *Meet the Challenge, Make the Change*. Submitted to the 1989 Conference it announced substantial programmatic innovations. The original function of the third phase was to finalize any outstanding policy issues and then concentrate on the promotion of the new programme. But the rather surprising ease with which *Meet the Challenge, Make the Change* was shepherded through Conference convinced the leadership that, on a number of issues, it had been unduly circumspect. Presented to the 1990 Conference *Looking to the Future* signalled a further significant shift to the right as did the fourth *Opportunity Britain*, delivered to the 1991 Conference. All four reports were endorsed overwhelmingly. The final definitive statement was the 1992 Manifesto *It's Time to Get Britain Working Again*.

The state and the market

The Party had traditionally been associated with the belief that a substantial measure of state regulation was required for a more rational and efficient organisation of economic life. This was now regarded as an outdated approach. To have any credibility with business and opinion-formers in the media, it was deemed vital that Labour expressly affirm its belief that 'the market and competition are essential in meeting the demands of the consumer, promoting efficiency and stimulating innovation, and often the best means of securing all the myriad, incremental changes which are needed to take the economy forward' (*Meet the Challenge, Make the Change*, 1989: 10). This left open the question of the degree to which the market ought to be regulated. In the early stages of the Policy Review there were considerable differences behind the scenes between the more interventionist-minded soft left and the market-oriented right. The former group included Bryan Gould, the convener of the main economic Policy Review group and *Meet the Challenge, Make the Change* represented an effort to strike a balance. Thus as well as affirming its confidence in the market it called for a Medium Term Industrial Strategy, to be administered by a strengthened Department of Trade and Industry (roughly modelled on the Japanese Ministry of Overseas Trade, MITI) and two new institutions, British Technology Enterprise and the British Investment Bank. The intention was to break the stranglehold of the City, which Gould held primarily responsible for the endemic weakness of the British economy. But the leadership was dubious about Gould's views and it was their thinking which eventually prevailed. In October 1989 Gould was replaced as industry spokesman by Gordon Brown who, together with the Shadow Chancellor, John Smith and John Eatwell, Kinnock's personal economic adviser pushed for a less interventionist approach and a more conciliatory stance towards the City. Thus in the later stages of the Policy Review plans for an enhanced state role in the investment process were dropped and the role of proposed new interventionist agencies downgraded. This drift away from economic collectivism reflected the widespread lack of confidence within Labour's senior echelons in the value of an active state role in the economy. They argued the state should confine itself to those tasks which the market was either unable or unwilling to discharge. On the supply-side this meant tackling inadequacies in training, R&D and regional development, and discouraging industrially damaging takeovers. In the macro-economic sphere it meant establishing an economic environment sufficiently stable to restore business confidence and, hence, raise the level of investment. The axis of such intervention was to be partnership with the private sector: a flourishing economy, *Opportunity Britain* explained, required '*co-operation* between government and industry, as well as *competition* between companies' (Labour Party NEC, *Opportunity Britain*, 1991: 4, emphasis in the original).

Public ownership and privatization

As recently as 1986 the Party had pledged a future Labour Government to 'an ambitious programme to move towards wider social ownership' (*Social Ownership*, 1986: 2). During the course of the Policy Review any surviving proposals to extend public ownership soon disappeared. For a pragmatic party seeking a rapprochement with business and endeavouring to win the approval of the exponents of official economic wisdom, nationalization was a dangerous irrelevance. However, the question of how to respond to the Conservatives' relentless privatization programme caused considerable difficulties. Public sector unions were keen to maintain some commitment to renationalize the major utilities where many of their members worked, a view shared by Gould and others on the soft left. This was not the view of the increasingly ascendant right and, as the political balance moved in their favour, the remaining commitments were progressively shed. By 1990 *Looking to the Future* limited the list of candidates to water, which was 'so fundamental that it should be a priority for a return to the public sector' (*Looking to the Future*, 1990: 17). By the time the manifesto was written about eighteen months later it had ceased to be so and the Party simply called for public control (*It's Time to Get Britain Working Again*, 1992: 21). The Party's traditional stance had been that the utilities, as essential services and as monopolies, ought to be owned by the community but for Kinnock 'the question is what an industry does, not who owns it. Ownership is a matter for the ideologists' (*Observer*, 7 September 1989).[1] In an earlier clash over public ownership Bevan had defined the debate as being 'between those who want the mainsprings of economic power transferred to the community and those who believe that private enterprise should still remain supreme but that its worst characteristics should be modified by liberal ideas of justice and equality' (Greenleaf, 1983: 470). By the close of the Policy Review the debate had been conclusively resolved.

Macro-economic policy

For a generation Keynesian thinking was the kernel of Labour's creed, but this was now ceasing to be the case. Gould was a staunch Keynesian, but increasingly found himself in a minority. Smith, in contrast, reflected the views of the right-wing majority in the leadership when he rejected the proposition that demand could still be managed in such a way as to sustain growth and cut unemployment, claiming that the inevitable consequences would be higher inflation and a pounding of the currency. In an increasingly interdependent world economy, with its deregulated currency and capital flows and liberalized trading arrangements, he argued, nationally-oriented Keynesian strategies were obsolete. In 1989, the clash over macro-economic policy centred on the issue of membership of the Exchange Rate Mechanism (ERM). In line with Gould's thinking, *Meet the Challenge, Make the Change* expressed reservations about ERM's deflationary bias, with its damaging effects on growth and employment.[2] Smith and Kinnock, in contrast, contended that membership of the ERM would contribute to what they regarded as the primary economic goal of price stability whilst also reassuring the money markets of the Party's fiscal rectitude. The matter was resolved after Gould's removal from the industry portfolio in autumn 1989 when Labour embraced the ERM with the zeal of a convert which was to survive until Black Wednesday and Britain's forced expulsion from the ERM in September 1992.

By 1992, Labour was pledged to a fixed and high exchange rate and fiscal and monetary orthodoxy. By committing itself to maintain sterling at its over-valued rate, and (as ERM rules stipulated) to use interest rate policy to protect that rate it was proposing to lock itself into a deflationary regime which – if carried through – would have made it extremely difficult to curb unemployment. The National Institute of Economic and Social Research concluded in 1990, after a detailed review of Labour's policies, that 'the economic policy differences between the two major parties are narrower now than they have been for about twenty years' (National Institute Economic Review, 1990: 52).

The welfare state

The welfare state lay at the very centre of Keynesian social democracy. By socializing consumption it aimed to ensure that basic human needs were met and access to vital resources such as health and education provided by the conscious will of the community rather than left to market forces. It was the essential means to realize the values of freedom, equality and solidarity. Influenced by opinion research conducted after the 1987 election, Kinnock was convinced that the Party's reputation as a high tax–high spend party was a major handicap.

According to its findings, most voters welcomed what they perceived as a substantial reduction of taxation under the Tories and whilst sympathetic to the principle of increased taxation to finance better education and health services, in practice they were reluctant to dip into their own pockets. There was a widespread belief that additional funds, especially if administered by a Labour Government, would be squandered on benefits for 'social security scroungers' (Hughes and Wintour, 1990). Equally the Party was fearful of an anti-tax backlash and, rather than defending the principle of public provision, it insisted that it would maintain a firm rein on public spending. Thus Kinnock stressed that 'stringent controls on both the scale and balance of spending is vital' (*The Guardian*, 9 May 1989) whilst the Shadow Chancellor endlessly repeated the injunction that 'we can't spend what we haven't earned. We intend to earn it before we spend it. That will be the guiding light of the next Labour Government's economic policy' (*The Guardian*, 2 October 1989). As the Policy Review proceeded, Labour steadily tightened its fiscal stance, confining itself to minimal pledges – an increase in pensions and child benefits, to be funded by higher taxes on the richest 10 per cent or so of tax-payers. Any further expansion of the public services would have to be financed from the increments of economic growth.

Industrial relations and the unions

Industrial relations was – defence apart – the most difficult area covered by the Policy Review. Since 1979 the trade unions had been the butt of a full-scale political assault from a fiercely hostile Conservative Government. By the late 1980s they were hemmed in by a formidable range of judicial restraints limiting their right to strike and subjecting them to a host of penalties. The unions pressed Labour to pledge itself to repeal at least the most iniquitous of Tory laws. Prior to 1987, the Party had been committed to the straightforward repeal of the Thatcher Government's industrial relations package. The problem with maintaining this stance was the popularity of this legislation, reflecting the fear sedulously stirred by the Tories and the tabloids of a revival of trade union power with its alleged consequences of rampant inflation and industrial chaos: the slumbering images of the Winter of Discontent could very easily spring to life. To Kinnock the issue was primarily one of strategy: Labour must convince the voters that it was not the lapdog of the unions and there was no better issue on which to be seen over-ruling the unions than one viewed by them as a matter of vital interest.

However, internal resistance had to be overcome, not least from Michael Meacher, frontbench spokesman on Employment and convener of the industrial relations Policy Review group who favoured restoring to the unions the ability to bargain effectively. At first his views prevailed but Kinnock, furious that he had been thwarted, replaced him by his able young protégé, Tony Blair, in October 1989. By this time, influential elements within the TUC and individual unions were prepared to collaborate with the Parliamentary leadership and Blair was able without undue difficulty to secure a sweeping revision of Labour's long-held approach to labour law. Much of the existing legal code, including the banning of the closed shop, would be retained, and picketing and secondary action would only be legal in strictly limited circumstances. By 1992 the manifesto was assuring voters that 'there will be no return to the trade union legislation of the 1970s . . . There will be no mass or flying pickets' (*It's Time to Get Britain Working Again*, 1992: 11).

Defence

For the Leader, there was no more sensitive issue than defence. He had been a passionate unilateralist throughout his political life, but had concluded that its abandonment was a condition of Labour's revival. Whilst the real reasons were electoral, the profound changes in the Soviet Union under Gorbachev, the advent of much friendlier relations between East and West, the disintegration of Communist regimes which was soon to culminate in German reunification and the end of the Cold War all provided sustenance to Kinnock's claim that new realities demanded new policies. The first intimations that he was contemplating a policy reversal, however, provoked such indignation throughout the left that he was forced into an embarrassing retreat. He then moved more cautiously, steadily building up support. Steps were taken to ensure that the defence Policy Review Group would be packed with an anti-unilateralist majority. Opposition was softened up by a series of stratagems, including visits to the USSR and the USA, careful wooing of doubters within the unions and the release of Shadow Agency research demonstrating beyond doubt the scale and intensity of public hostility to unilateralism. At the NEC meeting called to discuss the report compiled by Gerald Kaufman, the shrewd Shadow Foreign Secretary, Kinnock for the first time openly and unequivocally rejected unilateralism, implied he would resign if Labour stood by it – and swept aside all opposition. The turnabout in policy was then endorsed by Conference (Wintour and Hughes, 1990, 121–2, 126). The position initially taken was a multilateralist one, that is Labour would bargain away the UK's nuclear force in international negotiations with other nuclear powers but, under media pressure, this was soon abandoned. The 1992 manifesto affirmed that as long nuclear weapons existed anywhere in the world 'Labour will retain Britain's nuclear capability' (*It's Time to Get Britain Working Again*, 1992: 26). For the first time ever, Labour accepted that nuclear weapons should, in effect, remain a permanent part of Britain's armoury, ironically at a time when it was more difficult than ever to identify a coherent security or military rationale for an 'independent' deterrent. Yet the total renunciation of what was for the whole of the left virtually an article of faith – which would have only a couple of years previously precipitated an outburst of outrage within the Party – was digested, albeit unhappily, with remarkably little public protest. One reason was that the international situation was being transformed out of all recognition and the possibility of a nuclear conflagration had all but vanished. But the key factor was the acceptance by many that the policy could never be sold to the electorate: in the words of Henri of Navarre, the sixteenth-century Protestant contender to the French throne – 'Paris was worth a mass'.

Party Modernization, 1987–1992

Party modernization was both a condition of and a complement to programmatic change. Its main purpose was to modify rules and institutional arrangements that by dispersing power and enforcing accountability inhibited the leadership's strategic flexibility. Shifts in the internal balance of forces strengthened Kinnock's hand as the continuing drift to the right lessened the need to reach compromises with the soft left. Other developments, too, added to the stock of power resources available to the leadership. In the second half of the 1980s Labour's campaigning and communications effort was thoroughly professionalized. The orchestrated and cohesive promotion of the Party's case via the media and the extensive deployment of modern mass persuasion techniques entailed a much greater degree of centralized campaign management, a task which only the Leader and his inner circle could effectively discharge. Professionalization also reduced the perceived functional value of local campaigning by grass-roots activists whilst elevating that of the opinion pollsters, advertising executives, public relations specialists and associated Party officials (grouped together between 1986 and 1992 in the Shadow Communications Agency) whose primary allegiance was to Kinnock. The centralizing effect of these changes were further amplified by the increasingly gladiatoral aspect of media coverage. Given that so much attention was focused on the Party leaders and given that their leadership qualities were often measured in terms of their 'strength' and 'toughness' Labour's members felt increasingly reticent about acting in ways that might impair Kinnock's standing.

Senior communications officials had established close working relations with a number of political journalists, especially those from the broadcasting organizations and the more sympathetic newspapers, *The Guardian*, the *Daily Mirror* and the *Independent*. Because most of Labour's rank and file drew their political information from these sources the leadership was in a position to influence their understanding of Party events. Thus Party 'spin doctors' used informal briefings to friendly journalists to feed into the public domain the Leader's version of political happenings, helping to mould the way in which issues were defined and inner party debates depicted. An increasingly common stratagem employed to tighten leadership control was the use of off-the-record briefings to undermine and discredit figures regarded as causing 'difficulties'. The device was systematically deployed against soft left dissenters such as Gould, Meacher and Prescott to prepare the ground for their demotion.

Parliamentary selection

As we have seen, Kinnock had already made one abortive bid to alter parliamentary selection procedures in 1984. He tried again three years later, with a new round of selections in the offing. His favoured model was selection on the basis of individual member ballots, but he soon discovered that he still was not able to muster a majority due to opposition from left and centre unions. So once more, reluctantly, he opted for a compromise, the local electoral college. Under this arrangement, the unions were assigned up to 40 per cent of the total vote, depending on the degree of union representation at General Committee level, whilst the rest of the vote was to be cast by individually-balloted rank and file members. With the backing of most unions the college was overwhelmingly adopted by Conference by 4,545,000 votes to 1,608,000 (*The Guardian*, 29 September 1987). This achieved one major reform goal – the removal from activists of their right to determine the choice of Parliamentary candidate. For the leadership it had another decided advantage: the regular monitoring of the MPs' conduct, which made mandatory reselection a potentially formidable instrument of accountability, was effectively ended since the body that conducted the monitoring (the General Committee) lost the ability to hold the MP to account. A later constitutional change, which rendered the system less automatic, further helped insulate MPs from constituency pressures. The electoral college, however, was complex and cumbersome, overtaxing Labour's scarce organizational resources. All these defects were so obvious that in 1990 Conference voted to discontinue the system though the final shape of what was to replace it was not to be decided until 1993.

Party elections

Kinnock was more successful in extending 'one member, one vote' to Party elections. In its guidelines for the leadership and deputy leadership elections of 1988, the NEC encouraged constituencies to use direct membership balloting. As the results suggested a strong correlation between the use of OMOV and support for Kinnock and Hattersley against hard left candidates (*The Guardian*, 8 October 1988) the NEC the following year recommended that the method be applied to voting for its own constituency section.[3] OMOV appeared to be having the desired effect, as hard left members of the Executive were ousted, and the NEC in February 1990 voted to make direct membership balloting mandatory.[4] The results the three following years were even more reassuring for the leadership as all hard left representatives were eliminated (including Tony Benn, who had for years topped the section) mainly in favour of right-wingers, including Brown and Blair (in 1994, however, two members of the hard left were elected). In future, the new and larger 'selectorate' will be much more difficult for left-wing ginger groups to mobilize whilst the rising importance of television exposure in securing a seat is bound to profit establishment candidates holding senior frontbench positions: it is no coincidence that the NEC now contains an unprecedented number of Shadow Cabinet members.

The NEC

From the early 1970s to the early 1980s, under the leadership of the left, the NEC had operated as an institutionalized source of opposition to the frontbench. By 1987, Kinnock could generally rely on NEC approval for important policy departures but agreement still had to be negotiated and concessions made. The splintering of the left and the pronounced drift to the right after the 1987 defeat helped the Leader tighten his grip. Although the Policy Review process was formally jointly directed by the NEC and the Shadow Cabinet the frontbench was very much the senior partner. By the end of 1989 the NEC had been reduced to a subaltern status and Kinnock was able to overturn policy on even the most controversial issues such as unilateralism (Kinnock, 1993: 16–17). The Executive's independent policy-making capacity largely disappeared with the depletion of its research staff; its Home Policy and International committees (reduced to bi-monthly meetings with scanty agendas) were only marginally involved in the policy process and the growing prominence of senior frontbenchers on the Executive ensured that for the most part it did little more than rubber stamp decisions made elsewhere. By the 1990s, the dispersal of power at the centre which had so complicated the work of Kinnock's three predecessors had been replaced by a tightly integrated system in which control was effectively concentrated in the hands of the Parliamentary elite. In October 1990 *The Guardian* could report that 'Mr Kinnock appears in Blackpool, too, more perhaps than any of his predecessors, as the undisputed voice of the Labour Party. By cunning and patient strategies he has achieved a control of the Party which even Harold Wilson never matched. What he says usually goes. In the Party's National Executive he wins vote after vote by truly crushing majorities' (*The Guardian*, leader, 1 October 1990).

The 1992 Election and the Smith Interregnum

As Labour's opening shot of the 1992 election campaign John Smith presented his 'shadow budget' which proposed raising the higher income tax band from 40 per cent to 50 per cent and the abolition of the upper limit on National Insurance Contributions. The overall effect would have been to lift taxes for the richest 20 per cent and reduce them slightly for the rest whilst surplus funds would be used to meet the Party's commitments on child benefits and pensions. This mildly progressive package provided the opportunity for the Conservatives to launch a long-planned offensive and volley upon volley was released against Labour's 'tax bombshell'. Notwithstanding, Labour entered the 1992 election campaign in a mood of optimism, with the polls giving it a small but consistent edge over the Conservatives which it sustained until polling day – making the result an even more crushing disappointment. Despite a severe recession and a stream of poor economic statistics, Labour only managed to push up its share of the vote by 3.6 per cent to 34.4 per cent., below the percentage gained in 1979 when Callaghan was ousted from power. As a consolation prize, it secured an above average swing in the marginals, procuring it an extra 42 seats and cutting Major's majority to 21. Furthermore, it scored best in areas where previously it performed poorly, especially in the south-east. Overall its largest percentage gains were amongst ABs (professional and managerial), up 10 per cent compared to 1987 and 2 per cent to 1979, and the DEs (semi-skilled and unskilled) up 8 per cent since 1987, 2 per cent since 1979. However, amongst C1s (clerical workers) and C2s (skilled manual) the increase was only 4 per cent and in both cases down on 1979 (Crewe, 1992: 5; figures from Harris/ITN exit polls). Although the Conservative lead in seats was relatively small, for Labour to obtain an overall majority it still required a swing higher than it ever achieved. Tantalus-like, the prize seemed as elusive as ever.

Kinnock immediately signalled his intention to resign. The succession was disputed between John Smith and Bryan Gould, both men of impressive ability. However, Smith possessed the backing of all major union leaders, the bulk of MPs and even influential soft leftists like Robin Cook (his campaign manager) who might have been expected to rally behind his rival, and swept easily to victory winning all three sections of the electoral college.[5] A man of ruthlessly sharp intelligence, the new Leader had the supreme self-confidence his predecessor so obviously lacked. Convinced that he could regain for his Party the trust and confidence of the electorate, he favoured 'playing the long game', that is a calm and measured approach to rebuilding support for

Labour. The corollary of this was that sudden changes in policy and organization were not required whilst his consensual style of leadership also made him averse to actions that would alienate large sections of the Party. Ironically, on organizational matters, events pushed him into a confrontation with the centre-left unions that neither side really wanted. Smith had indicated in his campaign for the leadership that he favoured various organizational reforms, such as the extension of OMOV to parliamentary selection and the reduction of the union vote at Conference. Just prior to Kinnock's departure, the NEC had set up a 'Trade Union Links Review Group' composed of NEC and Shadow Cabinet members, trade union leaders, officials and an academic expert (Lewis Minkin) which aimed to foster compromise over organizational issues. The unions – by no means as averse to change as the media claimed – willingly agreed a reduction of their vote at Conference from 90 per cent to 70 per cent with a provision for a further cutback to 50 per cent if Party membership rose over the 300,000 mark. This was approved by the 1993 Conference to take immediate effect. However, the majority of unions refused to relinquish their role in leadership selection, believing that levy-payers had a right to participate. Smith initially wanted to phase out the union role entirely but, acknowledging the merits of the unions' case and to smooth ruffled feathers, he agreed to a compromise which was overwhelmingly endorsed by Conference. The union share of the electoral college fell from 40 per cent to 33 per cent (with the PLP and the CLPs also taking one-third each) and – the key reform – instead of unions casting a block vote, the right to vote was transferred to all those individual political levy-payers who were willing to declare themselves Labour supporters. This created a leadership electorate numbering in the millions, by far the largest of any party.

However, as in the past, parliamentary selection proved a tougher nut to crack. There was general agreement that the highly complicated and burdensome 1987 formula needed to be scrapped, but not over its replacement. A strong body of opinion pressed for a straightforward, simple to operate system of OMOV. But a powerful group of unions, including the TGWU, the GMB and NUPE, were insistent on preserving their role and a consultation exercise indicated that a majority of CLPs agreed with them. Eventually Prescott introduced a compromise, the so-called 'levy-plus' scheme by which political levy payers could participate in selections if they joined the Party at a discounted rate.

The NEC approved the scheme in July 1993, but the majority of unions continued to insist on separate union representation. To placate the unions, Smith reaffirmed his commitment to full employment – but he also raised the stakes by warning that, if beaten on the issue, he would resign

Why were so many unions – including those like the GMB with a tradition of loyalty to the leadership – so obdurate over an issue about which few voters cared, and fewer understood[6] whilst willingly compromising over others? Perhaps the main reason was that it had become a lightning conductor for a general sense of grievance. Trade union leaders were indignant over a spate of reports which appeared in the press the previous year highlighting private research conducted for Labour which allegedly blamed the Party-union link for the electoral defeat. Though the reports were inaccurate – the Party's post-election research hardly mentioned the unions and there was little evidence for the charge – they soon attained the status of conventional and endlessly recycled media wisdom. Union leaders, who had assiduously kept a low profile during the election campaign, greatly resented being scapegoated and suspected that the reports had been planted by the 'modernizers' (who were well-connected to the press). The modernizers, whose leading members included Brown, Blair and Mandelson, formed an influential new group on the right of the Party and had gained prominence with Kinnock's encouragement and patronage. They were also held at least partly responsible for the incessant flow of reports in the media depicting the unions as stubborn and die-hard traditionalists. Whilst the case for limiting parliamentary selection rights to individual members was a persuasive one, the GMB and TGWU officials were right in suspecting that more was at stake. To the modernizers, the unions represented a 'special interest' whose entrenched influence within the Party severely tarnished its appeal. It seems very likely that their ultimate intention was, as soon as state funding could be arranged, to snap the organizational tie between the unions and the Party. This reasoning was anathema to centre-left unions to whom the Party and the unions were integral parts of a single labour movement and who thereby held they had a wholly legitimate right to participate in the Party's affairs.[7] Whatever the reasons, the TGWU and the GMB were playing with fire and the Party only avoided a political disaster by a hair's breadth. The levy-plus option was carried by 47.5 per cent to 44.4 per cent, after a rousing speech by Prescott (known to be a strong upholder of the union link) and a last-minute switch by the Manufacturing Science and Finance union (MSF) produced by some neat political foot play.

Modernizers Triumphant: Labour under Blair

In the summer of 1994 Smith died suddenly from a heart attack, followed by a remarkable display of public grief. The two politicians most strongly placed to succeed were both modernizers as well as close friends (at the time), Blair and Brown. The former indicated that he was determined to stand, giving the latter little option but to give way to avoid splitting the modernizers' vote. With Gould out of the running, the strongest candidate from the soft left was Robin Cook. A man of razor-sharp intelligence and devastating debating skills, he was regarded by some commentators as the ablest frontbencher in the Party. A Scot like Smith and Brown, he was, however, advised that in a televisual age his alleged resemblance to 'a wee Scottish garden gnome' might alienate voters. For whatever reason, he decided not to stand. In the event, the two other contenders for the leadership were Prescott and Margaret Beckett and Blair easily prevailed, winning (under the new rules) a majority in all three sections of the electoral college.[8] The new Leader rapidly made a favourable impression upon the electorate: his looks and affability of manner appealed to voters whilst his self-confidence, lucidity and clarity of mind rendered him a highly effective communicator and lent him an air of authority which his predecessor but one (elected at the same youthful age of 41) was never able to acquire.

The shock of the Party's defeat in 1992 had persuaded the modernizers that the pace of change had been too slack, too weighed down by compromises. Behind the scenes they had become increasingly disturbed by Smith's cautious strategy, feeling that it lacked verve and urgency and it failed to grasp the dimensions of Labour's predicament. Martin Jacques, formerly editor of *Marxism Today* but latterly close to the modernizers, portrayed Smith as a politician 'tied by culture and background to the Old Labour universe' and rebuked him for 'breathtaking inactivity and complacency' (quoted in McSmith, 1994: 304). With Blair as leader the modernizers were now in the driving seat. With a crystal-clear idea of the direction in which he wanted the Party to move and, as he soon showed, a ruthless will, he was determined to complete the modernization of the Party that his mentor, Kinnock, had inaugurated. This strategy – or 'project' as his aides soon dubbed it – was rooted in an analysis of why Labour had lost in 1992.

The core problem, they argued, was that the Party had not adapted sufficiently rapidly or wholeheartedly to new social, cultural and economic realities. Its programme, organization and mentality were still coloured by an age which had now past: an age of mass production techniques, great sprawling industrial plants and tightly-knit occupational and residential communities. This was a time when workers composed the bulk of the population, class inequalities and class consciousness were pronounced and workers who flocked to the unions felt a natural affinity for collectivist ideals and institutions. However, economic and technological changes had brought about a steady contraction in the size of the working class, more workers were employed in smaller units, engaged in more specialized and a more varied range of tasks, enjoyed a higher status and earned better wages. Class barriers were loosening, with rising levels of social mobility as increasing numbers moved into white-collar occupations and service industries. Two-thirds of the population now possessed the means to purchase their own homes and live a reasonably comfortable and contented life.

In consequence class solidarity was rapidly diminishing and collectivist modes of thinking and behaviour were being displaced by more individualistic and instrumental ones. People were much less disposed to look to the state to supply minimum standards of life, resented the growing burden of taxation they were required to pay and were more sceptical of the benefits it procured. 'The new right,' according to Blair, 'had struck a chord. There was a perception that there was too much collective power, too much bureaucracy, too much state intervention and too many vested interests around it' (Sopel, 1995: 209). The Tories had succeeded in gaining new adherents – especially skilled workers in the South and Midlands employed in the private sector – because it was seen as a party which understood their desire to be freed from an intrusive state and to be allowed to rise in the world. Labour, in stark contrast, was seen as a party wedded to collective institutions like trade unions and the state, championing the interests of social security recipients, ethnic minorities and the downwardly-mobile and increasingly out of touch with the aspirations of the majority. 'We own our house, we've got good jobs,' a skilled engineer told opinion researchers in a post-election survey. ' We're doing all right and we want to do better. We're on the way up and Labour's for people on the way down' (Hewitt and Gould, 1993: 46). The Smith tax proposals had played into the Tories' hands, reflecting a failure to appreciate how many people aspired to better themselves. An egalitarian tag was a vote-loser, 'a fatal electoral handicap in a "two-thirds, one-third" society' (Radice, 1992: 17).

This assumption that Britain now was a 'two-thirds, one-third society' inhabiting (in J. K. Galbraith's phrase) a culture of contentment underpinned the modernizers' strategy. It was the rationale for the sustained efforts to woo to 'Middle England', the fulcrum of 'New Labour's' electoral appeal – although precisely who formed 'Middle England' was never made clear.[9] The modernizers' thinking derived from market research, as interpreted by professional communicators from the Shadow Agency who shared their perspective not by any searching scrutiny of the dynamics of social change or systematic empirical analysis. In fact, there were solid reasons to believe that the concept of a 'two-thirds, one-third society' was wholly inapposite, that, indeed, Britain was far closer to a '30/30/40' society. The first 30 per cent comprised the disadvantaged, the unemployed and economically inactive who lived in conditions of poverty; the second 30 per cent consisted of the marginalized and insecure, part-time and casual workers on low wages, deprived of most entitlements and at permanent risk of redundancy; and the remaining 40 per cent were composed not only of the well-off but also of the many receiving less than the median wage (Hutton, 1995: 105–9). Far from the majority of the population dwelling in contentment, more than half of people eligible to work 'are living either on poverty incomes or in conditions of permanent stress and insecurity' (Hutton, 1995: 109). Furthermore 'downsizing', the ruthless pressure on costs, and the widening remuneration gap between employers and employees, were threatening the jobs and living standards of an ever-growing proportion of white-collar workers. Job insecurity, a depressed housing market, a rising crime wave, evidence everywhere of a disintegrating social fabric – these were phenomena seized upon by Labour's leadership when lambasting the Tory record, but ones which sat uneasily with their depiction of a 'two-thirds, one-third' society.

However, modernizers were disinclined to contemplate the implications of such an analysis since it raised questions about the validity of their political strategy. The whole tilt of 'New Labour' was towards cultivating an image of 'moderation' and 'responsibility', abandoning 'old-fashioned' collectivist policies and values and accommodating too many of the institutional changes accomplished by the Conservatives. Its primary strategic objective was the essentially defensive one of winning the electorate's trust and confidence in its ability to govern and to manage the economy effectively. To achieve this it must reassure the voters that it would not overtax, overspend and overborrow; nor would it extend any 'favours' to the unions. All the old demons must be banished. It must 'make the mental leap that says that aspiring to be middle class is positive', wrote Mo Mowlam, a Shadow Cabinet member. 'People want more money, a decent house, a good car . . . ' (Mowlam, 1993: 6). It must transform itself into 'a broad-based national party, concerned with individual rights and opportunities' (Radice, 1992: 23–4).

Clause IV

On the basis of their analysis, the modernizers had concluded that Labour had both to complete its transformation and convince the voters that it had done so – that it had ceased being 'Old' and was now 'New Labour'. The way to accomplish both objectives was to succeed where Gaitskell had failed and revise Clause IV of the constitution, which pledged the Party to common ownership. This, two modernizers claimed in a Fabian pamphlet, would be 'a potent symbol of Labour's modernisation' (Radice and Pollard, 1993: 16). Scrapping the old clause would be almost a ritual purgation. The fact that the move would be bitterly fought by the hard left was all to the better, since without a fight the public would not be persuaded the change was authentic. Smith had opposed the move but Blair's first major initiative as Leader was to spring it on an unsuspecting audience at the 1994 Party Conference. More, however, was required than deleting the commitment to common ownership. The new clause must dramatize how different 'New Labour' was from the old. The best way to do this was not only to dump public ownership but to praise capitalism, and acknowledge 'that the market economy has been remarkable successful in bringing prosperity' and 'symbolically declare its support for the market economy' (Radice, 1992: 18–19).

But this raised a problem. A new clause would have to be approved by Conference. Left to themselves, the rank and file might jettison the old clause but opt for a new one highlighting Labour's attachment to social justice, equality, full employment and all the dated shibboleths of 'Old Labour'. In response the Blair camp adopted the following stratagem: curtail the choice to one of two options and – given that one would have to be the status quo – exercise tight control over the compilation of the alternative. Conference would be left the final choice: but the leadership would decide what the choice would be *between*. The new clause was thus drawn up by Blair: presented to the NEC with his full authority as Leader it was accepted after some minor amendments. Its most publicized section was the pledge 'to work for a dynamic economy, serving the public interest, in which the enterprise of the market and the rigour of competition are joined with the forces of partnership and co-operation . . . with a thriving private sector and high quality public services . . . '. Much of the rest was vague and anodyne, with calls for a just society, security against fear, equality of opportunity , a healthy environment and so on.

The next step was to secure the new Clause IV's acceptance. By the end of 1994, constituency resolutions appeared, ominously, to signal hardening support for the 1918 version, opening up the possibility that the amendment would only be carried on the backs of union votes. This would have been totally self-defeating since it would be seized open with glee by the Conservatives as showing that 'New Labour' could only be delivered with 'Old Labour' acting as midwife. Knowing that constituency General Committees could not be relied upon to rally behind him, Blair persuaded the NEC to urge CLPs to hold a ballot of all their members, and to fund a campaign – to be conducted mainly by youthful modernizing volunteers – to mobilize support for the new clause. Most boldly of all, Blair personally undertook an intensive round of meetings throughout the country, attended, he estimated, by no less than 30,000 Party members, a massive and unprecedented exercise in persuasion.

Political initiatives often have unintended consequences, and this was to be no exception. As the Conference drew near, it suddenly seemed that the project might capsize. It had been assumed that the TGWU would probably cast its hefty block vote against the new formula, but unexpectedly a Unison[10] conference overturned the recommendation of its leadership and voted narrowly to back the original clause. This meant that there was now a serious prospect that Blair might be defeated or win only narrowly. However, news from another quarter was highly encouraging. Over two-thirds of CLPs had decided to ballot their members and, with the results now flowing in, on average no less than 85 per cent were voting for the new Clause IV. Further, those unions who either balloted all their members or polled a representative sample of them uncovered equally firm support for revision. Blair immediately grasped that he could turn the situation decisively to his advantage by portraying the issue as a struggle between 'New Labour' and the trade union avatars of the 'Old', played out with a chorus – the media – chanting out his lines.[11] Primed by off-the-record briefings from Party sources, Blair's handling of the union 'barons' was depicted by the media as a test of his determination to 'stand up to' and 'out-face' union power in Government (see, for example, the *Independent*, 15 April 1995). The Leader accordingly insisted that there would be no deals in 'smoke-filled rooms' with union power brokers, no compromises: he would rely on the rank and file to beat the 'union bosses'. To ram the message home even union leaders who had actually urged their executives to accept the new clause – Morris from the TGWU (disparaged as 'confused, muddled and pusillanimous' – *The Guardian*, 22 January 1995) and Bickerstaffe from Unison – were portrayed as amongst the dragons to be slain.[12]

At a special Conference held on 29 April 1995 Blair swept to victory. He won just under two-thirds of the total vote, 54.6 per cent from the unions (with 70 per cent of the vote) and a massive 90 per cent from the constituencies (with 30 per cent) (*Observer*, 30 April 1995). To the modernizers this was proof of overwhelming endorsement for 'New Labour' but this seems doubtful. Most members realized that defeating Blair over Clause IV would have been interpreted as a personal repudiation – an electorally foolish snub to a leader riding high in the polls. In effect, the vote was a plebiscite – a vote of confidence in the Leader. And his strategy bore fruit. Media coverage was extensive and sympathetic, the message that a 'New Labour' party had arrived was effectively conveyed and he emerged with his popularity with the public and his supremacy over the Party consolidated. The reputation of his opponents, particularly in the TGWU and Unison, had been badly dented. Shortly after Jack Dromey, a staunch modernizer, husband of Harriet Harman, the shadow Employment Secretary and friend of Blair, exploited the opportunity to stand against Morris for leadership of the TGWU. Despite the fairly overt support Dromey received from Blair – and the help provided by Mandelson, Labour's canniest communicator – Morris repulsed the challenge with a three to two victory. If Dromey had triumphed, the TGWU, the pillar of the left for more than a generation, may well have moved closer to the mainstream, greatly consolidating the political mastery of the new Leader.

The Triumph of 'New Labour'

To many commentators the modernization of Labour marks its long-delayed conversion to European-style social democracy. In fact the real ideological significance of 'New Labour' is the abandonment of Keynesian social democracy in favour of pre-Keynesian orthodoxy. 'New Labour' has repudiated the basic Keynesian postulate that by manipulating the level of demand the state could promote growth and employment. 'Macro-economic policy,' Blair bluntly stated, 'can do little to change the underlying growth rate of the economy' (Sopel, 1995: 210). In his much-flagged Mais lecture in the City, he emphasized that the foremost objective of a Labour government would be price stability, 'the essential prerequisite' for achieving improved living standards and high employment. Variations in levels of borrowing, taxation and public spending as means of influencing economic performance were no longer realistic options since budget deficits and tax regime had to be kept broadly in line with those prevailing in other major industrialized countries (*The Guardian*, 23 May 1995). In a speech by Brown on monetary policy described by the *The Guardian* as 'by far the most fiscally orthodox and – in terms of government intervention – minimalist paper to have been issued by Labour in recent memory' the Shadow Chancellor insisted that inflationary pressures would be repulsed – whatever, by implication, the effect on employment. To ram the point home, 'New Labour' was prepared to augment the Bank of England's influence over interest rate policy, ensuring that whatever the rate needed to vanquish inflation would be applied (*The Guardian*, 18 May 1995). In effect, 'New Labour' was offering 'very much the same economic framework as that established by the right over the past fifteen years' (Will Hutton, *Tribune*, 26 May 1995). Macro-economic policy was once more an area of consensus but with the role of the state now a minimal one, confined largely to maintaining the monetary and fiscal conditions required to enable the market to maximize investment, output and employment

Keynesian social democracy had accepted the market as the most appropriate mechanism for organizing and co-ordinating economic trans-actions and responding to consumer preferences. But it also saw the market as plagued by serious defects. It was endemically unstable because of wide swings of the business cycle caused by perennial imbalances between savings and investment. The existence of externalities inevitably meant that 'private agents responding to the price system by seeking to maximize their own private gain will not at the same time act in accord with the social interest' (Hare, 1984: 120). Profit maximization, whilst often rational at the corporate level, often failed to benefit the economy as a whole. Corrective action by the state to stabilize the business cycle and operate as a custodian for the public interest was therefore essential.

'New Labour' thinking, in contrast, reposed a greater faith in the self-correcting mechanisms of the market and did not perceive any inherent tension between corporate profit-seeking and public welfare. Attempts by government to boost investment by means of regulation, tax allowances or subsidies would generate sub-optimal resource deci-sions: these matters were best left to the commercial judgement of private corporations. Government, in short, would achieve little by trying directly to affect levels of economic output. Its proper role should be to help business not seek to by-pass it. 'New Labour' does, nevertheless, envisage a significant role for government in eco-nomic matters. In place of the state as custodian of the public interest it expounds the notion of the 'enabling state' which would perform supply-side tasks the market tended to neglect but were vital to national competitiveness. It would operate as 'the lubricant in the engine of the British economy, oiling its wheels and allowing to run faster and more smoothly' (Brown, transcript of speech, 27 September 1994). Investment in collective goods – like research and development and, especially, education and training – enlarged the overall efficiency and competitiveness of the economy but for the individual enterprise might not be rational, for costs could well outweigh benefits. For example, it might be cheaper for a firm to purchase the skilled labour trained by others rather than sink resources into training its own workforce – which may then be poached by competitors. The role of government,

'New Labour' contended, was to create a framework which discouraged this tendency to free-ride by tax measures rewarding firms that undertook training schemes and penalizing firms that did not. The accent on the state's role in education and training was given a theoretical gloss by the thesis of the 'skills revolution' which claimed that the most valuable input into the productive process was no longer capital but labour. The Conservative strategy of seeking to enlarge British share of international markets by cutting labour costs, it was argued, would fail because the key to competitive success was product quality. Product quality, in turn, was primarily contingent on the expertise of the labour force. Furthermore since the quality of labour was a crucial factor determining market share, improvements in education and training – and not enlarging demand – was the best way to tackle unemployment. Supply-side measures, by expanding outlets for British goods, would encourage firms to build up productive capacity, thereby creating more employment opportunities. Conversely, since the bulk of the jobless were the inadequately educated and trained, a skills-oriented strategy would also facilitate their entry onto the labour market.

By contending that higher public expenditure was an effective way of maintaining demand and output, Keynesian economics had helped reconcile social and economic needs. 'New Labour' doctrine severed them, returning to the pre-Keynesian notion that social spending represented a drain on the economy and could only be increased when additional economic resources were available. Public investment – embracing spending on such items as education, training and R&D – was of direct benefit to the economy so it was justifiable to finance increased levels, if need be, by borrowing. Public consumption, that is most forms of social spending, constituted a net cost to the economy and should not, therefore, be funded by borrowing. Nor was financing higher public consumption by increased taxation feasible: it would be both extremely unpopular and potentially economically injurious by eroding work incentives. Indeed, rather than viewing a high level of social expenditure as a sign of a humane society, as Crosland had averred, the accent was placed on controlling its growth – 'a long and gruelling slog' Blair declared, but essential (*The Guardian*, 23 May 1995). Since progressive taxation was ruled out for electoral and economic reasons, since further a larger tax yield from the corporate sector would only deflect investment overseas, it followed that, for 'New Labour', the politics of distributional justice was at an end.

Notes

1 Ironically the behaviour of the privatized industries provided evidence that ownership *did* matter. Thus in the electricity industry 'since privatisation the increasing profits of the regional electricity companies, the ever-growing dividends, the high executive remuneration and the . . . ability of some companies to buy back their stock demonstrates that most of the benefits of privatisation had been enjoyed by the investor'. Whilst over the five years since privatization share values have soared 300 per cent the quality of service provided to 'those of modest means or in hardship' has deteriorated (Report of official electricity consumer committees quoted in *The Guardian*, 3 May 1995).

2 Gould was a long-standing critic of the EC as well as favouring the use of devaluation as an means to restore competitiveness to British industry.

3 Labour Party NEC Report, 1989: 28.

4 NEC minutes, February 1990.

5 Gould, whose relations with Smith had been uneasy for some time, shortly after resigned from the Shadow Cabinet over policy differences. A little later, he announced his impending return to his native New Zealand as a university vice-chancellor, explaining that he no longer had confidence in the leadership's willingness to pursue full employment policies in the face of resistance from the financial establishment. His removal from the scene meant that, when Smith died shortly after, Tony Blair was spared competition from the candidate who had perhaps the best prospect of defeating him.

6 Television news made its own contribution to public bafflement by persistently confusing the issue of parliamentary selection with that of the Conference block vote, a matter, as we have seen, amicably settled.

7 Another likely factor is that the ability to affect Parliamentary selections has been, for some unions, a useful source of prestige and influence. For example, the GMB has for many years enjoyed a considerable say in selections in the Labour heartland of the north-east. Given the union's traditionally right-wing complexion (until the arrival of Edmonds) the beneficiaries had been right-wing MPs, including, ironically, two enthusiastic modernizers, Giles Radice (a former head of research for the union) and Peter Mandelson.

8 Prescott defeated Beckett to become deputy leader.

9 'They are apparently a kind of advertising manager's grouping – middle-aged, middle-opinionated, worried by job insecurity, fed up with rising taxation and declining public services. Like most admen's categories, they will probably prove evanescent' (Patrick Dunleavy, *Tribune*, 28 April 1995).

10 Unison was a recent merger of three public sector unions, NUPE, COHSE and NALGO though, as the latter was not affiliated to Labour, only the levy-payers from the first two counted towards its vote at Conference.

11 *The Guardian*'s influential columnist (and chairman of its governing trust) Hugo Young denounced the trade union block vote as 'an excrescence on democracy, the alpha and omega of political death in modern times' (*The Guardian*, 14 January 1993). Even on broadcasting news programmes reporters routinely referred to 'union barons' and took for granted that the union link was a serious impediment to Labour voting (see, for example, *Today* Programme, 21 April 1995).

12 For example, Martin Kettle, a leader writer on *The Guardian* close to Blair charged the TGWU and Unison leaders with using 'corrupt' decision-making systems . . . They stand exposed as politicians who depend upon the lack of democracy to wield political influence. Their power was based on lies' (*The Guardian*, 29 April 1995).

9 Conclusion: Labour Old and New

'It is always dangerous for a political movement to repudiate its past.'
(Barbara Castle, *Tribune*, 28 April 1995)

'Nothing could be more remote from Socialist ideals than the competitive scramble of a society which pays lip-service to equality, but too often means by it merely opportunities of becoming unequal.'
(Tawney, 1964: 187)

'Old Labour'

The novelty of 'New Labour' has been defined primarily in terms of its contrast with 'Old Labour'. To the modernizers 'Old Labour' favoured (1) a large dose of planning which, constraining the operations of the market, enhanced the role of the state in allocating resources, co-ordinating economic activity and influencing corporate decision-making; (2) a steady expansion of public ownership; and (3) the occupation by the trade unions of a key position in the governmental machine. When measured against its actual record in office, however, this portrait of 'Old Labour' appears well off the mark.

Planning and state intervention

The post-war administration was, of all Labour governments, the keenest advocate of planning and public ownership. Yet although it inherited from war-time an apparatus of controls that gave to the state a power of the economy never subsequently matched this was retained primarily to manage the severe shortages caused by the dollar gap and the payments imbalance: 'Planning, in any meaningful sense, played no prominent part in the government's economic strategy' (Morgan, 1984: 492). By the same token, far from wishing 'to impose upon industry a preconceived government' Labour sought the co-operation of business so that 'both sides of industry should feel that what the government is trying to do is to help industry help itself' (Cripps, quoted in Tomlinson, 1992: 169). As Morgan comments, the rapid growth of exports was achieved by 'a more vigorous and efficient system of incentives to private industry within the mixed economy rather than through controlled planning, whether of the corporatist Monnet type that emerged in France in the late forties, or the more thoroughgoing mechanisms of socialist direction that Labour was supposed to favour' (Morgan, 1984: 369). Indeed, it has been argued that, at a critical historical conjuncture after the war, Labour *failed* to use the physical controls bequeathed to it to establish a planning system (Hall, 1986: 66). Keynesianism eroded support for planning by ending unemployment and 'an alternative planning agenda, aimed at industrial modernization, never cohered in this period' (Tomlinson, 1992: 173).

By the early 1960s planning had returned to fashion with Labour's National Plan presented as the centrepiece of its strategy for growth and modernization. In practice, however, little distinguished it from the approach devised by the Macmillan government aside from its 'evangelical language' (Middlemass, 1990: 123). It was primarily an exercise in persuasion which rested heavily on co-operation with the private sector. 'The DEA had none of the powers of economic sanction or inducement over industry, trade, scientific policy or state infrastructure, let alone fiscal policy which a full Ministry of the Plan required' (Middlemass, 1990: 122). The Plan sought to encourage investment and the expansion of productive capability by creating confidence in the determination of the Government to raise the level of growth. But when, because of the huge payments deficit inherited from the Conservative government and persistent speculative pressure, Labour had to choose between defending sterling or going for growth, it was the latter that fell by the wayside. Faced with the alternative in July 1966 of devaluation or salvaging the pound by a heavy dose of deflation the Wilson Cabinet opted for the latter, a step which 'destroyed not only growth, but also the Plan for growth and the very *idea* of planning for growth' (Opie, 1972: 171).

In reaction to the failures of the first Wilson Government, a left-led NEC in the 1970s developed a highly *dirigiste* scheme of planning and public ownership. Profitable firms in key industrial sectors were to be nationalized, compulsory Planning Agreements signed with all major corporations and a National Enterprise Board established with the function of acquiring an extensive share portfolio in leading manufacturing companies. However the leadership never had the slightest intention of putting these policies into effect. Planning Agreements, as originally conceived, never materialized whilst the NEB ended up primarily as a convalescent home for sickly private companies. The industrial strategy which the 1974–9 Government did implement was little more than a research and diagnosis exercise which relied wholly upon the voluntary co-operation of the private sector and which had little effect.

In all three Labour governments planning was 'never . . . more than a succession of isolated efforts . . . which have been temporary expedients rather than thoroughgoing reforms' (Leruez, 1975: 279). The collaboration of the private sector was always sought and usually obtained and there were rarely any sustained attempts to influence the commercial judgement of firms. Labour Cabinets certainly rejected laissez faire and the scale of government involvement grew, but the outcome was as much to augment the capacity of business to influence public policy as to extend state control. Little interest was displayed in developing a proactive industrial strategy and instigate state-sponsored modernization schemes on the French or East Asian models.

Public ownership

How high a priority did 'Old Labour' give to the expansion of public ownership? To the 1945 Government it was, ostensibly, the socialist kernel of their programme, but in reality it was difficult to detect any particular pattern in the choice of industries to be nationalized or any coherent set of objectives. One declared aim was to endow the state with the capacity to control the economy, but no effort was made to tie the public sector to any general economic plan or industrial strategy. Bountiful compensation paid to former owners, coupled with the financial frailty of those industries transferred from the private sector,[1] prevented nationalization from acting as an instrument of redistribution. After 1948 when the manifesto pledges had been implemented there was little enthusiasm outside the left for a further extension of the public sector. Public ownership, the foremost analyst of the Attlee Government's economic programme concluded, was introduced by 'a set of rather conservative politicians whose main anxiety was to secure efficient management and give it a fairly free hand provided it followed commercial precedents' (Cairncross, 1985: 494).

The ideological ascendancy won by Keynesian social democracy in the 1950s relegated public ownership to the status of a secondary goal. It contended that equipped with Keynesian macro-economic techniques, the state now had sufficient control over economic life to ensure growth, full employment and a more equitable distribution of resources. Subsequent Labour governments did extend the public sector, but on pragmatic grounds to save jobs and industries deemed strategically important, for example because of their contribution to the balance of payments or to sustaining the local economy. Thus in the 1960s and 1970s British Leyland, the shipyards, the docks and British Aerospace were all nationalized but this was in most cases with the approval of owners keen to extricate themselves and their capital from bankrupt or languishing concerns.[2] Beyond this, neither in the 1960s nor the 1970s was nationalization a significant instrument of policy (Ponting, 1989: 273; Donoughue, 1987: 148–9).[3]

Government and the unions

The role of the unions varied considerably in the three Labour Governments. In the first, the unions performed a largely supportive function and the question of their role only became controversial during the 1964–70 Wilson administration. The need for union co-operation arose from the Government's reliance on incomes policy to improve the balance of payments and to dampen inflationary pressures. This did not lead to the enlargement of the unions' role in the policy process because the Government made no move towards establishing a corporatist structure. The blocking of *In Place of Strife* in 1969 thrust the question of union power high onto the political agenda. For the unions what was at issue was their right to operate freely without state interference; but they were slow to recognize that voluntarism was no longer tenable in an economy where economic and industrial activities were so interdependent and, in retrospect, they would have been wiser to display greater flexibility.

In the 1970s Labour sought to surmount inflationary pressures, which had now reached destructive levels, by means of the so-called Social Contract. The effect of the initial Social Contract, during the first year of the 1974–9 Labour administration, was to give to the unions more political power then they had ever before wielded. The Government kept to its side of the bargain, introducing food subsidies, health and safety legislation, and repealing the Conservative Industrial Relations Act, replacing it by laws which incorporated much of what the unions wanted such as compensation for unfair dismissal, provisions for trade union recognition and access to company information for collective bargaining purposes. For their part, the unions failed to deliver the goods and the TUC guidelines agreed as part of the Social Contract 'provided a flimsy, inadequate protection against the suicidal consequences of the illusory pay bonanza' (Taylor, 1991: 192). But one must beware of exaggeration: for many critics, Labour's industrial relations legislation provided the prime piece of evidence of its subservience to the unions. But, as a Policy Studies Institute analysis in 1978 showed, the impact of these measures was marginal. They suffered from weak enforcement and highly restrictive judicial interpretation which, for example, rendered the statutory provisions for trade union recognition more or less ineffective (Taylor, 1993: 238–9).

In July 1975, as the Treasury was battling for a statutory policy, Jack Jones played a vital part in securing union assent to the £6 pay policy. But from this point on union influence waned as the Government came under mounting pressure from more formidable actors, such as the financial markets, the IMF and the US, as well as, within the domestic policy machine, from the Treasury and the Bank of England. Union visibility remained high: this was the period of 'beer and sandwiches' (or something tastier to the palate) as senior union leaders became frequent visitors to Number 10 but, in reality, 'this gave them little positive power or influence over key economic decision-making . . . even if it increased their sense of self-importance' (Taylor, 1991: 177). But more than anything else, it was the Winter of Discontent which has left an enduring image of a Labour Government impotent in the face of brute union power. In fact, the event has been absurdly misrepresented. The (predictable) effect of the huge wave of industrial unrest – the downfall of the Labour government – was certainly not what unions wished: an act which has as its consequence the outcome which the actor *least* wants is a peculiar illustration of its power. As some Labour ministers recognized at the time, the problem was not the exercise but the abdication of union leadership – the inability of union leaders, such as Moss Evans, to do much more than passively follow events. Insofar as a single causal factor can be identified, it was the deflationary strategy – enthusiastically endorsed by the money markets, the Treasury and the Bank – which stoked up such a head of frustration and resentment that spontaneous combustion, benefiting no-one and harming many, was virtually inevitable.

'Old Labour's' Record

In the seventeen years that it occupied office, Labour accomplished much in alleviating poverty and misery, and in giving help and sustenance to groups – the old, the sick, the disabled – least capable of protecting themselves in a market economy. Its employment record appears rather more praiseworthy after the experience of the last sixteen years than it did at the time. In particular, and without exaggerating the scale of the transformation it achieved, the post-war government remains for Labour a beacon of light. Class divisions and a highly unequal distribution of wealth and status may have survived intact but it constructed a welfare state, extended social citizenship and ensured that the hardships of economic change were shared more equitably than either before or since. In comparison, the first Wilson Government was a disappointment. Notwithstanding, it did raise pensions, family allowances and supplementary benefit, and spending on social services rose from 16 per cent of national wealth to 23 per cent. However, to finance these improvements taxation as a share of the national income rose from 32 per cent to 43 per cent, though the rich paid most and the poor least (Ponting, 1989: 392). This reflected the Government's main blemish, its mediocre economic performance, due above all to its decision to opt for a deflationary economic stance.

If Wilson was a politician who knew better how to attain power than what to do with it, so Labour, in the 1960s and 1970s, was a party which wanted to conserve and improve on past achievements but had little clear idea of what to do next. Bereft of any vision of an alternative social order it became the custodian of the post-war settlement. By

1974, that settlement was under siege and increasingly the Party's main task was to protect it from forces which wished to dismantle it. Under the harshest of conditions, it even registered some gains. Despite the rise in unemployment, the poorest improved their share of their national income slightly whilst that of the rich diminished. However claims that in this period, in its impulse towards equality, 'Old Labour' imposed a crushing burden of taxation – in Gordon Brown's inimitable idiom, that it 'taxed for taxation's sake' – were mythical. 'The much-touted higher marginal rates of income tax were paid only by an extraordinarily small proportion of taxpayers' (Artis and Cobham, 1991: 275), whilst the Capital Transfer Tax, an attempt to level out a little the vastly unequal distribution of wealth, had so many loop-holes that no one who could afford an accountant paid it (Healey, 1989: 404). Amongst the rich, as one wit put it, the weight of taxation fell most heavily on those whose dislike of accountants exceeded that of the Inland Revenue.

Overall, Labour's record in implementing social democracy was poorer than comparable north European sister parties (see, for example, Esping-Andersen, 1985; Padgett and Paterson, 1991). Why? One proposition suggests that the problem lay with the unions. It holds that 'social democratic parties are more capable of altering the distribution system and maintaining growth with full employment when they are linked with powerful and centralised trade union movements'. They can thereby shift distributional pressures from the market to the state, with organized labour trading market wages for a social wage and reaping the benefits of full employment, a comprehensive and effective welfare state and legislation enhancing workers' shop floor status (Esping-Andersen and van Kersbergen, 1992: 202). The conditions specified in the proposition clearly have not obtained in Britain with its decentralized and pluralistic union structures and its strong shop steward movement engaged in sectionalized and localized bargaining. The insistence of British unions upon the virtues of free collective bargaining, differentials and leap-frogging contrasts markedly with the solidaristic ethic of their Scandinavian counterparts. For this thesis the key test case is the 1964–70 Labour Government since this was the only time that Labour occupied office during the 'golden age of social democracy' in the 1950s and 1960s. Critically, the thesis assumes that the priorities of social democratic governments are growth, full employment and distributional justice. This was not, however, the case of the 1964–70 Wilson Government which gave preference to the defence of the pound and deflation, a choice which demolished hopes for a faster rate of growth and undermined its capacity to attain its social goals.

Why? The differences in behaviour between British and Scandinavian social democracy in part flowed from distinctive features of the UK's political economy, its pronounced international orientation and the hegemony of the financial interest, the City of London. Its close institutional ties with the Bank of England gave the City a uniquely privileged position in the heart of the economic policy-making machine as the Bank operated as spokesman for the financial community. Its overriding objective was 'to sustain London's position as an international financial centre . . . its basic credo that the promotion of the City of London's financial markets is synonymous with the public interest' (Hutton, 1995: 144). The impact of the Bank–City alliance was heightened by their close working relations with the Treasury. The Treasury bestrode 'the economic policy machine like a Colossus' (Keegan and Pennant-Rea, 1979: 81). Habitually giving precedence to the interests of finance, it helped engender a macro-economic policy approach which, with its bias towards deflation and a high exchange rate, was inimical to growth.

It would be inaccurate to conclude that Labour governments faltered simply because of institutional constraints. Goals and contexts interweave in complex ways and governments help to construct their own environments by the choices they make. At certain points Labour made strategic decisions which contributed at least as much as environmental constraints to retarding its progress in implementing social democracy. Established wisdom has assumed that insofar as the Party's creed differed from 'mainstream European social democracy' it was because of adherence to planning, public ownership and union power. In reality, the most striking aspect of what we have called Labour's operational code – the principles that animated its *actual behaviour* in office – was the extent to which the leadership's thinking was steeped in a highly traditional national culture. What is sometimes misleadingly entitled the post-war 'social democratic consensus' was in reality composed of a mix in which the commitment to full employment, growth and welfare was uncomfortably superimposed upon a traditional understanding of British interests and objectives. This we have called the global mind-set. It comprised a belief in the country's status as a world power, with extensive international interests and responsibilities; a willingness to maintain high levels of overseas spending to protect them; staunch advocacy of an 'independent deterrent' to buttress Britain's aspirations to great power status; and the maintenance of the City as a leading international centre and, as corollary of this, a strong pound.

The global mind-set had a ubiquitous influence upon the Attlee Government. The extremely influential Foreign Secretary, Ernest Bevin, 'took as axiomatic the preservation of British influence in south-east Europe and the eastern Mediterranean. He was also instinctively committed . . . to a permanent military and economic involvement in the Middle East . . . ' (Morgan, 1984: 235).[4] The scanty resources lavished so abundantly on financing a girdle of overseas bases, a million troops scattered over the continents and the construction of an atom bomb drained hard currency, manpower, and valuable research and development expertise all which could have been more profitably used to modernize the country's industrial base. The status of sterling as an international currency and the financial hegemony of the City supplied the financial muscle of British imperialism in the nineteenth century and their restoration were adopted as major policy objectives almost as reflex actions with little debate. These policy decisions did much to aggravate the problems of the domestic economy, since the balance-of-payments weakness stemmed essentially from the huge outflows of sterling caused by government overseas expenditure and mass capital exports (Tomlinson, 1991).

The apotheosis of globalism, with extremely deleterious consequences for Labour, was the decision in 1951 to embark upon a rearmament programme way beyond the economy's capacities. Senior Treasury advisers and officials reassured the Cabinet that a gargantuan rearmament programme was economically feasible,[5] but it was with the stubborn determination of Gaitskell and other senior ministers to press ahead that responsibility ultimately lay. The external account swung dramatically from surplus to deficit and a 'major assault' was mounted on the productive investment capacity of industry (Morgan, 1984: 458). The upshot was that the Government, which had striven with such resolve to rebuild the country's manufacturing base, squandered '*the* golden opportunity in the entire post-war period for a sustained export-led boom . . . our best hope for the kind of post-war economic miracle enjoyed by so many western European countries' (Hennessy, 1993:

415, emphasis in the original). The effects of piling on fresh taxes and a further tightening of the consumers' belt on the imminent election was all too predictable. Not only might Labour have triumphed in 1951 – as it was it won more votes than the Tories – but it would thereby have inherited and benefited politically from its association with the more affluent age of the 1950s whose foundation it had helped to build.

Despite Britain's post-Suez diminished status, and notwithstanding Wilson's modernizing rhetoric, the global mind-set persisted during the 1964–70 Labour Government. The post-war Bretton Woods monetary regime, with its fixed but alterable exchange rates, limited capital mobility and widespread use of exchange and other forms of controls to restrain capital movements gave national governments the economic freedom they needed to implement Keynesian social democratic policies (Schor, 1992: 1–3). Yet of all countries with strong social democratic movements Britain's progress was least impressive. As we have noted the historically much more open and internationally-oriented character of the British economy, and the strength of the City–Bank of England–Treasury complex, offers part of the explanation. The global mind-set supplies much of the rest. Wilson emphasized that 'he had not come into office to preside over the destruction of Britain's world role' (Whitehead, 1985: 4). He regarded the integrity of sterling as vital to the maintenance of Britain's influence abroad: it was, in the words of one of his biographers 'the most sacred Ark of the Covenant' (Ziegler, 1993: 191). The strength of sterling and its continuation as an international currency symbolized the UK's status as an international power and was deemed indispensable for the survival of the City as a principal financial centre – in turn accepted as a vital national interest. Britain's frontiers, the Labour Prime Minister proclaimed grandly, lay on the Himalayas and for four years strenuous efforts were made 'to keep Britain's world role by maintaining virtually all the commitments in the Far East and . . . the Gulf' (Ziegler, 1993: 211; Ponting, 1989: 397).

The effect of the global mind-set extended beyond the sacrifice of growth on the alter of the sterling parity and the wasting of scarce resources. It also heightened Britain's vulnerability to the speculative activity of the currency markets. As we have seen, financial crises between 1964 and 1970 – almost irrespective of the state of the current account – were triggered off by virtually anything: an industrial strike, a Middle East war, a weakening of the dollar, a strengthening of the

Deutschmark, a nose-dive by the franc, even false rumours of ministerial resignations. It took little for short-term holders of sterling balances to flee the currency (usually on the advice of their financial managers in the City) – it was all like 'a barrel of nitroglycerine which any sudden bump, any undue heat on the international scene, was liable to set off' (Strange, 1971: 301). The price of the ceaseless effort to hold or regain the confidence of the money markets was, as the Bank of England and the Treasury constantly spelt out, restrictive fiscal and monetary policies. Deflation, in turn, by discouraging investment, ensured that efforts to improve productivity, competitiveness and growth would be enfeebled and pushed up unemployment. The economy was stunted 'as a direct consequence of policies which gave priority to the preservation of sterling as an international currency and to the defence of particular exchange rates, and put these goals before the promotion of economic growth' (Strange, 1971: 300).

The more the Labour Government proceeded down this path, the more it found its options were foreclosed, its freedom of manoeuvre narrowed, the more indeed it was enmeshed in the consequences of its own choices from which ultimately it appeared almost impossible to escape. It was determined to sustain the double burden of sterling and the global role but an ailing pound could only be propped up with American help. The Johnson Administration was willing to help – at a price: devaluation must be avoided and deflation imposed, statutory wage restraint must be introduced, and the UK's global military commitments maintained (Ponting, 1989: 50–3; Ziegler, 1993: 205).[6] Statutory pay policy in the service of deflation alienated the unions and when inflation mounted, they were less prepared to co-operate. The abandonment of growth meant that Labour's social programmes had to be pruned – disappointing its supporters – whilst those that remained could only be financed by heavier taxation. Higher taxes on wage-earners in turn help set off a tax-wage spiral igniting stronger inflationary pressures which, lacking union backing, the Government was unable to curb. Eventually, it was forced to devalue and to begin the retreat East of Suez, but by then its course was irrevocably set and all hope of accelerated economic expansion squandered.

By Labour's return to office in 1974, the scale of Britain's global commitments had shrunken considerably, but sterling remained the world's second reserve currency and, indeed, received a new lease of life when, after the hefty oil price rise in 1973, short-term funds ('hot money') from oil-rich states poured into the London financial markets. The result was that the pound remained exceedingly susceptible to capital movements since 'changes of sentiment in the foreign exchange markets were often greatly exaggerated by the movement of reserves into or out of Britain' with currency rates determined by 'the faceless men who managed the growing atomic cloud of footloose funds' on the Eurocurrency markets (Healey, 1989: 411, 412). The retreat from Keynesian social democracy, symbolized by the IMF Loan, was not, we have suggested, the outcome of its own endemic flaws and contradictions but of the new constellation of power, formed by the money markets, the US and its ally the IMF and the world official financial establishments. But resistance was weakened not only by the belief held by the Bank of England and by the Treasury that public spending was out of control and the government would benefit from the iron discipline of the IMF – but by the fact that these sentiments were shared within the Cabinet.

From 'Old Labour' to 'New Labour'

This leaves us with a puzzle: why did the modernizers paint a portrait of their own Party in which accuracy was sacrificed not to enhance but to belittle the original? The answer was that the past was recreated to serve the present's strategic needs. To the modernizers the central problem was the inability of the Party – 'Old Labour' – to obtain the trust and confidence of the public. The term 'New Labour' was 'deliberately designed to distance the party from its past' (*Independent*, leader, 22 July 1995). To maximize the public impact of the new name, the contrast with the old had to be as stark as possible and to make sense to voters long accustomed to consume from the tabloid press caricatured images of past Labour governments and of the Party itself. It benefited the strategic purposes of the modernizers to engage in pre-emptive auto-strikes, acknowledging the truth of much of the tabloid version and then demonstrating that 'New Labour' had learnt its lessons and wiped the slate clean.

The very vocabulary employed – 'Old Labour' and 'New Labour', modernizers and traditionalists – was an essential part of the modernizing project. These concepts were in effect stereotypes, that is simplified and value-loaded mental images designed to project a particular view of reality and like most stereotypes they were misleading, squeezing and distorting complex reality by neatly parcelling up people into crude categories which did little justice to the diversity of views within the Party. As such, they were highly successful since they were quickly taken up by the media, becoming 'an effortless part of our vocabulary' (*Independent*, leader, 22 July 1995) and used to frame their reporting of Labour's internal affairs. Their value to the modernizers was that they asserted the superiority of the modernizing viewpoint by definitional fiat – new is better than old, being modern better than being traditional – relieving them of the more onerous task of demonstrating the validity of their ideas by the more conventional means of reasoning and substantiation.

What 'modernizing' actually meant was never defined but it can perhaps be best understood in terms of two concepts: a *detachment* from Labour's established values and objects and an *accommodation* with established institutions and modes of thought. In this sense, by the mid-1990s Labour had been thoroughly 'modernized'. Keynesian social democracy has been displaced as its ruling creed by a more market-oriented one which accepts much of the new institutional landscape created since 1979. The old objectives of full employment, equality and social justice have either been abandoned or diluted. How can we account for the modernizers' success? One can distinguish between those factors which enhanced the capacity of the leadership to engineer or removed hindrance to change, primarily matters of internal party politics and organization; and those, primarily external, factors which operated as pressures upon the Party to adapt to altered environmental conditions.

Cleavage patterns

Leadership capacity to secure change varies inversely with the ability of the rank and file to exert countervailing power. This, in turn, is a function of the shape of the internal cleavage system. All large parties will contain differences of interests and viewpoints. Where differences follow sharply-delineated lines, and where they are deep, bipolar and cumulative, and where, finally, they envelop the core principles of a party, then the potential for mass resistance to central decision-making exists. These conditions were present in the Labour Party from the mid-1970s to the mid-1980s and greatly hampered the leadership: as long as it faced a more or less united and organized left, its innovating capacity was limited. From the mid-1980s polarization began to unravel, cleavage patterns became more complex, lines of demarcation increasingly cut across each other, and attachment to factional groupings abated. The so-called 'realignment of the left' set in motion a process of fragmentation as the old 'Bennite' coalition of 1979–83 splintered into two increasingly hostile segments, the hard and the soft left. The soft left moved steadily towards a rapprochement with the leadership and their eventual inclusion into the governing coalition furnished Kinnock with overwhelming majorities in the PLP, the Shadow Cabinet and the NEC. However, the Party's steady shift to the right in time rendered them dispensable and those of their members who sought too vigorously to arrest the modernizing drive usually suffered demotion. Whilst their representatives on the frontbench occasionally chafed about the drift to the right, which accelerated under Blair, they lacked the means and – reluctant to rock the boat – perhaps the will to reverse it.[7]

At the same time, the hard left were increasingly marginalized: electoral defeats undermined the case for radical policies whilst their abrasive and often dogmatic style alienated support. The defeat of the miners' strike was an especially severe setback discrediting the belief that the Government could be brought down, or at least dealt a disabling blow, by extra-parliamentary mobilization and confrontation. The introduction of OMOV further undermined their influence and by 1990 they no longer had the capacity to mobilize effective rank and file protest against the leadership. The highly pluralistic party with an institutionalized dispersal of powers and uncertain central authority which characterized Labour from the late 1960s to the mid-1980s had been transformed into a tightly controlled one. This was the indispensable condition for the leadership's drive to accomplish the 'modernization' of the Party's doctrine.

Party culture

Whatever the wider aims of a party, none can be effectively realized without obtaining access to government. In the 1970s and early 1980s an intense suspicion of leaders had suffused Labour's internal culture. The shock of repeated electoral defeat persuaded many that 'the betrayal theory' had inflicted serious damage on the party by engendering 'a constant climate of suspicion and grievance . . . which makes it difficult for the Labour Party to maintain the unity and discipline rightly expected of a party seeking office' (Bryan Gould, *The Guardian*, 14 June 1988). Within the rank and file there developed a greater disposition to acknowledge the functional importance of leadership, a much enhanced sensitivity to the effects of their behaviour on Labour's image and a greater appreciation of the need (amidst an antagonistic and relentlessly probing press) for Party unity. Above all, a deep yearning to rid Britain of a government which had created mass unemployment, hugely widened social and economic inequalities and was steadily taking apart the welfare state fed a growing disposition to compromise and swallow unpalatable leadership decisions if this facilitated victory at the polls. This helped produce a reawakening of a sense of common purpose, a feeling once more that all Party members, whatever their views, were bound up in a common political enterprise, which inhibited challenges to the leadership.

A loss of ideological self-confidence has also helped render the rank and file more tractable. The Webbs' phrase 'the inevitability of gradualness' summed up the belief that at one time pervaded the Party, namely that society was moving ineluctably towards a more collectivist social order. In the second half of the 1970s, the progressive consensus crumbled with a paradigm shift from Keynesianism and welfare politics to neo-liberalism. 'A broad convergence in the acceptance of the major tenets of the new dominant paradigm was discernible across Western Europe' reflected in the adoption of policies 'rooted in individual choice, market-driven competition, targeting and private initiative' (Muller and Wright, 1994: 2). Coupled with the ideological resurgence of laissez faire individualism was the decline and then sudden and dramatic collapse of the Communist world in Europe. The countries of the former Soviet bloc all set about constructing free-market economies, loudly proclaimed to be the only feasible way of organizing economic life.

This message was highly unpalatable to those on the left of the Labour Party for whom socialism meant the replacement of the market economy by a fully planned and publicly-owned system. The powerful case (argued by market socialists as well as centrists and right-wingers) that the market had great strengths as well as admitted flaws, and that there were dangers of bureaucratization, lack of flexibility and limitation of consumer choice inherent in publicly-owned industries, shook the confidence of many socialists in traditional tenets of belief and hence facilitated the leadership's modernization drive.

The union connection

Until recently the unions commanded 90 per cent (at present 70 per cent) of the votes at the Party Conference, elected two-thirds of the members of the National Executive Committee, sponsored a large proportion of the PLP and furnished the bulk of Party funds. On the surface, this appeared to give the unions an effective veto over change, but in practice, this was rarely the case. The term 'the unions' is itself no more than a convenient shorthand. The union movement has very rarely acted as a homogeneous force. Unions have been divided in a multitude of ways – between left and right, public and private sector, craft workers and the semi- and unskilled. Further, and most crucially, the norms and conventions of the labour movement have inhibited union leaders from utilizing their structurally-advantaged position within the Party's organization to pressurize the Labour leadership (Minkin, 1991: 27–47). The precise extent to which the union stake in the Party has constrained the leadership has varied. Traditionally, on matters which impinged upon their core functions, such as labour law and pay policy, unions have stalled leadership initiatives – at various intervals there were major and highly publicized clashes over these issues. However, the relentless organizational decline of trade unionism gradually eroded its willingness to challenge the leadership. The return of mass unemployment, together with the imposition by the Conservatives of extremely restrictive labour laws, have led to a drastic fall in union membership, a sharp deterioration in union finances and organizational resources, a decline in morale and self-confidence, and the development of a more defensive mentality. The balance of mutual dependence between the unions and the Party altered as the former increasingly came to vest their hopes for a revival of their influence and the amelioration of the conditions of their members on the return of a Labour Government. The outcome was that even on the crucial issue of labour law, the unions who had previously dug in their heels became increasingly amenable.

Party competition

The sheer scale of the electoral collapse of 1983 imparted a powerful impetus to the professionalization of the Party's campaigning and com-munications. This involved the extensive use of modern communications methods such as opinion research, the pre-testing of language and slo-gans, the use of audio-visual techniques, rigorous image management, the projection of key messages through the mass media, and the consequent reliance on communications professionals (organized in the Shadow Communications Agency) to undertake these tasks (Shaw, 1994).

This process facilitated modernization in two ways. Firstly, opinion researchers were charged with identifying hindrances to Labour voting, market testing policy options and defining the strategic agenda. Their recommendations set the parameters of policy choice and eased the task of weeding out those policy commitments, inserted by the left, which were judged to be vote-losers, including planning, public ownership and the non-nuclear defence policy. Secondly, since the distribution of power in a voluntary organization varies according to the ability to command resources, supply appropriate specialized skills and undertake tasks vital to its welfare, professionalization had the effect of reducing the functional importance of Labour's constituency activists whilst elevating that of the opinion pollsters, advertising executives, public relations specialists and associated party officials (grouped together between 1986 and 1992 in the Shadow Communications Agency) whose primary allegiance was to the parliamentary leadership.[8] The competitive appeal of both the SDP–Liberal Alliance and of Thatcherite Conservatism operated more directly to pull Labour to the right. The success of the SDP in siphoning off millions of voters convinced Labour strategists that to fend off its challenge the Party had to reposition itself in the middle-ground.

The perceived need to accept many of the Conservatives' institutional innovations – privatization, tight regulation of the unions, lower income tax and so forth – exerted an even stronger magnetic pull to the right. A rationale for this strategy was furnished by opinion research findings which indicated dwindling sympathy for collectivist ideas and values, lack of trust in Labour and faith in its ability to deliver its promises, anxiety about its reputation as a 'tax and spend' party and fear of extremism. The inferences drawn by Party strategists were that Labour should cultivate an image of moderation and respon-sibility, abandon 'old-fashioned' collectivist policies and values, and accommodate to those elements of the Thatcherite revolution that ran with the popular grain (for a critical discussion, see Shaw, 1994).

The global economic environment

Crosland had, in 1956, argued that the advent of Keynesian techniques meant that the state now possessed the means to control capital (Crosland, 1964). However, he failed to appreciate the extent to which the capacity of government to determine economic and social policy rested upon its ability to insulate the economy from unfavourable international financial pressures. During the immediate post-war decades the availability of exchange and other forms of controls, coupled with the relative stability of the Bretton Woods system, created the space in which governments could pursue the Keynesian social democratic programme of growth, full employment and social welfare. However a combination of changes from the late 1960s onwards, such as the expansion of the Eurodollar market, the breakdown of Bretton Woods, the huge growth in speculative currency flows and the removal of exchange and other capital controls, massively increased the power of international financial markets. By 1988, the amount of money crossing exchanges in pursuit of speculative profit was fifty times more than was needed to finance world trade (Healey, 1987: 413). Labour's policy-makers were acutely aware of the fact that the financial markets were relentlessly squeezing their room for manoeuvre. In Healey's words, 'the markets in the end decide what is the appropriate level of interest rates, whatever the central bank wants to do, and the markets decide what is the value of your currency' (quoted in Whitehead, 1985: 187). Keynesianism in one country appeared no longer to be a feasible policy option: 'any demand increase by extra government borrowing in any state with open capital borders and markets partly leaks abroad whilst incurring risk that capital markets take fright, sell the currency and force up short-term interest rates – in which case the reflationary action becomes self-defeating' (Will Hutton, *The Guardian*, 27 June 1994).

To Keynesians the task has been to devise forms of international co-operation to tame the markets but this was not Labour's response. The markets needed to be reassured, not challenged - hence the so-called 'prawn cocktail offensive' of 1990–1 as John Smith and other frontbenchers strove to alleviate the financial institutions' worries about Labour's intentions. The leadership's decision to advocate membership of the ERM at the existing sterling parity despite its adverse effects on employment – as Bryan Gould and other soft left critics pointed out at the time – was intended in part to convince the City that Labour could now be trusted to behave with 'financial rectitude'. More broadly, the adoption of impeccably orthodox monetary and fiscal stances and the displacement of full employment by low inflation as the foremost objective of Labour's economic strategy were designed to reassure the markets. Fear of following policies that could precipitate a loss of confidence in the markets and a currency crisis has now emerged as perhaps the most important single factor shaping policy determination by the Labour Party in the crucial economic arena.

The Dilemmas of 'New Labour'

For more than a generation, 'Old Labour' had pursued, with varying degrees of success, the politics of distributional justice. This entailed a commitment to full employment, to a more extensive social citizenship through the provision of improved public services and welfare benefits, and to a more equitable distribution of income and wealth. 'New Labour', too, aspires – in the words of the new Clause IV – to 'a community in which power, wealth and opportunity are in the hands of the many not the few'. The challenge here facing an incoming Labour government will be awesome. Since 1979 inequality has been growing at a more rapid pace than in any comparable country in western Europe. By the mid-1990s the poorest 20–30 per cent of the population had experienced no improvement in their standard of living since 1979 and the proportion of those earning less than half the average income had trebled. The top 10 per cent possessed 27 per cent of the share of income and no less than 49 per cent of the share of wealth (that is including property, shares and savings) whilst the bottom 50 per cent held 25 per cent of overall income and only 8 per cent of wealth (Rowntree Foundation Inquiry into Income and Wealth, quoted in *The Guardian*, 10 February 1995, 13 February 1995). According to a report by the Institute of Fiscal Studies the gulf between the highest and lowest paid had become wider than at any time this century (*The Guardian*, 30 June 1994). There were a range of reasons for this including the skewed growth of remuneration, with those on highest salaries making the largest advances and those at the bottom of the ladder making none at all; privatization where the gains from sales of under-priced shares and rising capital values were in direct proportion to wealth at the cost of draining the Treasury;[9] the growth of unemployment, low wage and part-time jobs and attendant social deprivation; reductions in the value of benefits and, not least, a switch to a much more regressive tax system. Cuts in income tax and the multiplication of loopholes and allowances in inheritance and corporation taxes had greatly benefited higher income groups whilst Britain had one of the world's lowest levels of taxation on land and inherited wealth (*The Guardian*, 8 August 1994). Conversely, higher National Insurance Contributions and VAT rates plus the extension of VAT to fuel bore particularly heavily on those at the bottom of the ladder.

How does 'New Labour' propose to tackle this and promote a fairer distribution of opportunities and resources? After what was seen as the election-losing tax proposals in Smith's 'shadow budget' the modernizers became convinced that a dramatic break must be made with the 'tax, spend and borrow' practices of the past. Any further increase in the tax burden of those on middle incomes would be bitterly resented and was therefore ruled out whilst a more steeply progressive personal tax regime would reduce incentives. Although many of the biggest firms operating in Britain now pay little tax (*The Guardian*, 24 May 1993) any appreciable expansion of corporate tax levies – 'New Labour' argues – would be counter-productive either because profits would be squeezed, investment suffer and competitiveness undermined or because it would provoke a flight of capital seeking more profitable outlets. This left only the 'undeserving rich' as candidates for higher taxes and these were very narrowly defined as people who exploited loopholes and engaged in tax avoidance (Gordon Brown, *On the Record*, 2 October 1994; *Today* Programme 3 October 1994).

The unwillingness to consider any substantial appreciation of direct taxation on higher income groups, or any fiscal measures to make inroads into accumulated and inherited wealth, means that an incoming Labour government would not reverse the regressive tax regime established by the Conservative. Given that, also, little in practice could be done to control private sector remuneration practices and, most crucial of all, capital accumulation would be left primarily in private hands, it is difficult to envisage any alteration of the existing massive inequalities in the distribution of income and wealth. The corollary is that any significant expansion of social programmes will have to await higher economic growth. In theory higher economic growth will generate fuller tax revenues and reduce the burden of welfare payments caused by heavy unemployment and consequent privations and social decay. In practice, 'New Labour's' commitment to low inflation and fiscal orthodoxy means that sustained growth depends on the capacity of supply-side reforms to boost economic performance. Even if the rather implausible 'skills revolution' thesis is correct and the consequences of the enhancement of the quality of labour were as potent as claimed, a training-oriented supply-side policy would take time to come to fruition and much will still depend on the willingness, notably lacking in the past, of business to step-up investment.[10] Yet, at the same time, Labour has constantly upbraided the Government for starving the public services of money, for failing to fund teachers' pay awards and for hospital closures. However studiously Party spokesmen might refrain from making spending pledges, expectations have inevitably been raised that an incoming Labour Government would provide at least some of the resources which the Tories have withheld. This means that a Labour cabinet will be caught in a pincer – between mass pressure for improvements in health, education and other services, and a macro-economic policy rigidly limiting the scope for expenditure increases. Balancing the opposing pressures for fiscal and monetary 'responsibility' and the relief of cash-starved public services without incurring massive disillusion will be a Herculean task.

An incoming Labour government will also be expected to make sizeable inroads in the level of unemployment. However, given the priority the Party now assigns to combatting inflation by means of fiscal and monetary orthodoxy, given, further, its determination to reassure the financial markets it is very difficult to see how, in practice, it can attain this objective. 'New Labour's' belief that supply-side policies can be relied upon to bite deeply into the jobless totals is unconvincing. It is doubtful whether firms will risk expanding capacity unless they feel there is a good prospect of a matching level of demand materializing. In office 'New Labour' is likely to land itself in a Catch-22 situation, where it (or the Bank of England) will rein back demand for fear of capacity limitations leading to inflation but firms are afraid to expand capacity because demand prospects do not justify it (John Grieve Smith, *The Guardian*, 12 June 1995). The willingness of 'New Labour' to contemplate giving the Bank greater control over interest rates in fact casts doubt about the strength of its commitment to anything approaching a return to full employment (the following argument is drawn from E. Eshag 'Putting the Old Lady in Monetarist Jail', *The Guardian*, 28 October 1994). Given that the level of rates affects the management of the economy as a whole, given too that the Bank 'is openly and firmly committed to . . . orthodox monetarist and laissez-faire doctrines', 'New Labour' appears to be signalling that it is prepared to endorse the Bank's order of priorities, in which full employment comes a long way behind price stability.

A Conservative government prepared to preside over high levels of unemployment may be tolerated by those upon whose support it relies to stay in power, because it is not *expected* to give priority to the pursuit of full employment. With Labour, it will be different – expectations *will* be high that it will make substantial progress in cutting the jobless queues, not least because it has expended so much effort over the years in lacerating the Tories for failing to do so. The endeavour to end the blight of mass unemployment is so inextricably a part of the *raison d'etre* of the Labour Party, so much part of its history, ethos and traditions, that abandoning it is likely to provoke widespread resentment and disenchantment. The corollaries are equally grim. Persisting unemployment on the present scale will continue to soak up huge financial resources because of the sheer cost of unemployment benefits and all the other forms of social assistance needed to relieve the poverty, crime and dislocation that joblessness causes. Labour will confront a fiscal crisis which will present it with the same unpalatable alternatives as the present Government. But if it were to adopt the same response – reducing the amount and coverage of benefits – it will precipitate the type of rebellion within its constituency that the Conservatives need never fear.

For Keynesian social democracy, as Gaitskell once explained, the goal of extending opportunity was of little value if this meant no more than a state in 'which all start on the same line and proceed through life racing against each other to amass as much wealth as possible' (Gaitskell, 1956: 3). Socialism, Crosland had claimed, was ultimately about equality and it was this principle, however inconsistently applied, which has in the last half-century most distinguished Labour from its opponents. For the modernizers, however, equality is an outdated concept with (it is alleged) its connotations of levelling down and dull uniformity. The majority of the population aspire to improve their standard of living and acquire the means to advance themselves and it is these aspirations that Labour must show that it shares. It must unequivocally affirm that its real objective is enhancing individual freedom by extending opportunities (Radice, 1992: 17). Yet freedom, as a contemporary Keynesian social democrat has argued, is only effective to the extent that people have the resources to make real choices and this requires a substantial degree of redistribution (Hattersley, 1987). Or, as a socialist of more traditional stripe observed, the existence of opportunities to rise depends 'not only upon an open road, but upon an equal start' (Tawney, 1952: 106). The more liberal-oriented approach embraced by the modernizers has, in contrast, disconnected the concepts of freedom and opportunity from any egalitarian commitment. Indeed, modernizers have made it plain that they regard steep gradations in pay as wholly acceptable in companies operating in a competitive market[11] – Gordon Brown's strictures against huge salaries and bonuses have been reserved for privatized monopolies. 'New Labour' is, in effect, embracing the American vision of an economically and socially mobile society where everyone has the opportunity to procure for themselves the place in the social and economic hierarchy which their energy and talents merit.

Perhaps sensing a vacuum, modernizers have attempted to add communitarian themes to the individualistic ones. Individuals, it is argued, are socially interdependent and it is only within a strong and cohesive community that they can develop their talents to the full (Blair, 1994: 4). The growth of crime, drug abuse and random violence flowed from the decay of the sentiments of mutual obligation and social responsibility (Tony Blair, quoted in *The Guardian*, 23 March 1995). But what has been interpreted as a return to ethical socialism in reality reflects the tendency of 'New Labour' to accommodate to established modes of thought.[12] The ethical socialist espousal of community arose as a protest against the acquisitive and narrowly materialist spirit of the market. It embraced 'a desire to replace competitive social relations by fellowship and social solidarity and the motive of personal profit by a more altruistic and other-regarding motive' (Crosland, 1956: 90). It sought the creation of social and economic arrangements that institutionalized and strengthened the ties of mutual and reciprocal obligation and fellow feeling. For ethical socialism, the natural impulse of the market and economic individualism was to eat away at the bonds of community and mutual responsibility, to reduce all human relationships to the narrow calculation of the cash nexus, to treat people not as ends in themselves but as means for the furtherance of corporate gain. 'New Labour' thinking, in contrast, sees no link between the dynamics of the economic system and the enfeeblement of community and social solidarity: the new Clause IV waxes enthusiastic about 'the enterprise of the market and the rigour of competition'. In the ethical socialist tradition, collective organization can embody and sustain the spirit of public service and social solidarity: the classic example being the National Health Service. 'New Labour', in contrast, sees no intrinsic value in collective institutions: 'the only valid argument for community action is to enable individuals to achieve what they are unable to achieve themselves' (Radice, 1992: 15). Like economic liberalism, it places the individual at the centre of its moral universe, regards the ownership of economic property as a right no longer to be queried and treats the ability to scale the social heights as a mark of virtue and social esteem. How the new institutional order of the resurgent market, with its widening social disparities, its expanding underclass, its endemic sense of insecurity, frustration and alienation can be reconciled with a stronger community is a question 'New Labour' has yet to address.

The Conservative's massive loss of credibility after 1992 as they heaped-on taxes after claiming that only Labour would do so, and as public discontent welled up over cut-backs in education, the commercialization of the NHS and many other discontents, sent millions searching for another political home. Tony Blair, for his part, soon demonstrated remarkable ability as a communicator and helped push his Party's lead in the polls in 1995 to dizzying heights. His strategy of dispelling the fears of floating voters and convincing them that Labour was a safe boat upon which to clamber appeared to be succeeding. But this has been purchased at a price. 'Behind the brilliant façade' observed a journalist generally sympathetic to the modernizers, 'is a party riddled with self-doubt' (M. Kettle, *The Guardian*, 22 July 1995). 'Being without clear convictions as to its own meaning and purpose,' Tawney once wrote of Labour, deprives it 'of the dynamic which only convictions supply' (Lukes, 1984: 271).

230   *Conclusion: Labour Old and New*

Notes

1 The utilities like gas and electricity were already largely publicly (municipally) owned.
2 There were occasional exceptions, as with the establishment of the British
   National Oil Corporation which was designed to give the state a stake in
   North Sea oil.
3 Nor was the performance of the nationalized sector as poor as has often
   been represented. Thus between 1974 and 1979 gas and telecommunications
   showed a very large rise in productivity and output. The record of
   productivity growth in the transport and fuel sectors bore comparison
   both with private manufacturing in Britain and the same sectors in the
   US. Indeed, a key difference between the private and public sectors was
   that the former devoted considerable resources to marketing their products
   and associating their company name with qualities such as reliability and
   efficiency whilst the latter did not (Millward, 1991: 147, 153–4).
4 'Within twenty-four hours' of being appointed to succeed the mortally sick
   Bevin, Morrison asked for a life of Palmerston which he 'ostentatiously'
   carried around with him 'for weeks afterwards' (Donoughue and Jones,
   1973: 510).
5 One of the first acts of the Churchill Conservative administration was to
   scale it down. As the new Premier provocatively put it, 'the member for
   Ebbw Vale [Bevan]' happened to be right.
6 Another condition was diplomatic support for the deepening US engage-
   ment in Vietnam. Wilson was also under pressure to dispatch troops to
   Vietnam but he drew the line here.
7 'I just couldn't stand another five years in opposition,' one frontbencher
   confessed. 'I've done it all before – I've put down my Early Day Motions,
   mounted my campaigns, answered my letters. I know there must be more
   to politics than this' (*Independent on Sunday*, 28 May 1995).
8 This effect rested on the assumption that grass-roots electioneering is
   of marginal significance – an assumption that recent research has shown
   to be invalid (see, for example, Denver and Hands, 1993; Seyd and
   Whitely, 1992.
9 According to Bill Robinson, formerly Norman Lamont's economic adviser,
   since 1985/6 the loss to the exchequer in non-tax revenues resulting from
   of the privatization of electricity, gas, water was equivalent to no less
   than 2 per cent of GDP (Will Hutton, *The Guardian*, 29 November
   1993).
10 According to Andrew Dilnot of the Institute of Fiscal Studies such a
   strategy would take a considerable time to have an effect, as well as being

more costly than Labour appears to anticipate (interview, *On the Record*, BBC 1, 10 June 1995).

11 He 'welcomed high rewards for "excellence" and declined to criticise the 150 per cent pay increase awarded to . . . the chairman of Ford UK, which has taken his salary to £347,453' (*The Guardian*, 21 June 1995).

12 Economic and social policy should be designed to provide opportunities but equally a Labour Government should be prepared to take 'tough measures to ensure that the chances that are given are taken up' (Blair, 1993: 7).

Bibliography

Addison, P. 1977 *The Road to 1945: British Politics and the Second World War*. London, Quartet Books.

Aldcroft, Derek H. 1986 *The British Economy, Vol. 1. The Years of Turmoil 1920–1951*. Brighton, Wheatsheaf.

Allsopp, C. 1991 'Macroeconomic Policy; Design and Performance' in Artis and Cobham 1991.

Artis, M. 1972 'Fiscal Policies for Stabilisation' in Beckerman (ed.) 1972.

Artis, M. and Cobham, D. (eds) 1991 *Labour's Economic Policies 1974–79*. Manchester, Manchester University Press.

Bain, G., Coates, D. and Ellis, V. 1973 *Social Stratification and Trade Unionism*. London, Heinemann.

Banuri, T. and Schor, J. 1992 (eds) *Financial Openness and National Autonomy*. Oxford, Clarendon Press.

Barnes, D. and Reid, E. 1980 Governments and Trade Unions: the British experience, 1964–79. London, Heinemann.

Barnett, Joel 1982 *Inside the Treasury*. London, Deutsch.

Beckerman, W. (ed.) 1972 *The Labour Government's Economic Record*. London, Duckworth.

Beckerman, W. 'Objectives and Performance: an Overall View' in Beckerman (ed.) 1972.

Beer, S. H. 1965 *Modern British Politics*. London, Faber and Faber.

Beer, S. 1982 *Britain Against Itself*. London, Faber.

Benn Tony 1987 *Out of the Wilderness. Diaries 1963–68*. London, Hutchinson.

—— 1988 *Office without Power. Diaries 1968–72*. London, Hutchinson.

—— 1989 *Against the Tide. Diaries 1973–6*. London, Hutchinson.

—— 1990 *Conflict of Interest: Diaries 1977–80*. London, Hutchinson.

—— 1992 *The End of an Era. Diaries 1980–1990*. London, Hutchinson.

Blackerby, F. T. 1978 *British Economic Policy 1960–74*. Cambridge, Cambridge University Press.

Blair, Tony 1994 *Socialism*. London, Fabian Society.

Bosanquet, N. and Townsend, P. 1980 *Labour and Equality*. London, Heinemann.

Brooke, S. 1992 *Labour's War: the Labour Party during the Second World War*. Oxford, Clarendon Press.

Bulmer, M. 1975 *Working Class Images of Society*. London, Routledge and Kegan Paul.

Burk, K. and Cairncross, Alec, Sir 1992. *'Goodbye, Great Britain': the 1976 IMF crisis*. New Haven, Yale University Press.

Butler, D. and Stokes, D. 1974 *Political Change in Britain*. London, Macmillan.

Butler, D. and Kavanagh, D. 1992 *The British General Election of 1992*. London, Macmillan.

Byrd, P. 1984 *Social Democracy and Defence*. London British Atlantic Publications.

Cairncross, Alec, Sir 1985. *Years of Recovery: British Economic Policy 1945–51*. London, Methuen.

—— 1989 *The Robert Hall Diaries 1947–53*. London, Unwin Hyman.

Callaghan, James 1987 *Time and Chance*. London, Fontana.

—— 1990 *Socialism in Britain*. Oxford, Blackwell.

Castle, Barbara 1980 *The Castle Diaries, 1974–1976*. London, Weidenfeld and Nicolson.

—— 1984 *The Castle Diaries, 1964–1970*. London, Weidenfeld and Nicolson.

—— 1993 *Fighting all the Way*. London, Macmillan.

Castles, F., Lehner, F. and Schmidt, M. (eds) 1988 *Managing Mixed Economies*. New York, de Gruyter.

Caves, R. E. et al. 1968 *Britain's Economic Prospects*. London, Allen and Unwin.

Caves, R. E. and Kraus, L. B. (eds) 1980 *Britain's Economic Performance*. Washington, D.C., Brookings Institution.

Chick, M. 1991 'Competition, Competitiveness and Nationalisation, 1945–51' in Jones and Kirby 1991.

Coakley, Jerry and Harris, Laurence 1983 *The City of Capital: London's role as a Financial Centre*. Oxford, Blackwell.

Coates, David 1975 *The Labour Party and the Struggle for Socialism*. London, Cambridge University Press.

—— 1980 *Labour in Power?* London, Longman.

Coates, Ken (ed.) 1980 *What Went Wrong*. Nottingham, Spokesman.

Cooper, R. 1968 'The Balance of Payments' in Caves 1968.

Coopey, R., Fielding, S., and Tiratsoo, N. 1993 *The Wilson Government 1964–70*. London, Pinter.

Cousins, J. and Brown, R. 1975 'Patterns of Paradox: Shipbuilding Workers' Image of Society' in M. Bulmer 1975.

Crafts, N. F. R. and Woodward, N. (eds) 1991 *The British Economy since 1945*. Oxford, Clarendon Press.

Craig, F. W. S. 1982 *Conservative & Labour Party Conferences 1945–80*. Chichester, Parliamentary Research Services.

—— (ed.) 1975 *British General Election Manifestos, 1900–1974*. London, Macmillan.

—— (ed.) 1990 *British General Election Manifestos, 1959–1987.* Aldershot, Dartmouth Publishing Company.

Crosland, Susan 1982 *Tony Crosland.* London, Cape.

Crosland, Tony 1964 *The Future of Socialism.* London, Cape.

—— 1974 *Socialism Now.* London, Cape.

Crossman, Richard 1963 *Introduction to Bagehot's The English Constitution.* London, Fontana.

Crossman, Richard 1975 *The Diaries of a Cabinet Minister. Vol. I 1964–66.* London, Hamilton Cape.

—— 1975 *The Diaries of a Cabinet Minister. Vol. II 1966–68.* London, Hamilton Cape.

—— 1977 *The Diaries of a Cabinet Minister. Vol. III 1968–70.* London, Hamilton Cape.

Cunningham, O. 1993 '"From the Ground Up?" The Labour Government and Economic Planning' in Fryth 1993.

Dalton, Hugh 1962 *High Tide and After.* London, Muller.

Denver, D. and Hands, G. 1993 'Measuring the Intensity and Effectiveness of Consistuency Campaigning in the 1992 British General Election' in Denver, Norris, Broughton and Rallings (eds) 1993.

Denver, D., Norris, P., Broughton, D. and Rallings, C. (eds) 1993 *British Elections and Parties Yearbook 1993.* Hemel Hempstead, Harvester Wheatsheaf.

Donoughue, Bernard 1987 *Prime Minister: the conduct of policy under Harold Wilson and James Callaghan.* London, Cape.

Donaghue, B. and Jones, B. W. 1973 *Herbert Morrison: Portrait of a Politician.* London, Weidenfeld.

Drucker, H. 1979 *Doctrine and Ethos in the Labour Party.* London, Allen and Unwin.

Durbin, E. 1985 *New Jerusalems.* London, Routledge.

Duverger, M. 1964 *Political Parties.* London, Methuen.

Elbaum, B. and Lazonick, W. 1986 *The Decline of the British Economy.* Oxford, Clarendon Press.

Elliott, G. 1993 *Labourism and the English Genius.* London, Verso.

Ellison, Nicholas 1994 *Egalitarian Thought and Labour Politics: Retreating Visions.* London, Routledge.

Epstein, Leon 1980 *Political Parties in Western Democracies.* London, Transaction Publishers.

Esping-Andersen, G. 1985 *Politics Against Markets.* Princeton, NJ, Princeton University Press.

Feinstein, C. H. (ed.) 1982 *The Managed Economy: essays in British economic policy and performance since 1929.* Oxford, Oxford University Press.

Floud and McCloskey, D. 1994 *The Economic History of Britain Since 1700: 1939–1992.* Cambridge, Cambridge University Press.

Foot, Michael 1975 *Aneurin Bevan 1945–1960*. St. Albans, Paladin.

Foote, G. 1984 *The Labour Party's Political Thought*. London, Croom Helm.

Foster, J. 1993 'Labour, Keynesianism and Welfare State' in Fryth 1993.

Freedman, L. 1980 *Britain and Nuclear Weapons*. London, Macmillan.

Fyrth, J. (ed.) 1993 *Labour's High Noon: The Government and the Economy 1945–51*. Lawrence and Wishart.

Gaitskell, Hugh 1956 *Socialism and Nationalisation*. London, Fabian Society.

Gardner, Richard N. 1969 *Sterling-Dollar Diplomacy*. New York/Maidenhead, McGraw-Hill.

Gamble, A. 1984 'Stabilisation Policy and Adversary Politics' in Gamble and Walkland 1984.

Gamble, A. and Walkland, S. A. 1984 *The British Party System and Economic Policy 1945–1983*. Oxford, Clarendon.

Giddens, A. 1994 *Beyond Left and Right*. Cambridge, Cambridge University Press.

Goldthorpe, J. H. (ed.) 1984 *Order and Conflict in Contemporary Capitalism*. Oxford, Oxford University Press.

Gorst, A., Johnman, L. and Lucas W. S. 1991 *Contemporary British History 1931–1961*. London, Pinter.

Graham, A. and Beckerman, W. 1972 'Introduction: Economic Performance and the Foreign Balance' in Beckerman (ed.) 1972.

Grant, W. 1982 *The Political Economy of Industrial Policy*. London, Butterworth.

Greenleaf, W. H. 1983 *The British Political Tradition Vol. Two The Ideological Inheritance*. London, Routledge.

Haines, J. 1977 *The Politics of Power*. London, Jonathan Cape.

Hall, P. A. 1986 *Governing the Economy: the politics of state intervention in Britain and France*. Oxford, Oxford University Press.

Ham, A. 1981 *Treasury Rules*. London, Quartet Books.

Hare, P. G. 1985 *Planning the British Economy*. Basingstoke, Macmillan.

Haseler, S. 1969 *The Gaitskellites*. London, Macmillan.

Hatfield, M. 1978 *The House the Left Built*. London, Gollancz.

Hattersley, R. 1987 *Choose Freedom*. London, Penguin.

Healey, D. 1989 *The Time of My Life*. London, Michael Joseph.

Heath, A. et al. 1991 *Understanding Political Change*. Oxford, Pergamon Press.

Heffernan, R. and Marqusee, M. 1992 *Defeat from the Jaws of Victory: Inside Kinnock's Labour Party*. London, Verso.

Helleiner, E. 1994 *States and the Reemergence of Global Finance: from Bretton Woods to the 1990's*. Ithaca, New York, Cornell University Press.

Hennessy, P. 1989 *Whitehall*. London, Secker and Warburg.

—— 1993 *Never Again*. London, Vintage.

Hennessy, P. and Seldon, A. (eds) 1987 *Ruling Performances: British Governments from Attlee to Thatcher*. Oxford, Blackwell.

Hill, M. 1993 *The Welfare State in Britain*. Aldershot, Edward Elgar.

Holland, S. 1975 *The Socialist Challenge*. London, Quartet.

Howard, A. (ed.) 1991 *The Crossman Diaries*. London, Mandarin.

Howell, D. 1980 *British Social Democracy*. London, Croom Helm.

Hughes, C. and Wintour, P. 1990 *Labour Rebuilt*. London, Fourth Estate.

Hutton, W. 1995 *The State We're In*. London, Jonathan Cape.

Hyman, Richard 1989 *The Political Economy of Industrial Relations: Theory and Practice in a Cold Climate*. Basingstoke, Macmillan.

Jackson, P. M. 1991 'Public Expenditure' in Artis and Cobham 1991.

Jay, Douglas 1980 *Change and Fortune*. London, Hutchinson.

Jefferys, K. 1993 *The Labour Party since 1945*. London, Macmillan.

Jenkins, Roy 1991 *A Life at the Centre*. London, Macmillan.

Jenkins, Peter 1970 *The Battle of Downing Street*. London, Knight.

—— 1987 *Mrs. Thatcher's Revolution*. London, Cape.

Johnman, L. 1991 'The Labour Party and Industrial Policy, 1940–45' in Tiratsoo (ed.) 1993.

Johnson, P. 1994 'The Welfare State' in Floud and McCloskey (eds).

Jones, G. and Kirby, M. (eds) 1991 *Competitiveness and the State in Twentieth Century Britain*. Manchester, Manchester University Press.

Jones, M. 1994 *Michael Foot*. London, Gollancz.

Kavanagh, D. 1982 *The Politics of the Labour Party*. London, Allen and Unwin.

Keegan, W. and Pennant-Rea, R. 1979 *Who Runs the Economy?* London, Temple Smith.

Keohane, D. 1993 *Labour Party Defence Policy Since 1945*. Leicester, Leicester University Press.

Keohane, R. O. 1984 'The World Political Economy and the Crisis of embedded Liberalism' in J. H. Goldthorpe 1984.

King, A. et al. 1992 *Britain at the Polls 1992*. Chatham, New Jersey, Chatham House.

Kinnock, N. 1986 *Making Our Way*. Oxford, Blackwell.

Kircheimer, O. 1966 'The Transformation of the Western European Party Systems' in La Palombara and Weiner 1966.

Kramer, D. C. 1988 *State Capital and Private Enterprise: the Case of the UK National Enterprise Board*. London, Routledge.

Kogan, D. and Kogan, M. 1982 *The Battle for the Labour Party*. London, Fontana.

La Palombara, J. and Weiner, M. (eds) 1966 *Political Parties and Political Development*. Princeton, Princeton University Press.

Lane, T. 1974 *The Union Makes Us Strong*. London, Arrow.

Leapman, M. 1987 *Kinnock*. London, Unwin Hyman.

Lehmbruch, G. 1984 'Concertation and the Structure of Corporatist Networks' in J. H. Goldthorpe (ed.) 1984.

Lehner, F. 1987 'The Political Economy of Distributive Conflict' in Castles,

Lehner and Schmidt 1988.

Lemke, C. and Marks, G. (eds) 1992 *The Crisis of Socialism in Europe*. London, Duke University Press.

Leruez, Jacques 1975 *Economic Planning and Politics in Britain*. London, Robertson.

Loewenberg, G. 1959 'The Transformation of the British Labour Party Since 1945' *Journal of Politics* 21 (1).

Lowe, Rodney 1993 *The Welfare State in Britain since 1945*. Basingstoke, Macmillan.

Lukes, S. 1984 'The Future of British Socialism' in Pimlott (ed.) 1984.

McKenzie, R. and Silver, A. 1968 *Angels in Marble*. London, Heinemann.

McSmith, A. 1993 *John Smith*. London, Verso.

—— 1994 *John Smith: A Life*. London, Mandarin.

Marquand, D. 1988 *The Unprincipled Society*. London, Jonathan Cape.

—— 1991 *The Progressive Dilemma*. London, Heinemann.

Meadows, P. 1978 'Planning' in Blackaby (ed.) 1978.

Mercer, H. 1993 'The Labour Government and Private Industry' in Tiratsoo (ed.) 1993.

Mercer, H., Rollings, N. and Tomlinson, J. 1992 *Labour and the Private Sector: the Experience of 1945–51*. Edinburgh, Edinburgh University Press.

Middlemas, K. 1986 *Power, competition and the state. Vol. 1. Britain in search of balance, 1940–1961*. Basingstoke, Macmillan.

—— 1990 *Power, competition and the state. Vol. 2. Threats to the postwar settlement: Britain, 1961–74*. Basingstoke, Macmillan.

—— 1991 *Power, competition and the state. Vol. 3. The end of the postwar era: Britain since 1974*. Basingstoke, Macmillan.

Miliband, Ralph 1973 *Parliamentary socialism*. London, Merlin Press.

Millward, R. 1994 'Industrial and Commercial Progress since 1950' in Floud and McCloskey 1994.

Milner, H. 1989 *Sweden: Social Democracy in Practice*. Oxford, Oxford University Press.

Minkin, L. 1991 *The Contentious Alliance: Trade Unions and the Labour Party*. Edinburgh, Edinburgh University Press.

—— 1978 *The Labour Party Conference*. Manchester, Manchester University Press.

Mitchell, A. 1983 *Four Years in the Death of the Labour Party*. London, Methuen.

Morgan, K. 1984 *Labour in Power, 1945–1951*. Oxford, Clarendon Press.

Mullard, M. 1992 *Understanding Economic Policy*. London, Routledge.

Newman, M. 1989 *John Strachey*. Manchester, Manchester University Press.

Nichols, D. and Armstrong, P. 1976 *Workers Divided*. Glasgow, Fontana.

Nordlinger, E. A. 1967 *The Working Class Tories*. London, MacGibbon and Kee.

Opie, R. 1972 'Planning' in Beckerman, W. (ed.) 1972.

Padgett, S. and Paterson, W. E. 1991 *A History of Social Democracy in Postwar Europe*. London, Longman.

Panebianco, A. 1988 *Political Parties: Organisation and Power*. Cambridge, Cambridge University Press.

Panitch, Leo 1976 *Social Democracy and Industrial Militancy*. Cambridge Cambridge University Press.

Pierson, C. 1995 *Socialism after Communism*. Cambridge, Polity.

Pierson, S. 1973 *Marxism and the Origins of British Socialism*. Ithaca, Cornell University Press.

Pimlott, Ben (ed.) 1984 *Fabian Essays in Socialist Thought*. London, Heinemann.

Pimlott, Ben 1985 *Hugh Dalton*. London, Jonathan Cape.

—— 1992 *Harold Wilson* London, Harper Collins.

Pimlott, B. and Cook, C. 1991 *Trade Unions in British Politics*. London, Longman.

Piven, F. F. (ed.) 1991 *Labor Parties in Postindustrial Societies*. Cambridge, Polity.

Pliatzky, Sir Leo 1982 *Getting and Spending: Public Expenditure, Employment and Inflation*. Oxford, Blackwell.

Plowden, E. 1989 *An Industrialist in the Treasury*. London, André Deutsch.

Ponting, C. 1990 *Breach of Promise*. London, Penguin.

Porter, D. and Newton, S. 1988 *Modernisation Frustrated: the Politics of Industrial Decline in Britain since 1900*. London, Unwin Hyman.

Przeworski 1985 *Capitalism and Social Democracy*. Cambridge, Cambridge University Press.

Radice, Giles 1992 *Southern Discomfort*. London, Fabian Society.

Radice, Giles and Pollard, S. 1993 *More Southern Discomfort*. London, Fabian Society.

—— 1994 *Any Southern Comfort?* London, Fabian Society.

Robinson, J. 1962 *Economic Philosophy*. London, Penguin.

Rogow, A. with Peter, S. 1956 *The Labour Government and British Industry*. London, Blackwell.

Saville, R. 1993 'Commanding Heights: the Nationalisation Programme' in Fryth 1993.

Sawyer, M. 1991 'Industrial Policy' in Artis and Cobham 1991.

Scharpf, F. W. 1987 *Crisis and Choice in European Social Democracy*. London, Cornell University Press.

Schor, J. 1992 'Introduction' in Banuri and Schor 1992.

Seyd, P. 1987 *The Rise and Fall of the Labour Left*. London, Macmillan.

Seyd, P. and Whiteley, P. 1992 *Labour's Grass Roots*. Oxford, Clarendon Press.

Shaw, E. 1974 *British Socialist Approaches to International Affairs 1945–51*. Unpublished M.Phil Dissertation, University of Leeds.

—— 1988 *Discipline and Discord*. Manchester, Manchester University Press.
—— 1994 *The Labour Party since 1979: conflict and transformation*. London, Routledge.
Shlaim, A. 1978 *Britain and the Origins of European Unity*. Reading, University of Reading.
Shonfield, A. 1959 *British Economic Policy Since the War*. London, Penguin.
Skidelsky, R. (ed.) 1977 *The End of the Keynesian era: essays on the disintegration of the Keynesian Political Economy*. London, Macmillan.
Smith, M. J. and Spear, J. (eds) 1992 *The Changing Labour Party*. London, Routledge.
Sopel, J. 1995 *Tony Blair, Moderniser*. London, Verso.
Stewart, M. 1972 'The Distribution of Income' in Beckerman (ed.) 1972.
—— 1977 *The Jekyll and Hyde Years: politics and economic policy since 1964*. London, J.M. Dent.
Strange, S. 1971 *Sterling and British Policy*. Oxford, Oxford University Press.
Stubbs, R. and Underhill, G. R. D. 1994 *Political Economy and the Changing Global Order*. London, Macmillan.
Tawney, R. H. 1961 *The Acquisitive Society* (1921). London, Fontana.
Taylor, I. 1991 'Labour and the Impact of War' in Tiratsoo (ed.) 1991.
Taylor, R. 1991 'The Trade Union "Problem" in the Age of Consensus' in Pimlott and Cook (eds) 1991.
Taylor, R. 1993 *The Trade Union Question in British Politics*. Oxford, Blackwell.
Thompson, W. 1993 *The Long Death of British Labourism*. Oxford, Pluto.
Tilton, T. 1990 *The Political Theory of Swedish Social Democracy*. Oxford, Clarendon University Press.
Timperely, S. R. and Woodcock, G. L. 1971 'Shopfloor Attitudes to Industrial Relations Change' *Industrial Relations Journal* 2 (4).
Tiratsoo, N. (ed.) 1993 *The Attlee Years*. London, Pinter.
Tiratsoo, N. and Tomlinson, J. (eds) 1993 *Industrial Efficiency and State Intervention*. London, Routledge.
Tomlinson 1993 (b). 'The Labour Government and the Trade Unions, 1945–51' in Tiratsoo (ed.) 1993.
Turner, H., Clack, G. and Roberts, G. 1967 *Labour Relations in the Motor Industry*. London Allen & Unwin.
US Foreign Relations 1977 *US Foreign Economic Policy Issues*. Washington, Government Printing Office.
Walker, D. 1987 'Harold Wilson' in Henessy and Seldon 1987.
Williams, Philip M. 1982 *Hugh Gaitskell*. Oxford, Oxford University Press.
Wilson, Harold 1971 The *Labour Government, 1964–1970: a personal record*. London, Weidenfeld and Nicolson.
Wilson, Harold 1979 *Final Term: the Labour Government*. London, Weidenfeld and Nicolson.
Whitehead, P. 1985 *The Writing on the Wall*. London, Michael Joseph.

Whiteley, Paul 1983 *The Labour Party in Crisis*. London, Methuen.
Woodward, N. 1993 'Labour's Economic Performance 1964–70' in Coopey et al. (eds) 1993.
Ziegler, P. 1993 *Wilson*. London, Weidenfeld and Nicholson.
Zysman, J. 1983 *Governments, Markets and Growth*. Oxford, Robertson.

Articles

Alderman, K. and Carter, N. 1994 'The Labour Party and the Trade Unions: Loosening the Ties?' *Parliamentary Affairs* 47 (3).
Andrews, D. M. 1994 'Capital Mobility and State Autonomy: Toward a Structural Theory of International Monetary Relations' *International Studies Quarterly* 38 (2).
Barker, R. 1986 'Civil Service Attitudes and the Economic Planning of the Attlee Government' *Journal of Contemporary History* 21 (3).
Blair, Tony 1991 'Forging a new Agenda' *Marxism Today*, October.
—— 1993 'Why Modernisation Matters' *Renewal* 1 (4).
Brooke, S. 1989 'Revisionists and Fundamentalists: The Labour Party and Economic Policy during the Second World War' *The Historical Journal* 32 (1).
Burk, K. et al. 1989 'Symposium: 1976 IMF Crisis' *Contemporary Record* 3 (2).
Cairncross, A. 1992 'Economic Policy After 1974' *Twentieth Century British History* 3 (2).
Crewe, I. 1987(a). 'A New Class of Politics' *Guardian* 13 June.
—— 1987(b). 'How Labour was Trounced all Round' *Guardian* 14 June 1987.
—— 1992 'Why Did Labour Lose (Yet Again)? *Politics Review* 2 (1).
Cronin, J. E. and Weiler, P. 1991 'Working-Class Interests and the Politics of Social Democratic Reform in Britain, 1900–1940' *International Labor and Working Class History* 40.
Dow, G. 1993 'What do we Know about Social Democracy?' *Economic and Industrial Democracy* 14 (1).
Drucker, H. 1981 'Changes in the Labour Party Leadership' *Parliamentary Affairs* 34 (4).
Esping-Andersen, G. and van Kersbergen, K. 1992 'Contemporary Research on Social Democracy' *Annual Review of Sociology* 18.
Fay, S. and Young, H. 1978 'The Day the £ Nearly Died' *Sunday Times*, 7, 14, 21 May 1978.
Fielding, S. 1992 'Labourism in the 1940's' *Twentieth Century British History* 3 (2).
Hewitt, P. and Gould, P. 1993: 'Learning from Success – Labour and Clinton's New Democrats' *Renewal* 1 (1).
Jones, Tudor 1991 'Labour Revisionism and Public Ownership' *Contemporary Record* 5 (3).
Kelly, R. 1993 'Taxing the Speculator' *Fabian Review* 105 (4).
Keman, H. 1993 'Theoretical Approaches to Social Democracy' *Journal of*

Theoretic Politics 5 (3).

Lovenduski, J. and Norris, P. 1994 'Labour and the Unions: after the Brighton Conference' *Government and Opposition* 29 (2).

Ludlam, S. 1992 'The Gnomes of Washington: Four Myths of the 1976 IMF Crisis' *Political Studies* 40 (4).

Martin, F. 1991 'Old Realisms: Policy Reviews of the Past' *Labour History Review* 56 (1).

Media Research Group, 1987 Goldsmiths' College 'Media Coverage of London Councils: Interim Report'. Unpublished paper.

Mowlam, Mo 1993 'Why Labour Should Learn to Love the Middle Class' *Fabian Review* 105 (1).

Muller, W. 1994 'Political traditions and the Role of the State' *West European Politics* 17 (3).

Muller, W. and Wright, V. 1994 'Reshaping the State in Western Europe: The Limits to Retreat' *West European Politics* 17 (3).

National Institute of Economic and Social Research, 1990. 'Policy Options Under a Labour Government' *National Institute Economic Review*, November.

Notermans, T. 1993 'The Abdication from National Policy Autonomy: Why the Macroeconomic Policy Regime Has Become So Unfavourable to Labour' *Politics and Society* 21 (2).

Robinson, E. A. G. 1986 'The Economic Problems of the Transition from War to Peace' *Cambridge Journal of Economics* 10.

Rose, R. 1979 'Ungovernability: Is there Fire Behind the Smoke?' *Political Studies* 27 (3).

Rose, B. and Ross, G. 1994 'Socialism Past, New Social-Democracy, and Socialism Futures' *Social Science History* 18 (3).

Samuel, R. 1986 'The Cult of Planning' *New Socialist* January 34.

Tobin, J. 1994 'Taxing Speculators Makes Sense' *New Economy* 1 (2).

Tomlinson, J. 1989 'Labour's Management of the National Economy 1945–51' *Economy and Society* 18 (1).

—— 1991 'The Attlee Government and the Balance of Payments, 1945–1951' *Twentieth Century British History* 2 (1).

—— 1992 'Planning: Debate and Policy in the 1940's' *Twentieth Century British History* 3 (2).

—— 1993a. 'Mr Attlee's Supply-side Socialism' *Economic History Review* 46 (1).

Turner, J. E. 1981 'The Labour Party: Riding Two Horses' *International Studies Quarterly* 25 (3).

Webb, M. 1991 'International Economic Structures, Government Interests and International Coordination of Macroeconomic Adjustment Policies' *International Organisation* 45.

Wilks, S. 1981 'Planning Agreements: the Making of a Paper Tiger' *Public Administration* 59.

Index

New Brunswick Free Public Library

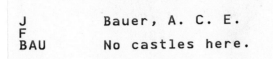

3 9309 00188464 2

J
F
BAU

Bauer, A. C. E.

No castles here.

$15.99

DATE			

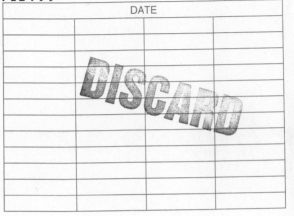

NEW BRUNSWICK FREE PUB LIBY
60 LIVINGSTON AVE
NEW BRUNSWICK NJ 08901

BAKER & TAYLOR